# Support Your RV Lifestyle!
## An Insider's Guide to Working on the Road
### 3rd Edition

# Support Your RV Lifestyle!
## An Insider's Guide to Working on the Road
### 3rd Edition

By Jaimie Hall Bruzenak

Pine Country Publishing

# Support Your RV Lifestyle!
## An Insider's Guide to Working on the Road
by Jaimie Hall Bruzenak

Published by:
**Pine Country Publishing**
127 Rainbow Dr., #2780
Livingston, TX 77399-1027 U.S.A.
www.rvlifestyleexperts.com

Unattributed quotations are by Jaimie Hall Bruzenak
Graphics in the text ©2002-2011 *www.ArtToday.com*.
In order to protect privacy, some names have been changed.
Cover design by Robert Aulicino *(www.aulicinodesign.com)*
Photos: George Bruzenak, Eric Steilberger, Jim & Marcie Cumberland

Copyright © 2002- 2011
ISBN: 0-9716777-1-9; 978-0-9716777-1-5
First printing, 2002
Second printing, 2002
Third printing, 2003, revised
Fourth printing, 2004, revised
2nd Edition, 2006, completely revised
Sixth printing, 2007, revised
Seventh printing, 2011, completely revised
Printed in the United States

### Library of Congress Cataloging-in-Publication Data
Bruzenak, Jaimie Hall
Support Your RV lifestyle! : an insider's guide to working on the road / Jaimie Hall Bruzenak — 3rd ed., completely rev.
p. cm.
Includes bibliographical references and index.
LCCN 2001099204
10- digit ISBN 0-9716777-1-9; 13-digit ISBN 978--0-9716777-1-5
1. Recreational vehicle living--United States.
2. Temporary employment--United States. I. Title.
TX1110.H35 2002
796.7'9'0973                              QBI02-200025

This book is dedicated to my late
husband, Bill. We began our RV adventure
in 1992. His support and encouragement
were instrumental in creating this book.
(1945-2004)

This book is also dedicated to the many
Workampers who have led the way by
following their dreams.

# Table of Contents

## SECTION IV. RV LIFESTYLE CONSIDERATIONS

## SECTION V. APPENDICES

## SECTION V. RESOURCES

# Acknowledgments

This book is the culmination of ten-plus years on the road and many experiences and sharing. Two incidents were instrumental in even conceiving the idea of *Support Your RV Lifestyle! An Insider's Guide to Working on the Road*:

✔ The first was when we pulled Grand Teton National Park for our first seasonal jobs. Snow still covered the ground and the jagged Teton peaks. Being there was a dream come true. Both Bill and I were excited. We had actually gotten seasonal jobs with the National Park Service. I wanted to share how we had done it with anyone else who wanted to know.

✔ The second took place at a "Boomerang" in October of 1994 in Pena Blanca, Arizona. Alice Zyetz invited several women RVers to participate in writing exercises a la Natalie Goldberg's *Writing Down the Bones*. Little did I suspect that day that this book would result. Alice's book, *You Shoulda Listened to Your Mother: 36 Timeless Success Tips for Working Women,* was also yet to be written and Alice and I have since teamed up to write another book and two eBooks.

Besides the hours of personal time, this book would not have been completed without the generous help of many people.

I would especially like to acknowledge and thank Alice Zyetz, my editor and friend, for her tireless work. I actually got a package deal. Chuck Zyetz, too, spent considerable time editing, the book benefitting from his logical, engineering mind.

Also giving editorial assistance and encouragement were Stephanie Bernhagen, Phyllis Frey, Judith Waite Allee, Janice Lasko, Joe and Kay Peterson, Greg and Debbie Robus, Paul Bernhagen, and Hope Sykes. Carol Richards, David Loring, Alfred Lutz and Ron Chance provided invaluable assistance with the chapters on legal and financial issues facing working RVers and managing RV expenses. Friends Shaneen and DeAnna willingly shared valuable information they have gathered in dealing with health issues on the road. Heidi Young assisted with the chapter on e-mail. Sue Bizek helped verify websites and other information for this edition.

Stephanie Bernhagen, author of *Take Back Your Life! Travel Full-Time in an RV*, wrote her book on the road and gave invaluable assistance and encouragement with the publishing process. She also contributed "Working with the Mouse" and the budget worksheet she developed for Life on Wheels.

Several individuals contributed pieces to the book: Hope Sykes, Janice Lasko, Virginia Heitman, Lou Schneider, and Chuck Wright. Their experiences and contributions added valuable information. Janice's "Whistle While We Work" originally appeared in 1994 *Camperways* and was updated for this book. I am also grateful to Dorothy Ayers Counts and David E. Counts for the use of their survey data from their classic ethnography, *Over the Next Hill: An Enthnography of RVing Seniors in North America.*

It would be impossible to list all who helped. I thank the many working RVers who have shared their stories with me over the years; you will see many of their names throughout the book. Ron and Val Jones deserve special mention. They are the consummate working RVers; their work experiences are mentioned in several chapters. They represent what this adventure is all about, having expertly used working on the road to achieve their travel and life goals. Terry and Joe Sweeney are another special couple. Their skill and determination in making this lifestyle work has been an inspiration too.

I also owe a big thanks to George Bruzenak, for his ongoing support and for sharing his life with me.

Bob Aulicino created the cover for this edition, capturing the essence of the book. George Bruzenak took the photo of Becky Reiger's truck and 5th wheel coming up Highway 87 out of Strawberry, Arizona and that of the Red Car Tour. Eric Steilberger photographed his wife, Denise, driving the tractor hauling the Airstream. Jim and Marcie Cumberland provided the photo of the two of them in period costume.

And finally, I would like to thank you, dear readers, for your openness and willingness to create your own lives!

*Jaimie Hall Bruzenak*

# Preface

**S**upport Your RV Lifestyle! is written for three groups of readers:

✔ You're new to RVing and are considering working on the road.
✔ You've had some work experience on the road and you're not entirely satisfied.
✔ You're experienced working RVers who would like some new ideas and tools for making money on the road.

When we first became full-time RVers in 1992, my husband Bill and I knew we would need to work on the road to support our RV lifestyle. Could we do it? Where could we find jobs? Could we find jobs to make enough money to live on? Unfortunately, there was no manual to help us answer these questions.

Because of this void, I began listening for and collecting information about working on the road. Since then, I have been sharing this information with other working RVers through articles, newsletters, seminars and personal contact.

**Support Your RV Lifestyle!** is the result of more than ten years of research and sharing. This is the "how-to" manual that we wished we had when we started out. *Support Your RV Lifestyle! An Insider's Guide to Working on the Road* provides the necessary tools and resources to find jobs that pay well and enhance your experiences on the road.

*Update:* My husband Bill passed away in 2004. I am continuing to travel and meet many RVers working and volunteering on the road. As the editor for Workamper Viewpoint, a division of Workamper News®, and moderator of its online forums, I am privileged to interact with experienced Workampers and help and encourage those thinking about or new to this lifestyle. Since 1992, technology has changed and health insurance costs are a growing concern for many. Costs like campground fees and fuel prices are rising too. Finding ways to supplement income or reduce travel expenses is even more important today than when Bill and I started.

# Why you need this book:
# 14 mistakes working RVers can avoid

Talk to RV workers about their work experiences and you'll find many who have had at least one job doing things they didn't like. Others have paid out more money to get there than they earned or quit their jobs mid-season because it was nothing like what they expected. Contrast these with other RV workers who always seem to get wonderful jobs. They get free tickets to area attractions, see things that only locals know about, and save more money now than before they hit the road. I want to help you become part of the second group of working RVers.

This book provides the tools to:

✔ make the money you need or desire

✔ get the most out of your RV lifestyle

Too many RV workers are not achieving these goals because they make one or more of the following avoidable mistakes:

## MISTAKE #1: TAKE THE FIRST JOB YOU ARE OFFERED.

RV workers have told me they talked to one employer and got hired. They were so excited about getting a job, they jumped at it. Later on they confessed that it wasn't what they were expecting. It is a piece of cake to find a job. The trick is finding a job that makes the money you want and adds to your travel experiences.

To do this you will examine your income needs and wants. (Chapter 3) You'll identify what you want to do and what you don't want to do. (Chapter 2) You'll find out how to prepare for an interview to find out about a job before taking it. (Chapter 10)

## MISTAKE #2: UNDERVALUE YOUR SKILLS AND WHAT YOU HAVE TO OFFER.

If you are new to a field, you may have no idea what the going rate for a position is or how your skills compare to those of other RV workers.

Many RV parks and other seasonal employers advertise very low wages so you figure that's what you must accept, even if you bring more value to the job. This often goes with Mistake #1, grabbing the first job offer.

You will learn how to do your research to enable you to negotiate from strength and knowledge. (Chapters 8 and 10)

## MISTAKE #3: NEED A JOB SUDDENLY.

Suddenly needing a job could happen for any number of reasons: an expected job falls through, the stock market declines, or you have unexpected expenses like vehicle repairs or a medical emergency. Being in a position where you need a job and have nothing lined up does not put you in a good bargaining position.

You'll learn how to have several options, how to develop your job contacts, and what to do to find a last-minute position. (Chapters 8 and 9)

## MISTAKE #4: WORK 20 HOURS/WEEK FOR A "FREE" RV SITE.

You may get an RV site as all or part of your compensation. Remember, your time is valuable. The site is not free. Depending on the monthly rate, you may be "earning" the equivalent of $2 or $3 an hour.

You'll learn several ways to value your "free site" to determine if you are working for a fair amount. (Chapter 11)

## MISTAKE #5: PAY TAXES ON YOUR "FREE" RV SITE.

You could end up owing income taxes on your "free" RV site. The IRS looks at your site as income unless certain conditions are met.

You will learn about the letter you must get from your employer to avoid such taxes. (Chapter 13)

## MISTAKE #6: GET CHARGED OUTRAGEOUS AMOUNTS FOR YOUR "FREE" SITE.

You may have an employer tell you the site you are getting is worth $750 dollars a month. However, the employer based it on the daily rate of $25 per night. You are entitled to the much-reduced monthly rate.

You'll learn how to determine a fair value for your RV site, even if the employer does not have a published rate. (Chapter 11)

## MISTAKE #7: WORK 50-60 HOURS, GET PAID FOR 40.

Salaried employees are usually expected to work beyond the standard work week. Accepting a salary for your work instead of an hourly rate is inviting trouble. If you are not paid for extra hours, you can find yourself donating lots of time to an employer.

You'll learn how to set limits and make sure you get paid appropriately for your work. (Chapter 12)

## MISTAKE #8: WORK FOR THE "BOSS FROM HELL."

Let's face it, some bosses are wonderful and working for them can be a joy. Others are not. They make you wonder how they ever stayed in business this long.

You'll learn how to use networking, sharp interview techniques, communication skills and a good sense of self-worth to avoid being victimized by a difficult boss. (Chapters 10 and 12)

## MISTAKE #9: OWE BIG BUCKS IN STATE INCOME TAX.

In each state where you have earned W-2 income, you must file a state income tax return — if that state requires it. What you may not know is that some states want a proportional share of all of your income based on the length of time you spent there. If you worked for six months in such a state, for example, then they would consider that you earned half of your total income (counting retirement, investments, etc.) in that state and tax you accordingly. Don't get surprised at tax time.

You'll learn why you should check your tax situation before accepting a job offer and how to do so.(Chapter 13)

## MISTAKE #10: SPEND MORE MONEY THAN YOU MAKE BY TAKING A JOB.

More than one RV worker has driven hundreds of miles to a job, earned barely minimum wage, and then realized this was a losing proposition. Expenses were higher than income, especially considering the travel costs to get there.

You'll learn to make a good estimate of your expenses and learn how to evaluate the true income from your work.(Chapters 3 and 13)

## MISTAKE #11: RETURN TO THE SAME PLACE, SAME JOB EVERY YEAR.

Inertia, staying in your comfort zone, can find you going back to the same place year after year. It may be your best choice, but is it? You are missing out on the very reasons that most people RV — to have new experiences and see new places. You may be underpaid and overworked and never know it. And you could be suddenly left with no job if there is a change of ownership or management, or if the business folds.

You'll have many more possibilities to consider after reading this book. (Chapter 4 and Chapters 14-22)

## MISTAKE #12: COUNT ON A "SURE" THING.

The employer told you he wanted you back next year. Then he changes his mind, dies or sells the business. You are left without a job.

You'll learn the importance of keeping abreast of the job market and how to do it. (Chapters 4 and 8)

## MISTAKE #13: PURSUE MONEYMAKING OPPORTUNITIES WHERE YOU LOSE YOUR SHIRT.

A business opportunity can sound like you will rake in the dough yet end up costing you money. If you only look at the income side and fail to consider your expenses, it could be a disaster.

You'll learn factors to consider in starting an enterprise and how to determine if you can "afford" this business. (Chapter 21)

## MISTAKE #14: HAVE NO TIME TO PLAY.

One RV worker and her husband accepted a job requiring 24 hours/ week each, then found out after they arrived, they'd be working six four-hour days. They didn't have time to explore the area since they had to drive a long way to get anywhere. Other couples have said they didn't get two days off back-to-back, or their days off weren't the same. Some employers expect 6-day weeks during the busy parts of the season. One day off when you have grocery shopping and laundry to do leaves very little time for adventures.

You'll learn to ask the right questions and negotiate what is important to you. (Chapters 10 and 11)

Whether you have made any of these mistakes, are new to RV work, or are looking for new ideas for earning or making money, the chapters ahead will position you to avoid these mistakes. You'll find more than 350 job and moneymaking categories and a whole world of possibilities.

# How to use this book

## HOW THIS BOOK IS ORGANIZED

### Section I: Know Yourself
Introduces possibilities for working and volunteering on the road. You'll determine how much income you need, think about the kind of work you are qualified to do on the road, and decide what types of jobs you'd like to do.

### Section II: Nitty-gritty of getting work to support your RVing
Gives you the tools for getting a well-paying job. You'll find out
✔ How to locate seasonal and temporary job openings and volunteer positions
✔ How to write a résumé for working on the road
✔ How to prepare for an interview
✔ How to negotiate for good pay and perks

### Section III: Job List and more than 350 moneymaking opportunities
Starts with a job list that itemizes actual jobs, job categories, as well as volunteer and moneymaking opportunities that dovetail with the RV lifestyle. You'll learn where to locate them and what they entail. You'll read the stories of working RVers doing many of these jobs.

In each chapter you'll see several partial ads in boxes. These are ads from actual publications or jobs that working RVers have had.

Included are chapters on

✔ How to get jobs with a campsite
✔ How to get jobs traveling in your RV
✔ How to get jobs within the RV industry
✔ How to get seasonal federal jobs
✔ How to get jobs working in the outdoors

✔ How to get jobs at resorts and travel destinations
✔ How to get temporary jobs and work at special events
✔ How to be your own boss
✔ How to help your budget by volunteering

## Section IV: RV lifestyle considerations

Covers managing RV expenses and additional issues you may face on the road.

## Section V: Appendixes

Appendix 1: State tourism offices
Appendix 2: National Park Service offices
Appendix 3: U.S. D.A. National Forest Service regional offices
Appendix 4: State parks
Appendix 5: State revenue offices and tax information
Appendix 6: State motor vehicle and driver's licensing bureaus
Appendix 7: Janice's grocery shopping list
Appendix 8: Budget worksheet
Appendix 9: Stephanie Bernhagen's budget worksheet
Appendix10: Three RV worker stories

## Section V: Resources

Lists resources by chapter. Included in resources are

✔ Specific job search sites
✔ Employers
✔ Resources for locating job openings

## HOW TO GET THE MOST OUT OF THIS BOOK

### Planning stage

If you are still in the planning stage, go through the entire book. You will have a clearer picture of what you are getting into and be able to make better plans. For instance, you might want to begin now to develop a current job or business, or even a new one, that will support you as you travel. You could take classes to sharpen or acquire skills that will make you more valuable.

Before you begin full-timing, subscribe to *Workamper News,* check websites listed in **Resources** for Chapter 9, look at ads, and talk to potential employers to get an idea of what you can make per hour. Read RV publications and talk to any RVers you meet. If you have not already done so, I also recommend that you read at least one general book on full-time RVing to use in conjunction with *Support Your RV Lifestyle!* See the beginning of **Resources**.

### On the road but limited or no work experience

If you are already on the road and haven't worked, or are not satisfied with your current work experience, you should start with **Section I**. You'll take a look at work ideas and what it is you would like to get out of working or volunteering. Take advantage of the knowledge other workers have shared. Make sure you read "Why you need this book:14 mistakes Working RVers Can Avoid." Begin getting familiar with the job market as well. Subscribe to *Workamper News* and check websites listed in **Resources.**

### Seasoned RV workers

You may have experience and be looking for some new ideas. Look at **Section III** with more than 350 job categories and moneymaking opportunities that fellow working RVers are already doing. If you haven't done so, be sure to use "Why you need this book:14 Mistakes Working RVers Can Avoid" as a checklist and review the appropriate chapters in **Sections I and II** if needed. You may pick up helpful ideas and information and you'll have a handy reference you can turn to whenever you are job hunting.

### Volunteers

If you are thinking of volunteering, or would like additional ideas, read Chapter 22. Since highly desirable volunteer positions can be competitive, you'll benefit from information in other chapters that will help you locate and obtain positions.

## HOW TO MAKE THIS BOOK YOURS

You'll see **Your turn!** in many of the chapters in the first two sections. Here you can apply the chapter information to your unique situation. I know many of us hate exercises, but to get the most out of this book, do them!

Start a **Job Notebook** to keep job and volunteer information in one place. A three-ring binder is ideal so you can add additional pages or even job applications easily. (If you use your computer instead, be sure to back up your data!) I recommend these sections:

### Section 1:
**Your turn!** Keep your answers here.

### Section 2:
**Contacts:** Include contacts you make. Anytime you meet people who are working or volunteering on the road, jot down their names, contact information, and what you learned. Include contacts you have gleaned from RV-related discussion forums on the Internet, newsletters, and mutual friends.

### Section 3:
**Potential Employers:** As you travel and see areas where you'd like to work or if you stay at an RV park you enjoy, write down contact information and the date you were there. Introduce yourself to potential employers during your visit and find out about the application process. Take notes so that if you later apply for a job with those employers, you can remind them of your visit. If you pick up an application, file it here along with your notes. Include ads from *Workamper News* and other publications. Don't forget to write down employers mentioned in discussions with other working RVers.

---

### Go for it!
We have met lots of RVers in our travels. Most have one regret: They didn't hit the road sooner!

---

# The author's work story

## HOW WE GOT STARTED

In 1991, Bill and I took a typical tourist vacation, a three-week whirlwind trip from Pennsylvania out west and back. This trip took us as far west as Yellowstone, south to the Grand Canyon, then back home by way of Colorado. We drove 14 hours the first day. Once we slowed down a bit we started meeting full-time RVers. We knew people vacationed in RVs. But live in one?

Some of these full-timers were working. We were tent camping out of our Chevy Cavalier station wagon in Custer State Park, South Dakota. Ward came up and started talking to us and insisted on showing us his RV. He and his wife were working there and living in their motorhome, which was set up to be totally self-contained. When not working, they could park on BLM (Bureau of Land Management) or Forest Service land without hookups, lowering their yearly expenses drastically. Ward also introduced us to *Workamper News,* a publication with employment ads for RVers. Intrigued, I copied down the address.

At Old Faithful in Yellowstone, we met two more full-time RVers, salesladies in the gift shop who started telling Bill all about this lifestyle, their work experiences and the Escapees RV Club. Escapees? From what? We wrote that address down too.

**Some of our work and volunteer experiences:**
- worked at seven national parks
- volunteered at one national forest and one national park for our site
- volunteered at one national park to get experience
- provided tax season help
- sold Christmas trees
- remodeled houses
- worked at tourist businesses in Alaska

In the Grand Tetons we met a couple headed back for their third season in Yellowstone. We also talked to a seasonal maintenance worker for the National Park Service about her job and how she got it. She was a college student with no real maintenance background. Fascinated, we stopped in Personnel to find out how to apply. Maybe we could work at a beautiful place like this.

All the way back across Kansas, Indiana, Ohio and western Pennsylvania, we talked about the pros and cons of this lifestyle. In Kansas we were leaning towards giving it a try; in Indiana, how could we think of such a thing? By the time we got home, we had decided to send for books on full-time RVing by Joe and Kay Peterson (founders of the Escapees RV Club), order a sample issue of *Workamper News,* and call our realtor.

We went back and forth. Could we get jobs that paid enough? How would we handle banking and getting cash? Should we get a motorhome, a 5th wheel or pull trailer? We went to RV shows, visited RV dealers and answered RV ads. We put our house on the market. If it sold, that would decide it—we were meant to go. Houses in our area usually took a year or more to sell, yet the first person who looked fell in love with it. "I've been looking for this house for five years," she exclaimed. Sold!

We had found a barely used Pace Arrow Motorhome that came with a CJ7 Jeep, which the owners agreed to hold until the house sold. We moved in with a recently separated friend I worked with, saved some more money and held yard sales. The big day came Election Day, 1992. We voted and left!

That winter, when the announcements came out for maintenance workers at the Tetons, we worked our way through the tedious application process for jobs there as well as at ten or eleven other national parks. We got our wish. We were both hired to work at the Tetons and set off on our odyssey.

Since then we have also worked at national parks in Colorado, Utah, California, Arizona and Alaska. We've had a variety of other work and volunteer experiences as well.

## FLEXIBILITY

What this lifestyle has given us is a great deal of flexibility. When my mother was terminally ill with cancer, we were able to drive our motorhome to California to help her and my dad. We stayed for seven months. We could never have done that in our old way of life.

Unless we have made another commitment, we can stay as long as we like if we are enjoying an area. The weather gets bad? Want a new view? We simply move our rig elsewhere. It's wonderful.

In 2004 Bill passed away. What we loved, and I still do, is that each of us defines our own lives. If it doesn't work or isn't fun anymore, we can make new choices. While we both saw this as a wonderful lifestyle and were passionate about RVing, we were never evangelical about it.

My work now consists of book publishing, freelance writing, and working as the Workamper Viewpoint editor for *Workamper News*®. I also publish a twice monthly online newsletter, *RV Lifestyle Ezine* , produce Webinars on RV lifestyle and Workamping topics. I am enjoying seeing new places and meeting people working on the road and writing about them. A mobile brandband modem enables me to moderate the forums at Workamper.com while traveling and send in articles and photos for publication. I am traveling part time now and have found someone with whom to share my life. We plan to do a few more working and volunteering stints in the future.

## THE RV LIFESTYLE

On the road, Bill and I had some wonderful experiences and great adventures. Bill used to watch old World War II movies and think how exciting it would be to see Pearl Harbor or the mothball fleet near San Francisco. He saw them both. Alaska was my special dream. We spent a fantastic summer in Skagway. On a weekend trip to Glacier Bay we kayaked among the dolphins and whales. Things we never in our wildest dreams thought we'd do, we saw and did.

We made countless friends through RVing and working over the years and I have quite a support network. I've found RVers to be accepting and generally judge people for what kind of person they are rather than by their material possessions.

Working RVers are able to have a community of friends and new adventures as well as freedom and control of their lives. They can create their own lives and live the dreams they have. What more can we ask?

## SUPPORT YOUR RV LIFESTYLE!

You, too, can live the life you dream. Working can keep you on the road and take you to places you want to visit. It can give you the freedom and flexibility to be where you want, when you want. There is no right or wrong way. *Support Your RV Lifestyle!* will give you the resources and tools to create the future of your choosing.

# Warning - Disclaimer

This book is designed to provide information on making money and working on the road as a full-time RVer. It is sold with the understanding that the publisher and author and contributors are not engaged in rendering legal, financial or other professional services. If legal or expert assistance is needed, the services of a competent professional should be sought.

It is not the purpose of this book to reprint all the information that is otherwise available, but to complement, amplify and supplement other books and resources. You are urged to read all the available material, print and Internet, and learn as much as possible about full-time RVing and working on the road and to tailor the information to your individual needs. For more resources, see Resources at the end of this book and the appendices.

Every effort has been made to make this book as complete and accurate as possible. However, there *may be mistakes,* both typographical and in content. Therefore, this book should be used only as a general guide and not the ultimate source for making a major lifestyle change. Furthermore, this book only contains information on making money and working on the road up to the printing date.

The purpose of this book is to educate and entertain. The author and Pine Country Publishing shall have neither liability nor responsibility to any person or entity with respect to loss or damage caused, or alleged to be caused, directly or indirectly by the information contained in this book.

If you do not wish to be bound by the above, you may return this book to the publisher for a full refund.

# Section I. KNOW YOURSELF

# Chapter 1
## What do you bring to the job market?

You will be amazed at what you already bring to the job market. Attitude and perseverance, not experience, are the main keys to job success on the road. Employers are crying for responsible workers and increasingly prefer retired or semi-retired people. Therefore, they advertise in publications and websites aimed at RVers.

Working at Lake Powell one summer, we heard a college-aged woman complain to her co-worker, *"I have to go back to school in three weeks and I haven't even had a chance to see my friends."* She quit the first part of August. For many employers, this is all too typical. Is it any wonder that many prefer RV workers who don't have school commitments and will honor their agreements?

This chapter will help you identify what you bring to the RV job market, but first, let's look at some of the things you could do.

## HOW CAN YOU MAKE MONEY ON THE ROAD?
Working and making money on the road usually fall into one of the following categories. Which ones interest you?

### Seasonal temporary work
If you want to work only part of the year, many seasonal and temporary positions are tailor-made for you. Resort areas have RV parks that need help. What better source of labor than RVers who understand the needs of their visitors?

> **There are any number of ways to make money on the road.**

In national parks, concessionaires hire hundreds of seasonal workers to run hotels, stores, restaurants, and other tourist activities and services. They've learned that RVers are good workers. About one-third of the workers for Yellowstone National Park Lodges are "mature" workers (meaning not college-aged kids), many living in their RVs. In fact, many openings occur in mid-season. A retired couple stopped by Flagg Ranch, between Yellowstone and Grand Teton National Parks just to check it out. They were asked to start work the next day.

## Jobs that include travel

"Home is where you park it," reads an Escapees RV Club bumper sticker on the back of our motorhome. RV workers bring their houses with them so jobs that require moving from site to site are natural for them. Working at craft fairs or shows, checking gas pipelines, house-sitting, or leading caravans are just a few possibilities.

## Your own business

If you have the entrepreneurial spirit, you can have your own business as you travel. From making money on the Internet to supplying and servicing the burgeoning RV subculture, there are many ways to make a buck. Some RV entrepreneurs use their creative abilities like writing, performing, and making arts and crafts to earn money.

## Skills from your former life

You may be able to take skills from your previous work life and use them to earn money on the road. RVers have returned and worked a few months a year for former employers, started consulting businesses, or given seminars. Handy people and mechanics can pick up jobs wherever they find RVers parked. Some of these options take planning before you leave if you want to earn money right away.

**Acquire jobs skills for the road by volunteering.**

## Volunteering and exchange of services

Reducing your expenses is money in the bank. Volunteers for federal and state agencies generally get a full hookup site in exchange for their efforts. You won't be spending money on gas to travel or for a space in an RV park, two of the largest items in most RVers' budgets.

You could work out an exchange of services for a place to park. Some options are to provide security by your presence, housesit, take care of mail, plants or pets. For example, Ardith and Page worked ten hours a week for their site in Anchorage, Alaska, having plenty of time for paying jobs and exploring.

If you want a paying job in a new field, volunteering is an excellent way to get experience and references. Jim worked as a volunteer at Acadia National Park in Maine, doing the same tasks that rangers did. After volunteering two seasons, the rangers encouraged him to apply and he was hired for the following year. Nick and Joanne were campground hosts at a state park. They asked for a letter of reference that they used to get paying jobs at a state park in another state.

## WHAT DO I HAVE TO OFFER?

I bet you are qualified for more seasonal jobs than you would imagine. Your skills and abilities can translate to cash in your pocket. Remember, you have life experience! That counts for a great deal.

Most seasonal jobs are front-line jobs, like cash register operation or registering campers. These skills can be learned on the job. Employers will want to train you in "their way."

Key attributes needed for nearly all jobs are ones you probably have:

✔ People skills — with customers, co-workers, management
✔ Willingness to follow directions
✔ Sense of responsibility
✔ Common sense
✔ Flexibility
✔ Reliability

> **Include non-paid as well as paid experience on your application.**

For positions requiring a trade, you must show that you have the necessary skills, but they don't need to be from paid experience. For example, Bill had worked in steel fabrication and management. He was applying for maintenance positions where skills in several trades were needed — carpentry, plumbing, etc. On applications, Bill listed the house he remodeled and the addition he built, plus high school summer jobs as a plumber's helper. He received several job offers in maintenance.

I applied for maintenance worker and motor vehicle operator positions for my first seasonal job. My background was in teaching, sales, and customer service. However, I had done many aspects of the job. As a teenager, I had driven trucks pulling horse trailers. I'd been driving both our motorhome and 4-wheel drive Jeep. I am an excellent assistant, having helped Bill and my dad with their projects. Because I highlighted my *relevant* experience, I was hired.

As you inventory your skills, knowledge, and abilities, be sure to consider all your activities outside work as well as past jobs. Hobbies, home maintenance, travel, and community activities should be evaluated and included.

## YOUR TURN!

Start your **Job Notebook** now. (Refer to instructions in "How to use this book.") Record your answers to **Your Turn!** in section one of your three-ring binder, beginning with the activity below. You could also put your **Job Notebook** answers on your computer. *Caution: Make sure you back up your computer periodically.*

Now it's your turn to identify what you can bring to the job market. Be specific. Brainstorm to uncover all the skills and abilities you have. Don't edit. This will help you focus your job search. We'll be returning to this list several times. If you have a spouse or travel partner, each of you should make a separate list.

### My skills and abilities:

List jobs you've had, including part-time and summer jobs and the main skills you used. Then do the same for the other categories. Three examples are provided: one for jobs, one for home maintenance, and one for community activities.

| Activity | Skills |
|---|---|
| *Receptionist:* | Used people skills for handling complaints. Followed company procedures. |
| *Remodel house:* | Hung drywall and kitchen cabinets, installed dishwasher, rewired, painted. |
| *Lions Club:* | In charge of annual fund-raiser, over $10,000 raised. Sold refreshments, collected money. |

Jobs:

Hobbies:

Volunteer and Community activities:

Home and vehicle maintenance:

RV maintenance:

Tools/equipment I can use:

People skills:

Skills that could be taken on the road: computer skills, management skills, selling, writing, art, teaching a skill, nursing, massage, hairdressing.

## BEGIN FOCUSING:

Start getting acquainted with the job market for RVers. I suggest you look at the Job List in the beginning of **Section III** (page 127). You can also scan through chapters in **Section III** that interest you. Look also at issues of *Workamper News* and the Internet at employer and job-search websites listed in Resources for ideas. In your **Job Notebook:**

- List some jobs you could do on the road.
- List another two or three jobs you *would like* to do.
- As you come across specific jobs or employers that interest you, list them in Section 3, under Potential Employers.

Finding a job will not be a problem. To take advantage of the opportunities and flexibility this lifestyle affords, you need to stop and think about your dreams and goals. What have you always dreamed of doing? What kind of work would you like to do? Where would you like to work? In the next chapter, we'll focus on identifying your dreams and goals.

---

### Key points

✍ **Attitude and perseverance are keys to job success on the road.**

✍ **RV workers have many different options for earning money.**

✍ **Most seasonal jobs require good people skills, responsibility, and common sense.**

✍ **You have acquired marketable skills in all aspects of your life: jobs, hobbies, community activities, and chores.**

# Notes

*"Do what you can, with what you
have with where you are."*
*Theodore Roosevelt*

*"Would you tell me, please, which way I ought to go from here?" asked Alice. "That depends a great deal on where you want to get to," said the Cheshire Cat.*
*Alice in Wonderland*

# Chapter 2
# What do you want to do for the rest of your life?

If you want to earn top dollar, you would probably do better staying put in your 9 to 5 job with a two- or three-week vacation. However, you are considering, or have chosen the RV lifestyle because you want freedom and adventures.

## WORKER ADVENTURES

As a working RVer you will have the opportunity for experiences you never would have had in your old life. I encourage you to look at job opportunities not only in terms of your former skills, but what you want to accomplish in your travels. Let's look at some adventures other workers have had on the road.

### A chance to really see it

Llorene and her husband worked several months one winter at Death Valley National Park. Death Valley has many fascinating and wondrous spots but they are miles and miles apart. Most tourists visit Furnace Creek and Scotty's Castle, but usually have to skip remote or less accessible sites like the Ubehebe Crater, the race track or Titus Canyon, to name a few. Since Llorene and her husband worked there, they could visit one location at a time on their days off.

> **Is there a place you have always dreamed of seeing?**

"Pristine Death Valley has many different moods. Sunrises and sunsets transform it like a kaleidoscope. Overall, it was our most enjoyable job and one we will never forget," says Llorene.

*Is there a place you have always dreamed of seeing or wanted to explore?*

## Experience the unusual

An extended stay often gives workers and volunteers opportunities to experience the unusual. Sue and Coby volunteered at Yosemite National Park. Sue's assignment was Search and Rescue (SAR).

> **An extended stay often gives workers and volunteers opportunities to experience the unusual.**

One time Sue's team was called on to rescue a man suffering from abdominal problems. Suited up in flight suit, helmet, earplugs, goggles and leather gloves, Sue was helicoptered from the valley floor to the top of Nevada Falls — a spectacular ride. That rescue was barely completed when two more hikers in the same area required evacuation. Sue ended up being helicoptered off the valley floor, flying alongside the rugged cliffs, and landing at the top of the waterfall three times in one day! Since planes are not allowed to fly low over the park, this was an experience a park visitor could not buy. Coby, not to be outdone, assisted in the release of a bear that was being relocated. It will take quite a bit to top these adventures.

*Does experiencing the unusual appeal to you?*

## Beautiful places

Working can take you to beautiful places and enhance your experience. Betty and Lin worked as freelance photographers and took photos to accompany Betty's articles. They once visited Bryce Canyon in the dead of winter to photograph the snow on the red rocks. They enjoyed the winter solitude and left with spectacular photos and memories.

For Betty and Lin, writing and photography dovetailed with RV travel. They sought places that have scenic beauty and interesting history, both natural and human. Says Betty, "The writing and photography enhance these places and help fix them in our minds." Article and photo sales rewarded their efforts with income and allowed for tax deductions as they traveled.

*Would you like to capture beautiful places in a creative way and be paid to do so?*

## Perks of the job

Workers and volunteers in tourist areas may have the opportunity to experience expensive area attractions at little or no cost. Ron and Val worked at an RV park in Haines, Alaska. Local tour operators offered them free or reduced-rate tours, providing direct experience with area attractions. This enabled them to better advise campers staying at their park. As a result, Ron and Val rafted down the Valley of the Eagles, rode the White Pass and Yukon narrow gauge railroad, and flew over Glacier Bay National Park. These experiences certainly added to their summer's memories.

*Do your travel dreams include taking special excursions like these?*

## YOUR DREAMS AND GOALS

If you stop to think about it, there are probably things you have always wanted to do but have not done. You could see Niagara Falls, visit Alaska, paint a picture, be in a play, volunteer for a national park, or work at Disney World.

---

### YOUR TURN!

Using your **Job Notebook**, brainstorm about things you'd like to do. List them with no thought to their importance or whether they are realistic. Just focus on getting them written down.

Take several days to add to your list. You might want to compare lists with your spouse or travel partner after you have exhausted your own ideas. Then, identify those items you want to focus on.

---

Don't underestimate the power of writing down your goals. Coach Lou Holtz read *The Magic of Thinking Big* by David Schwartz at age 28. Inspired, he wrote down 107 goals he wanted to achieve in his lifetime; many were lofty goals like having dinner at the White House, meeting the Pope, becoming the head coach at Notre Dame, and jumping out of an airplane. He has achieved 81 of those goals — so far.

> **Don't underestimate the power of writing down your goals.**

## Why are you working?

Work can enable you to achieve your goals and enhance your RV travels. How will working or volunteering fit into your RV lifestyle? Here are some reasons working RVers mention:

✔ **Maximize money earned:** Earning the most money in the least amount of time is a goal often mentioned. If you can work for $10.00/hour rather than $5.00/hour, it will take half the time to meet your income goal. For example, Wally & Patsy have chosen sales because they have found it makes the most money per hour for them.

✔ **Work as a way to see the country or a location:** Lester and Audrea make it a point to never work in the same location twice. In six years, they have worked in eight different states. Sometimes working RVers take less pay to work in an area they have always wanted to experience.

> **Lester and Audrea never work in the same location twice.**

✔ **Time for an avocation:** Love boats and fishing? Work at a lake or marina. Jerry loves golf. He has taken several lower paying jobs at golf courses so he has golf privileges. Paul went back to the Grand Tetons to work year after year because of the excellent fishing in Jackson Lake and other lakes in the nearby national forests.

✔ **New experiences:** Ron was a policeman in his former work life. The RV lifestyle has given him the opportunity to work at a marina and at two NASCAR races. He's done maintenance at campgrounds and sold Christmas trees. Page and Ardith explain they look for jobs that "…give us a chance to live in different places and meet different people; we like learning new things and doing different types of work."

✔ **Renewed purpose in life:** Having a sense of purpose and contributing something to the world are important for many people. Al always leaves an area better than he found it. For example, he will haul rocks to fill potholes and pick up litter. Many of our RV friends participate regularly in Habitat for Humanity builds, constructing decent affordable homes for low-income families.

✔ **Reduce expenses:** Gas and campground fees are big expenses for most RVers. Working and volunteering can reduce both. While you are in one place, your fuel costs for traveling will be zero. The money you spend on fuel will depend on how much you explore. You may get your site as part of the job or pay a reduced rate. Some employers supply shirts or entire uniforms, allowing you to save on clothing.

In addition, you may receive free or discounted propane, laundry, recreation, meals and other items. This effectively adds to your income.

✔ **Be your own boss:** Some people prefer to set their own schedules and do things their own way. They often seek ways to be entrepreneurs or independent contractors on the road.

✔**Be near family:** Working or volunteering in an area near your family can work well. You have time for visits with grandchildren or other special people while having a place to park in the area. Parking in a relative's driveway for a summer may be too close. Roy and Pat volunteer many summers at a state park not far from their daughter so they can spend time with their grandchildren.

✔**Obtain perks:** Sometimes the perks you receive on a job can help you experience an area. Besides the wonderful perks they got while working in Alaska, Ron and Val took jobs in Branson, Missouri, where they received free or reduced-price tickets for any show they wanted to see. They saw more than 20 shows in their month in Branson.

✔ **Provide for extras:** A job, or even a volunteer position, can provide money to supplement your regular income. Some RVers work for extras like a new tow vehicle or a special trip, or work when unexpected expenses leave a dent in the budget.

---

**YOUR TURN!**

Using the above reasons for working as a starting point, add your own reasons to your **Job Notebook.**

Consider also: Are you comfortable working for someone else or do you want to be your own boss?

Look at your lists. Are there any travel destinations you can achieve by meeting your goals for work? You will probably find overlap. If you do, that's great.

---

How long do any of us have to travel? Think about it and get cracking!

---

### Key points

✍ **As a working or volunteering RVer you can have unique and wonderful experiences.**

✍ **To focus on what is important to you, write down your dreams and goals.**

✍ **Working as an RVer can help you achieve your dreams and goals.**

✍ **You are in control of your life.**

---

*"The secret of success lies never in the amount of money, but in the relation of income to outgo."*
*Ralph Waldo Emerson*

# Chapter 3
# How much money will you need?

That's a good question. The answer is *very* individual. However, chances are you will need less money on the road than you did previously. While it is difficult to know exactly what your budget will be until you get out there and get some RVing time under your belt, this chapter will give you the tools to estimate how much money you will need.

## WHAT RVERS SPEND

In 2001, Stephanie Bernhagen and I polled full-time RVers, asking what they spend on average per month on the road. Results were spread out but were similar for the 324 respondents. Our poll showed that 58 percent live on less than $2,000 a month. Pages 42-44 show six different budgets that were shared with us by RVers.

For this revision, we asked several RVers to submit their budget. The six budgets included on pages 42 to 44 range from $1,098 per month for a solo who received a free RV site where she worked, to a high of $5,046 per month. This last couple had an RV payment of $2,765 per month. The other couples, who had no RV payment, had monthly totals of $1,653, $1,703, $2,505, and $3,168. (See pages 42-44 for details.)

In another poll, most RVers did say that they spend less living the RV lifestyle than they did living a "stix 'n brix' life.

| As a full-time RVer, how much money do you spend on average in a month? | |
|---|---|
| Under $700 | 11% |
| $700 -$1400 | 21% |
| $1500 -$1999 | 27% |
| $2000 - $2499 | 17% |
| $2500 - $2900 | 5% |
| Over $3000 | 18% |

Poll taken online Jan-April 2001

The cost of living the RV lifestyle varies tremendously. Working as you travel allows you to reduce many budget categories as we will see.

## MAJOR BUDGET CATEGORIES

The following are the categories I suggest you use to estimate your expenses on the road.

### RV payment

Costs for an RV can range from a few thousand dollars (secondhand) to more than a million dollars. I recommend you talk to your tax consultant about the implications of financing versus buying your RV outright. While an RV payment may decrease your flexibility, the tax benefits could make financing a better choice for you.

### Food, including restaurant meals

There are two basic ways you spend money on food: eating out or buying groceries to prepare meals in your rig. (You do have cooking facilities!) The best way to control your expense is to limit restaurant meals. Your grocery bill will probably be similar to what you spent prior to full-time RVing. However, there are factors to consider. You will not be able to buy in bulk due to lack of storage space. Grocery prices and availability will vary depending on where you are.

> **Some RVers go without any health insurance while others have complete coverage.**

### Health insurance

If you are currently covered by your employer, you can continue coverage under COBRA for at least 18 months after you leave your job. You can use this COBRA amount as a starting point to calculate your budget. If you will not have coverage, you must research what is available to you. Some RVers go without any insurance while others have complete coverage. Health care expenses vary widely because they are dependent on many factors:

✔ Your age
✔ The state where you have coverage
✔ Amount of your deductible

✔ Your pre-existing conditions and general health
✔ Smoker or nonsmoker
✔ Type of coverage

In this budget category also include any out-of-pocket expenses for items such as prescription drugs, dental work, eyeglasses, your deductible, and co-payments.

For additional information and references for finding and checking on health insurance, see Chapter 23, and **Resources.**

## Camping fees

Private RV parks charge $25-40/night, a killer on a limited budget. You can decrease this expense in several ways. If you stay a week or more, you should be able to get a reduced weekly or monthly rate. You can work for an employer who provides a free or low-cost campsite as part of the job. Two other ways to reduce this budget item are staying at federal or state campgrounds and boondocking (camping without hookups).

Some RVers purchase a membership in an RV park organization to reduce their camping fees. After the initial purchase, they pay annual dues and then reduced daily fees each time they stay at one of their member parks. I recommend waiting to join a membership park until you know your travel patterns. If you are

> **Wait to join a membership park until you know your travel patterns.**

working, you may not be able to use it enough to justify the expense. Also, before you purchase, make sure their parks are located where you plan to travel. If you are seriously considering a membership, see Alice Zyetz' column for Road Trip America. (See **Resources**.)

However you plan to camp, make sure you list all your fees, whether annual, monthly or daily. (See Chapter 23.)

## Transportation

✔ **Fuel:** Your fuel costs will be directly proportional to how many miles you drive. Take the mileage you expect to drive and divide it by your RV's miles per gallon (mpg). Take that result and multiply by an average price per gallon. If you don't know your mileage, figure that an RV with a gasoline engine gets about 5 mpg and one with a diesel engine gets about 8. For example: You have a motorhome with a gasoline engine and will travel 1000 miles per month. You expect the purchase price of gasoline to average $3.00/gal. The calculations would be the following: 1000 ÷ 5 = 200 x $3.00 = $600 per month for fuel.

When you are working in one location for several months, you will probably do less driving, and your fuel costs will be reduced.

✔ **Insurance:** Insurance will be higher for your RV than for a car. If you no longer own a house, you will need insurance designed for full-timers that covers your RV as well as its contents. If you do not have your RV yet, you can still get estimates from insurance companies on the type of rig you want. Be sure to check prices in all the states you are considering for your domicile. (See Chapter 13) Some companies listed in **Resources** for this chapter give "quick quotes" at their websites. If your policy does not include a roadside assistance service or towing package, you can purchase these coverages separately.

✔ **License and registration:** Fees for license and registration vary widely from state to state. See **Appendix 6** for contact information for all state motor vehicle departments.

✔ **Maintenance and repairs:** Be sure to set aside money for maintenance and repairs. The amount of money you spend will vary based on the age and condition of your rig, as well as your ability to maintain and repair it. Your driving habits also have an effect. The best way to minimize this expense is to take care of anything that goes wrong right away and follow your manufacturer's instructions for periodic preventative maintenance.

## Communication

For potential employers to reach you, at a minimum you need a mailing address ("snail mail"), voice mail for messages, and long distance calling cards. Occasional Internet access (free at public libraries) is almost a requirement nowadays for obtaining jobs. Most RVers have cellular phones and some Internet or e-mail access and consider these necessities. They do add to your overall expenses. Not only is there the initial cost of purchasing them, but monthly fees for phone and data plans accumulate. You may want to look at your travel and spending patterns before purchasing these extras if you don't already use them. See Chapters 5 and 6 for a complete discussion of communication alternatives.

> **Occasional Internet access is almost a requirement nowadays for obtaining jobs.**

## Other

All other expenses go here. These can include federal and state taxes, life insurance, clothing, propane, cable or satellite TV, gifts, entertainment, membership in clubs, laundry and other miscellaneous expenses. List your anticipated expenses for each item. Your RV lifestyle may decrease your costs for some of these. For example, since many jobs provide uniforms or allow you to wear casual clothes, you will save the expense of dress clothes and dry cleaning. If your RV site will be near your work place, you can walk or bicycle instead of drive, eliminating commuting

> **RVers buy fewer souvenirs and knickknacks.**

expense. Because of limited space, you will buy fewer souvenirs and knickknacks, thus spending less. In addition, you can eliminate state income tax by working in a state that has none. (See Chapter 13.)

## Some comments from RVers about expenses:

✔ It costs me more money sitting in one spot than it does on the road, mainly because of the electricity and phone hookups.

✔ We work to save up one year's money. When we get down to six month's worth, we get jobs again.

✔ House-sitting for a month saved us money.

✔ If we stay in one place for awhile, we eat out more. When we travel, fuel consumption goes up.

✔ Camping fees can vary: a monthly rate is cheaper than daily and if we volunteer, we get a free site.

✔ We have (and pay for) a storage shed for all the household items I refuse to give up!

## Sample budgets

To help you estimate your own budget, on the next three pages are several different budgets that are broken down into the seven categories we have been discussing. These budgets were submitted by five RVing couples and one solo woman RVer. They illustrate several different spending levels. Only one couple has an RV payment. It adds a considerable amount to a budget. In the case of the solo woman, working has reduced her camping fees and propane to zero as that is a job benefit. She also has free Wi-Fi, which reduces her Internet expenses, and free cable TV.

### Sample budgets

| Budget between | $1500-$1999 per month | $3000-$3500 per month |
|---|---|---|
| **RV payment/housing** | $ 0 | $ 0 |
| **Food, including restaurants** | $ 160 | $ 760 |
| **Health** | | |
| Medical insurance | $ 124 | $ 377 |
| Other medical expenses | $ 118 | - |
| **Camping Fees** | | |
| Membership parks & campground fees | $ 300 | $ 392 |
| **Transportation** | | |
| Fuel | $ 150 | $ 116 |
| Insurance, incl. towing | $ 157 | $ 244 |
| License & reg. | $ 17 | - |
| Maintenance | $ 200 | $ 271 |
| **Communication** | | |
| Telephone and Internet | $ 20 | $ 135 |
| Mail service | $ 17 | $ 38 |
| **Other** | | |
| Clothing | - | $ 135 |
| Gifts | $ 0 | $ 105 |
| Laundry | $ 20 | - |
| Life insurance | $ 47 | - |
| Memberships- clubs | $ 20 | - |
| Federal/state taxes | $ 21 | - |
| Propane | - | - |
| TV/satellite | $ 36 | $ 60 |
| Misc. | $ 20 | $ 589 |
| **Total** | **$ 1,653** | **$ 3,168** |

Note: Not each couple specified the same budget categories. Where you see a "dash," the couple did not break out an amount for that particular category. I suspect that Couple 2 lumped spending on several categories under "Miscellaneous."

## Sample budgets

| Budget between | Less than $1500/month | $1500-$1999 per month |
|---|---|---|
| RV payment/housing | $ 0 | $ 0 |
| Food, including restaurants | $ 200 | $ 563 |
| **Health** | | |
| Medical insurance | $ 120 | $ 106 |
| Other medical expenses | $ - | $ 94 |
| **Camping Fees** | | |
| Membership parks & campground fees | $ 0* | $ 260* |
| **Transportation** | | |
| Fuel | $ 100 | $ 45 |
| Insurance, incl. towing | $ 100 | $ 110 |
| License & reg. | $ 10 | $ 32 |
| Maintenance | $ 20 | $ 60 |
| **Communication** | | |
| Telephone and Internet | $ 60* | $ 80 |
| Mail service/PO box | $ 6 | $ 12 |
| **Other** | | |
| Clothing | $ 20 | $ 17 |
| Gifts | $ 2 | $ 29 |
| Laundry | $ 12 | $ 30 |
| Life insurance | $ 0 | $ 81 |
| Memberships- clubs | $ 18 | $ 6 |
| Federal/state taxes | $ 400 | $ 100 |
| Propane | $ 0* | $ 20 |
| TV/satellite | $ 5* | $ 58 |
| Misc. | $ 25 | - |
| **Total** | **$ 1,098** | **$ 1,703** |

* Workamper benefits reduce or eliminate this cost.
Note: The first budget is a solo Workamper's, the second is a couple's budget.

## Sample budgets

| Budget between | $2500-$3499 per month | More than $3,500/ month |
|---|---|---|
| **RV payment/housing** | $  0 | $2,765 |
| **Food, including restaurants** | $  454 | $  500 |
| **Health** | | |
| Medical insurance | $  472 | $  54 |
| Other medical expenses | $  162 | $  84 |
| **Camping Fees** | | |
| Membership parks & campground fees | $  112 | $  142 |
| **Transportation** | | |
| Fuel | $  215 | $  608 |
| Insurance, incl. towing | $  220 | $  185 |
| License & reg. | $  23 | $  32 |
| Maintenance | $  327 | $  158 |
| **Communication** | | |
| Telephone and Internet | $  74 | $  200 |
| Mail service/PO box | $  20 | $  - |
| **Other** | | |
| Clothing | $  13 | $  58 |
| Gifts | $  - | $  42 |
| Laundry | $  - | $  - |
| Life insurance | $  - | $  - |
| Memberships- clubs | $  - | $  17 |
| Federal/state taxes | $  - | $  84 |
| Propane | $  2 | - |
| TV/satellite | $  - | $  50 |
| Misc. | $  411 | $  67 |
| **Total** | **$2,505** | **$ 5,046** |

Note: Where you see a "dash," the couple did not break out an amount for that particular category. Couple 1 lumped spending on several categories under "Miscellaneous."

## YOUR TURN! DEVELOP A BUDGET FOR WORKING ON THE ROAD

A budget is essential for knowing how much money you require. This, in turn, will determine how much you need to work. (See instructions on the next page.)

| (Per month) | Now | Full-timing |
|---|---|---|
| **RV payment/housing** | $ | $ |
| **Food, including restaurants** | $ | $ |
| **Health** | | |
| Medical insurance | $ | $ |
| Other medical expenses | $ | $ |
| **Camping Fees** | | |
| Membership parks & campground fees | $ | $ |
| **Transportation** | | |
| Fuel | $ | $ |
| Insurance, incl. towing | $ | $ |
| License & reg. | $ | $ |
| Maintenance | $ | $ |
| **Communication** | | |
| Telephone and Internet | $ | $ |
| Mail service | $ | $ |
| **Other** | | |
| Clothing | $ | $ |
| Gifts | $ | $ |
| Laundry | $ | $ |
| Life insurance | $ | $ |
| Memberships- clubs | $ | $ |
| Federal/state taxes | $ | $ |
| Propane | $ | $ |
| TV/satellite | $ | $ |
| Misc. | $ | $ |
| **Total** | $ | $ |
| | X 12 = _____/yr | x12=_____/yr |

**YOUR TURN!**

**Instructions for developing a budget for working on the road:** To develop your budget, complete the chart on the preceding page. In column one, use figures for what you are currently spending per month. Use estimates if you don't have exact figures. Next, refer to the budget categories on the previous pages to estimate what your full-time RVing expenses will be and enter them in the second column. If you don't have a firm number for a budget item, use a range based on your research to date and spending patterns from column one. *Hint:* One RV couple noted, "We kept track of our expenses for 18 months and found that the minor things we hadn't thought about are what add up in expenses." (Some examples would be postage, newspapers, and snacks.)

*Note:* If you want a more detailed budget or further explanation see **Resources.** An additional Budget Worksheet is provided in **Appendix 8. Appendix 9** is a comprehensive budget worksheet Stephanie Bernhagen used in her seminar for Life on Wheels. Full-time RVing books cover budgeting for RVing in more detail as well.

## HOW MUCH DO YOU NEED TO MAKE PER HOUR?
## WORK 25 INSTEAD OF 50 WEEKS A YEAR

An almost universal goal for working RVers is to have more time off than the standard two-week vacation. In fact, most RVers would like to only work 25 weeks a year. There are three factors to consider to achieve that goal: amount of annual income needed, hourly rate earned, and number of weeks worked.

Now that you have an estimate of how much money you need, let's look at the **Earning Charts** on the following page that show the relationship between the hourly rate and the number of weeks worked. The amounts in the first chart are based on one worker; the second shows the amounts for two workers.

| Earning chart: One person working | | | | |
|---|---|---|---|---|
| Hourly rate | 1 week | 25 weeks | 37 weeks | 50 weeks |
| $6.00/hr | $240 | $6,000 | $8,880 | $12,000 |
| $7.00/hr | $280 | $7,000 | $10,360 | $14,000 |
| $8.00/hr | $320 | $8,000 | $11,840 | $16,000 |
| $9.00/hr | $360 | $9,000 | $13,320 | $18,000 |
| $10.00/hr | $400 | $10,000 | $14,800 | $20,000 |

| Earning chart: Two people working | | | | |
|---|---|---|---|---|
| Hourly rate | 1 week | 25 weeks | 37 weeks | 50 weeks |
| $6.00/hr | $480 | $12,000 | $17,760 | $24,000 |
| $7.00/hr | $560 | $14,000 | $20,720 | $28,000 |
| $8.00/hr | $640 | $16,000 | $23,680 | $32,000 |
| $9.00/hr | $720 | $18,000 | $26,640 | $36,000 |
| $10.00/hr | $800 | $20,000 | $29,600 | $40,000 |

Suppose you have determined that the two of you will need to earn $18,000 a year. Looking at the above chart for two people working, you can earn this amount by each working for about $6.00/hour for 37 weeks, or by each working for $9.00/hour for 25 weeks.

If the chart does not fit your exact situation, here are three methods you can use. Substitute your own numbers for the ones used below.

### I want to work 25 weeks. How do I figure the hourly rate I will need?

1. Divide your total income needed by 2 to figure the amount each person will need to earn. ($18,000 ÷ 2 = $9,000 each)
2. Divide by the number of weeks you want to work. ($9000 ÷ 25 weeks = $360 per week)
3. Divide that result by 40 hours. ($360 ÷ 40 hours/week = $9.00/hour)
4. You will each need to earn $9.00/hour.

**We each have job offers earning  $7.50/hour. How many weeks will we need to work to earn $15,000?**
1. Divide your total income by 2 to figure the amount each person will need to earn. ($7,500)
2. Divide by the hourly rate. ($7,500 ÷ $7.50 = 1,000 hours)
3. Divide by 40 hours/week. (1,000 hours ÷ 40 = 25 weeks)
4. You will need to work 25 weeks or half a year.

**We each have job offers earning $6.50/hour. If we work 21 weeks, how much will we earn?**
1. Multiply the hourly rate by 40. ($6.50 x 40 = $260/week)
2. Multiply the result by the number of weeks you will work. ($260 x 21 = $5,460)
3. Double the amount to get the total for two. ($5,460 x 2 = $10,920)
4. Together you will earn $10,920 at these jobs.

You can earn the amount you need from one job or work at two or more jobs for shorter amounts of time. Alternatively, you can throw in an extra short-term job. For example, we sold Christmas trees for three weeks and made a quick $3,000. Our other jobs provided the rest of what we needed to earn for the year.

## YOU CAN DO IT!

This chapter demonstrates that you have many options. A reasonable budget doesn't mean you can't have any fun. One couple who spends about $1500 a month parked a week in Tucson taking in a concert, a play, the movies, eating Thai, Chinese, Middle Eastern, Ethiopian and Italian food. After they left, they boondocked out in the desert to bring their budget back into balance.

If you want to take a job that pays a bit less because it fulfills a dream, work a little longer. On the other hand, you might settle in for awhile and work at a higher-paying job to build up your savings or to take a special trip. You may want to work a few hours a day or just a couple of days a week so you have plenty of time to relax or explore. The beauty of this lifestyle is the flexibility. There is no right or wrong way. If you don't like a job or a location, you can leave. If you are having fun, you can stay longer. Put together the life that works for you.

## Key points

✍ **Full-time RVers can live on less than $2500 a month.**

✍ **You can control or reduce expenses in all budget categories.**

✍ **How much you earn is a function of how much per hour you make and how many weeks a year you work.**

# Notes

*"Money is better than poverty,
if only for financial reasons."*
*Woody Allen*

# SECTION II. NITTY GRITTY OF GETTING WORK TO SUPPORT YOUR RVING

## Chapter 4
## Finding jobs that fit your lives: Getting started

I want you to have the money you need while making the most of your RV lifestyle. That means finding well-paying jobs or moneymaking opportunities located in areas where you want to be so you can explore or do the things you enjoy. Working and volunteering should add to the enjoyment of your lifestyle.

The first step is to know what you want or need. If you have skipped the first three chapters and haven't identified what you want out of your travels, you may end up disappointed in your RV lifestyle. As Ben Stein (writer/actor/game show host) said, "The indispensable first step to getting the things you want out of this life is this: decide what you want."

### YOUR TURN! FOCUSING EXERCISE
Look at your income goal, dreams and skills that you identified in **Section I.** Select the ones that are most important to you in each category. To focus your thinking, in your **Job Notebook,** consolidate this information into a short chart:

| | |
|---|---|
| **Type of work you can do** | |
| **Type of work you want to do** | |
| **Travel goals: hobbies** | |
| **Travel goals: places** | |
| **Income: annual amount** | |
| **Number of weeks to work** | |

## A JOB THAT FITS YOUR LIVES

Finding a job on the road is easy if you will take any job. Getting a job that fits all your needs and goals will take effort on your part, but can be done. You may not satisfy all your goals in your first job, especially if you need to earn more than minimum wage; however, if you work at it, you can eventually achieve the goals you summarized in the above chart.

> **"We wanted a job that fit around our lives."**

Rob and June's search for employment illustrates this process. Both were very definite about what they wanted to do. They figured the income they needed each year, what parts of the country they wanted to be in, and what dates they wanted to be there. Then they contacted many, many companies before they found a match. "There is a ton of work out there," says June, "but many jobs were in locations where we didn't want to be or at times that were inconvenient for us. More often than not, the companies wanted a greater time commitment from us than we wanted to give." They did find a match. Adds June, "After having spent years in corporate America making our lives fit around a job, we wanted a job that fit around our lives."

### Focus:

✔ *Is there a particular job or location you want to focus on next season? Circle or highlight your choices on your chart.*

If you still aren't clear on what you'd like to focus on, spend some additional time familiarizing yourself with the job market. Use the **Job List** and examples in the chapters in **Section III**. Also look through *Workamper News* and take a look at websites listed in **Resources** (Chapter 9). You will get the most benefit from the next chapters in this section if you select one job to focus on.

✔ *Is there a match between what you want to do and what your skills support?*

**Yes, you have a match:** For example, if you want to work in maintenance and have done these types of tasks in maintaining your own home, then *someone* will hire you as a maintenance person. If you'd like to deliver RVs with your pickup truck and you have some road time, you will find job opportunities.

**No, you don't have a match yet:** You may want to do something for which you lack qualifications, training or experience. You can still get started on the path to earning money and getting that job. Some companies provide training. For example, Princess Land Tours and Gray Line Bus Tours provide training for their bus drivers each year. If you would like to deliver RVs and do not have enough experience pulling an RV, you can get another driving job, one without hauling, while you acquire road time. Do some investigating. Courses in the skill you need may be available. **Section III** includes information about a number of training courses available.

## Getting started

To find a job that meets your goals, you want to apply to enough jobs so you have two or three job offers to choose from. Look at the process of finding a job like an inverted pyramid or funnel:

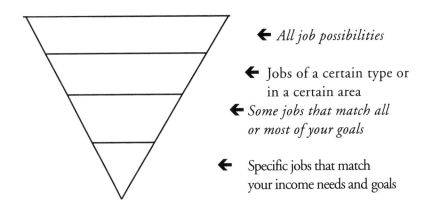

← *All job possibilities*

← Jobs of a certain type or in a certain area

← *Some jobs that match all or most of your goals*

← Specific jobs that match your income needs and goals

In order to get the job you want, you must set criteria and then narrow down the available jobs to find those that match your goals and income needs. As you work through job possibilities, most will fall by the wayside because they don't meet one or more of your criteria. Remember, employers go through a similar selection process, screening out employees who aren't a match to find the best candidate.

You must start with many job prospects to make this process work so that you have two or more good job offers to consider. The next story illustrates the importance of having many options and what can happen if you don't.

## OUR DREAM JOB: THE JOB THAT FIT AROUND OUR LIVES

When Bill and I hit the road, we began looking for summer jobs in December. Our dream job was to work in maintenance for the National Park Service (NPS) at Grand Teton National Park. Our second choice was to work in a national park in any location.

We figured that the larger parks with campgrounds would hire more seasonal maintenance workers, so using AAA trip planning books, we identified 20 western national parks with campgrounds. I made up a chart, listing each park and their telephone numbers. I started calling to find out if they hired seasonal maintenance workers and when they put out their job announcements. I recorded the date to call back, crossing those off who weren't hiring. As I followed up, I recorded the action I took and the step of the process we were in. (Now job announcements for the National Park Service can be found at USAJOBS website *www.usajobs.gov* or via NPS website *http://home.nps.gov/applications/digest/usajobs.cfm*)

> **Our dream job was to work in Grand Teton National Park.**

At the same time, we subscribed to *Workamper News.* For any job that looked like it might pay more than $6/hour, we followed up with either a résumé or telephone call. We also participated in the Workamper Referral System (replaced now by the Awesome Applidants database), making our résumé available to employers through *Workamper News,* and received several calls as a result. We contacted and screened an additional 30-plus employers. We narrowed this list down to acceptable job offers at two locations in case a park job didn't come through.

As each job announcement from a national park came, I completed the paperwork. We applied to twelve parks. We both got offers at the same two parks and one of them was the Tetons!

### Year 2

Our second year on the road, we learned the hard way why lots of contacts are important. We assumed we would go back to the Tetons so we applied to only two other parks. We missed a step in the re-hire process and there were changes in management. We weren't going back.

Then it was a mad scramble. We applied to employers advertising in *Workamper News* and checked their hotline. We had a number of offers but not in the same pay range we had earned our first summer. We took a position in Minnesota, driving all the way from California. It didn't work out. Right after we quit, Bill was offered a position in a national park in Colorado. We spent a lot of money driving halfway across the country twice, as well as losing time traveling and working for lower wages.

How much effort you need to put into your job search depends on how closely your experience matches the job requirements, how important your goals are, and how much you need to earn. In our case, with no experience working for the government, and determined to get positions with the National Park Service, we were willing to put in a lot of effort. We had offers at state parks and RV parks that first year, but the pay wasn't as good and those locations weren't our first choice. Now that we have experience with NPS, getting positions is much easier. However, we have learned to never count on just one possibility.

The remainder of **Section II: Nitty Gritty of Getting Work to Support Your RVing** will prepare you for acquiring the position you want and cover the mechanics of getting a job on the road.

### Key points

✍ **Apply for many jobs that meet your criteria so you have a better chance of getting job offers to choose from.**

✍ **Start with jobs that meet both your income and your travel goals.**

✍ **Keep your options open.**

# Notes

*"Persistence is what makes the impossible possible, the
possible likely, and the likely definite."*
*Robert Hall*

*"For every obstacle there is a solution — over, under, around or through."*
*Dan Zadra*

# Chapter 5
# How employers and family can reach you: Getting mail and phone calls on the road

To get jobs, you must be able to contact and be contacted by employers. You'll need to be able to receive employment information and applications in a timely manner.

## RECEIVING MAIL ON THE ROAD

How do you get your mail when traveling? RV clubs as well as private businesses provide mail forwarding services to RVers.

### Mail forwarding

While some RVers have family members forward their mail, many prefer a professional mail forwarding service so that mail is sent out the day requested, rather than at a family member's convenience. You pay a fee for the service as well as for postage and supplies.

When you sign up for a mail forwarding service, you have all your mail sent to their address with your personal mailbox number (PMB) on it. You then instruct the service where and when to send your accumulated mail.

Mail forwarding services vary. Some forwarding services send out mail according to a set schedule. Others require one or two days' notice. More personalized services will check at your

> **Correct formatting of PMB addresses:**
> *PMB 251*
> *113 South Way Dr.*
> *or*
> *113 South Way Dr., #251*

request to see if certain pieces of mail have arrived or even read that letter to you.

RV clubs like Family Motor Coach Association (FMCA), Good Sam, and Escapees RV Club provide mail forwarding for members. Private mail box providers like PostNet will also forward mail, but are usually more expensive than services set up exclusively for this task. You can find advertisements in RV publications for other mail forwarding services geared to full-time RVers.

Before signing up for a mail service, compare costs and services. Talk to RVers using them and see if they are doing a good job. Consider also the state you will choose as your domicile. This address will be part of establishing your domicile.

## Where do you pick up your mail?

If you will be in a location long enough for your mail to reach you, you can have your mail forwarded to the nearest post office in care of General Delivery. If you are working there for the season, you may need to rent a post office box or find an alternative place for mail delivery. Post offices vary on how long you can receive General Delivery mail; it can be as little as 10 days to more than 30 days. You might be able to have mail delivered to your employer or the RV park where you are staying, with their permission. Unless the RV park or employer has separate tenant or employee mail boxes, we prefer renting a mail box at the post office so we receive our mail as soon as it arrives, rather than have to track down our mail each week.

> **When traveling, forward your mail to the nearest post office in care of General Delivery.**

If you are traveling and decide to have your mail forwarded to you, figure out where you'll be in five to seven days and have it sent to that post office in care of General Delivery. Verify whether that post office accepts general delivery mail by calling the location or the toll-free U.S.P.S. number below. Some locations don't. If a town has several zip codes, only one will accept general delivery mail. To obtain the correct zip code, or verify that a post office accepts general delivery mail, call the U.S.P.S. toll-free number, 800/275-8777 or check at *www.usps.com*.

If your travel plans change and you can't be at that town when you expected, call or drop the Postmaster a card so that post office holds your mail until you arrive. We have had mail returned to sender because the mail handler didn't recognize our names or we didn't pick it up in a few days. If your mail forwarding service has already sent out your mail and now you won't be going to that location—or you will not be able to wait for its arrival—complete and turn in a change of address card. Your mail will be forwarded to the new address. Unfortunately, it may take a couple of weeks or more for your mail to catch up with you when you do this.

Mail at best can be iffy, as I'm sure we've all experienced. Be prepared for frustrating waits. If you are on a tight time schedule and waiting for something important, you may want to pay extra to have it sent Express Mail, Federal Express, or by another overnight carrier. Be aware that Express Mail can take two days to arrive at many rural locations.

To use Federal Express, UPS or other carrier, you need a physical address. You could use an RV park or perhaps a relative's address. A mail store, like PostNet, might accept it also, perhaps charging a fee. In small towns, the general store may agree to accept your pack-

> **The general store may agree to accept your UPS or FedEx package.**

age. And if there is a UPS or FedEx office in that town, make arrangements to have your parcel sent to their office and held until your arrival. You will need to have the package properly labeled. Contact the local office or call their toll-free number. (See **Resources.**) In any case, make sure it is expected so the delivery isn't refused and returned to sender.

If time is important, have mail sent from an employer directly to your current location or to a location where you will arrive in a few days. Going through your mail service could delay your mail for up to two weeks, taking you out of contention for a position.

For an even quicker response to a job opening, you could have the application faxed or sent by e-mail. For a fee, you can receive a fax at businesses like Kinko's or PostNet. You can receive the faxed application via the Internet if you have occasional access or can stop at a public library with Internet access. Sign up for e-Fax *(www.efax.com),* RapidFax *(www.rapidfax.com)* or other services that provide a personal fax number. You receive the fax as an e-mail attachment. Another option is receiving an e-mail directly from the employer, which is even faster if you can get online. (See Chapter 6 for information about e-mail on the road.)

Make it easy for employers to send applications or information to you. However you get employment information or applications from an employer, be very clear about where to send it, spelling out anything that might get misspelled. If mail is being sent to general delivery, don't apologize. Explain that you are traveling and that you will get it more quickly this way. Make sure you return applications or other requested materials as soon as possible. Clear communication is a way to sell yourself to an employer.

## RECEIVING TELEPHONE CALLS AND MESSAGES

The two main options for working RVers for getting messages from potential employers are cellular telephones and e-mail.

### Cellular telephone service

Companies like AT&T, Sprint and Verizon have national or one-rate plans that allow you to call anywhere in the U.S. for a low rate per minute. Many of these plans charge for roaming if you use your phone in an area that is not in their coverage or do not allow you to make a call at all.

> **Most RVers travel with one or more cell phones.**

✔ **Your budget:** Pick a plan that matches your budget. Be realistic. If you exceed your alloted minutes, extra minutes can cost a lot. If your plan offers free evening and/or weekend minutes, take advantage of that time to make most of your calls.

✔ **Voice mail:** Be sure you know how to access your voice mail. Check messages regularly when you are job hunting, even if your phone doesn't prompt you. In some areas, you may not receive a message alert.

✔ **Roaming charges:** Calls that cannot be completed on the supplier's network may have roaming charges so find out when and if you will be charged for roaming. Read the fine print.

✔ **Internet capable:** If you plan to use your cellular phone for retrieving e-mail and accessing the Internet, you need an Internet-capable phone or smart phone. You'll also need a data plan at an extra charge.

✔ **Service area:** Will you be traveling and working primarily in areas that have service? RVers who work or travel a lot in remote locations may find they have to drive a distance or climb hills to make calls or retrieve messages. Many plans require a one- or two-year contract. Check to see if you can suspend your plan in the event you spend several months working in an area with no coverage.

## Voice mail

At one time RV clubs provided voice mail service for members. With fewer pay phones and the availability of cell phones, most have dropped their service. A Google search on the Web *(www.google.com)* is one way to locate a voice mail service.

## E-mail

More and more RVers are relying on e-mail as their main way to keep in touch. Many RV parks have Wi-Fi so RVers have Internet access and can check e-mail or

> **Make it easy for employers to reach you.**

post on Facebook and other social networking sites. You can send a résumé as an attachment to an e-mail. With a high speed connection, you can use Skype *(www.skype.com)* to have a conversation over the Internet without using cell phone minutes. You can also send and receive e-mail on smart phones. See Chapter 6 for more information on Internet access and e-mail.

Make it easy for employers to reach you. If you will have limited access to your phone or the Internet, let the emplouyer know that on your cover letter, your voice mail greeting or via e-mail before you are without access. If other applicants are easier to reach, some employers may give up trying to reach you. Whatever method you decide upon should be easy to use and sound professional. Make sure you check your messages daily and return calls or e-mails promptly. How you handle calls and messages gives an employer an impression about the kind of employee you will be. Make sure the impression you leave is a positive one.

---

### Key Points

- ✍ **Have a professional-sounding way employers can leave a message for you.**
- ✍ **Return calls and reply to e-mails promptly.**
- ✍ **Comparison shop and talk to other RVers about cell phone and mail forwarding services.**

---

# Notes

*"We are what we repeatedly do. Excellence then,
is not an act but a habit."*
*The Goals Guy at www.goalsguy.com*

*"A computer lets you make more mistakes faster than any invention in human history — with the possible exceptions of handguns and tequila."*
*Mitch Ratcliffe*

# Chapter 6
# How to use a computer in your job search

Do you need a computer to find and get jobs on the road? The answer is both yes and no. Yes, it will make the job search process easier and no, you can get by without your own computer. While paper and pen can work if you decide not to get one right away, it is a real asset in organizing and tracking information as well as enhancing the materials you send out to employers. Some computer literacy is now essential for many jobs.

## ADVANTAGES OF USING A COMPUTER

### Professional looking résumés and cover letters

While you could use a typewriter to type your résumé and cover letter, computers make it much easier. You can easily update your information and tailor your résumé and cover letter for a particular job without having to retype the entire document again or pay someone to do it. Since your documents are saved, you simply make the revisions you want and print out the revised document. You can print out a crisp copy of your résumé whenever you need one.

> **You can revise your résumé easily without having to retype it.**

### Error reduction

The spell-check feature of most word processors reduces typographical and grammatical errors. However, you still need to proofread carefully so that *there* isn't a *their* or *they're*. When the spelling is correct, but the word is wrong, your spell checker will not catch it.

### Time-saving software

You can purchase résumé software programs at computer or office supply stores that provide templates for résumés. One may come with your word processing program. This will allow you to present your information in a professional format and easily update it. Plus you can save copies for future reference.

### Internet job searches

When you have Internet access through mobile broadband or using Wi-Fi at an RV park or coffee shop, you can use your own computer for job searches. (See Chapter 9.)

## COMPUTER LITERACY—KEY TO MANY JOBS

The companion question to "Do I need a computer?" is "Do I need to be computer literate?" Computer literacy gives you an advantage in the job market. It not only opens up new and effective job search techniques, but can also improve your marketability and help you get many jobs.

> **Many jobs require computer knowledge.**

More than half of jobs nowadays require some computer skills. Computer use is growing in service industries. Many more jobs now require the use of a computer, computerized machines or data input devices than a few years ago. More and more RV parks and campgrounds are using computerized reservation software. The ability to use one or more programs helps in obtaining jobs.

Computer programs are easier to learn now. Microsoft's Windows has become the industry standard. Software programs written for Windows have the same menus and toolbars. Once you've learned one program, others will be easier to learn. Having your own computer allows you to learn software programs at your own pace.

Other ways you can learn about computers or specific software packages like reservation software:

✔ **Use built-in tutorials** that come with some software. Books and CDs for specific software are often available at computer stores.

✔ **Take any company-offered training** that is available.

✔ **Ask a fellow employee** to help you learn a computer application for work when it won't interfere with productivity.

✔ **Volunteer** where you will be able to pick up new skills.

✔ **Check with your temporary agency.** Larger agencies offer courses to employees working for their agency.

✔ **Check at a community college** if you will be in the area for the length of a course.

✔ **Investigate training through state job service offices.** Every state has a job service. Counselors may be able to connect you with training classes to upgrade your skills, particularly if you are on unemployment.

✔ **Locate a Senior Net Center.** Senior Net is a nonprofit organization that provides adults aged 50 and over with education for and access to computer technology with 240 Learning Centers in 38 states.

✔ **Purchase a training CD or video.** Learn a reservation system on your own. Check online for the software; many companies have a downloadable training program.

✔ **Ask your computer vendor** if they offer any free or low-cost computer training if you purchase a new computer.

---

### Other uses

These computer applications can make your traveling easier or more enjoyable:

- **Mapping programs** like Street Atlas USA or Streets and Trips will map out routes, and compute mileage.

- **Databases** or listings of free places to park have been developed by RVers. Instead of carrying reams of paper or a book, it is all on the computer and easily updated.

- **Financial programs** like *Quicken* keep records of the money you spend.

- **Software for hobbies** like genealogy and photography store and organize your information.

- **Correspondence** with family and friends is easier with a computer. Some RVers produce family newsletters.

- **Writing or graphics programs** could be used to earn money; for example, designing and printing business cards.

- **Save photos** from your digital camera or scanned prints. This saves space in your RV. You can even post your photos in a personal website or blog for family and friends to view.

## CHOOSING A COMPUTER
With so many kinds and models of computers, how do you choose one?

### PCs or MacIntosh computers?
Both PCs (personal computers) and Macs have their advantages. There are more programs written for PCs than Macs, though Macs are easier to learn. Most employers, however, use PCs, which tend to be cheaper.

### Laptop vs desktop computers
Laptop computers are portable and take up little space. You can also send and receive e-mail more easily with a laptop.

Desktop computers take up more space and need to be anchored while traveling. As of this writing, you can get started with a desktop or a laptop for under $500 that will be suitable for e-mail and word processing. You do get more for your money with a desktop than a laptop.

The main advantage of a laptop is that you can carry it into a place that

> **You can send and receive e-mail with a laptop ...**

has wireless Internet access (or Wi-Fi.) Businesses like Starbucks, Barnes and Noble, Kinko's, and many public libraries and truck stops are Wi-Fi "hotspots" or provide wireless Internet access. The signal could be available for a few hundred yards so RVers with a desktop computer could pick up the signal if they can park within range. A laptop offers more options. A netbook is even smaller, though does not have a CD drive.

Power needed to operate your computer is a consideration, especially if you are boondocking. You will need to use an inverter or run your generator to operate your desktop. The size inverter needed will depend on the power draw of your computer. Make sure the invertor supplies adequate power or you could damage your computer. A laptop can be run off its battery though it must be periodically charged by plugging the laptop into a small inverter while traveling, or with any 110 volt electrical source. A second battery would be handy.

### Selecting a model
If you have never owned a computer, a good resource that covers basic knowledge about computers is *Campin' and Computin' — The Second Editon: A Basic Guide for RVers New to Computers:* by Eric Anderson. *The*

*Digital RV* by Richard Charpentier covers choosing a laptop computer, computer maintenance, and getting Internet on the road. To learn more about connecting on the road see RVer's Computer Help (*www.rverscomputerhelp.com*). Do a Google search (*www.google.com*) for "RVing and computers" for more information.

You can get started with a basic model, but if you plan to use a digital camera or work with graphics, you will need more of everything, especially hard drive space and memory. Nearly all new computers have built-in Wi-Fi or a wireless networking card, which enables you to access the Internet at a hotspot. Since what is considered minimum in the way of hard drive and memory changes rapidly, it would be a good plan to check with a reputable dealer or have a knowledgeable friend help you make your decision.

### Before you buy

The decision to purchase a computer is an individual one. If you have never used one, I'd suggest using the computers in libraries to see how they work and find out if you are "computer-compatible." You will have much more information at your fingertips and be able to apply for positions more easily; however, do research before you buy. Talk to others and see what features you might use and what fits your budget.

> **Before you buy, find out if you are "computer compatible."**

If you decide not to buy a computer right away, simple supplies like a pen, paper and a box of CDs will work. You can store your résumé on a CD and then use a computer at a copy shop to print out copies as you need them.

## USING YOUR COMPUTER FOR E-MAIL

E-mail is a low-cost way to keep in touch and another method for communicating with employers, many of whom are now online. If you have a laptop computer, you can get e-mail on the road. Many truck stops and RV parks have a Wi-Fi hot spot. If you are within a few hundred yards or so of a hot spot, you can connect to the Internet. Some Wi-Fi access requires paying a fee; access to others is free.

You first need an e-mail address, then access to your e-mail.

## E-mail options

**Web-based e-mail:** You can sign up for a free e-mail account at Hotmail, GMail or at Yahoo. When you are on any computer, you can go to their website and check your e-mail.

**Internet provider:** Some RVers still subscribe to an Internet provider like Earthlink or AOL. These can be useful if you need to access your e-mail or the Ineternet using a landline. If you have satellite Internet or a smart phone, you can have an e-mail account with them. A Web-based e-mail gives you the most flexibility, though, and stays with you if you change providers.

## Access:

**Public computers:** Most public libraries now offer free Internet access to the public or you can pay to use a computer at businesses like Kinko's.

**Cell phones:** You can send and retrieve e-mail on your laptop computer using your digital cellular telephone as a modem or you can purchase a separate modem along with a connectivity kit. Most newer laptops have a built-in cellular-capable modem card. To purchase one may run as high as $300, though you can find one for less by shopping on the Web. The adapter or cable could range from $30 to $100.

> **Get a free Hotmail or Yahoo e-mail address.**

Newer PCS or tri-mode phones can connect digitally to the Web and retrieve e-mail, with or without a computer. The phone acts as the modem so your computer does not have to have one. To connect to your computer, you use a connectivity kit ($50 to $75).

Verizon, AT&T, Sprint and T-Mobile have small cellular devices that are PC cards that slide into a slot in your computer or that plug into a USB port. These mobile broadband modems replace what Verizon called the Aircard. Verizon also has a "MiFi" unit or compact wireless router, which receives a signal and allows up to five Wi-Fi enabled devices to access that signal.

**Smartphones:** 3G phones such as iPhones, Droids, BlackBerry and similiar products have been developed so people could have a small portable phone that would be like a mini-computer for storing information and working with documents. They can act as a GPS device if that service is activated. They can send and receive e-mail and retrieve webpages. More webpages are being formatted for mobile applications and are easier to read and download. All sorts of applications or "apps" have been developed and are being developed for these phones, things like receiving real-time traffic reports, weather reports and much more. To access the Web using a 3G phone, you will need to subscribe to a data plan in addition to a cell phone plan.

**Wireless connections:** Wi-Fi (Wireless Fidelity) offers high-speed access to the Internet and is becoming more available. Most networks are not secure so you should take precautions before making a transaction over it. The main drawback with Wi-Fi is that there are so mny providers. Each business offering Wi-Fi can require a password so you must pay several dollars per day before using it. Subscribing to one service won't give you access on another's. Fortunately, Starbucks, McDonald's, Borders, Barnes and Noble and even many RV parksare now offering free Wi-Fi.

You may be able to pick up a Wi-Fi signal that is not secured and doesn't reauire a password. If you are in range, you can use that signal. You can purchase a Wi-Fi detector for this purpose so you don't have to turn on your computer first. Note: Some locations have made picking up an unsecured Wi-Fi signal illegal.

> **Wi-Fi and satellite Internet offer high-speed Internet access.**

**Satellite Internet:** High-speed, two-way satellite Internet is also available. DataStorm includes automatic targeting software. Hughes (formerly DirecWay) and Starband offer a service that requires aiming your dish to find the satellite each time you set it up—much like satellite TV. Hughes and Starband are more reasonably priced than DataStorm.

Some RVers with satellite Internet use a wireless router that broadcasts a signal not only within their own RV but into the surrounding area. Other RVers can piggyback on that signal. If a password is required, the owner must give permission. However, remember the satellite Internet owner is paying for the service you are asking to use free of charge so they may say no.

> **Several small devices can be used for e-mail.**

**iPad and other devices:** People are also using the iPad device to send and retreive e-mail. It is small, making it easily carried to locations where you can access a signal. Netbooks are small versions of laptop computers and are also easy to carry around. In both cases, the keyboard takes some getting used to. You can obtain a netbook at low or no cost from a cellular provicer, but in that case, you must also purchase a data plan.

The Peek device is a mobile device strictly for e-mail and texting. It can be synched with a regular computer.

## COMPUTER WORK AREA

While newer RVs often come with computer work areas, ours did not. We modified our motorhome to accommodate our desktop computer. We replaced the dinette with a desk made of Formica placed on two two-drawer file cabinets. I had a nice place to work and file cabinets to store our records. A side benefit was more space in the kitchen-dining area.

Our 5th wheel was designed with a work area but we added a tray for a keyboard, which we can use with a laptop. We also have a Wilson antenna and booster for our Internet signal.

The other modification we made was to install several 12-volt fluorescent lights. They are much brighter for computer use and for reading, and pull less power. We also installed a 110-volt fluorescent light above my computer to use when our RV is plugged into an electric source.

---

### Key Points
✍  **Make your job search easier with a computer by storing résumés and cover letters that can easily be revised, updated and printed out as needed.**
✍  **Computer literacy is an advantage in finding jobs.**

---

*"Efforts and courage are not enough
without purpose and direction."*
*John F. Kennedy*

# Chapter 7
# How to prepare résumés and cover letters for working on the road

## RÉSUMÉS

Although it is unlikely you will need a fancy, detailed résumé, you will still need a written summary to show the employer why you are the right person for the job.

You can prepare a résumé on a computer or typewriter that will work for most positions and look professional, or you can have one professionally done. If you have a computer, you can target your résumé for each job.

You can purchase résumé software and books with models or templates to use. (See **Resources**, or save money by checking out books at the public library.) A model for a functional résumé is on page 77.

Before sending out your résumé, be sure to check it over carefully for errors. Misspellings and grammatical errors indicate sloppy work habits to a prospective employer. Ask a friend or spouse to proofread your résumé.

**In a survey of human resource managers, respondents gave this advice for résumés:**

- ◆ **Grammar and spelling 100% correct**
- ◆ **No typos**
- ◆ **Personalized cover letter**
- ◆ **No more than two pages**
- ◆ **Emphasize accomplishments**
- ◆ **Concise and well-written**

*1999 Résumé Survey Report by Morris Assoc.*

## Résumé categories

Categories you often see on résumés, usually in capital letters and bold type, are

✔ Objective
✔ Work Experience
✔ Skills (or Computer Skills)
✔ Education
✔ Remarks or Interests
✔ Foreign Languages
✔ References

Choose the categories that match the position and your background. For most jobs on the road, I recommend omitting "Education" unless it directly correlates to the job at hand. Having a Master's degree in biology is not relevant to working as a cashier in a retail establishment and might make the employer wonder whether you'd be happy doing such work. On the other hand, a college degree or courses in accounting should be listed if you are applying for a bookkeeping or accounting position. Other categories like foreign languages would be appropriate if you might be dealing with customers speaking this language in this particular position; otherwise omit it. Sign language skills make you more valuable and should be noted.

## Objective

Start with your objective:

*"Work as a maintenance man, using skills from a variety of trades."*
*"Work as cashier or sales staff in a retail establishment."*

For a couple seeking a position together, "Couple seeks assistant manager position at an RV park or campground."

If you are having someone else prepare your résumé and won't be able to customize it to fit each job, leave the objective rather general, unless you will only be applying for one type of job.

> **Use a chronological résumé when your work experience matches the position.**

## Chronological or functional résumé

There are two types of résumés: chronological and functional. Use a chronological résumé when your work experience showcases or matches the skills you need for the position. For example, you are applying for a night auditor position and you have worked for an accounting firm or other establishments in the accounting department. You would also use a chronological résumé when you are applying for a campground manager position and you have several years of working on the road as manager or assistant manager.

**Use a functional résumé when your work experience does not match the position.**

With a chronological résumé, "Work Experience" would be your next category. List your work experience from most recent back at least ten years. Key accomplishments are listed or briefly described. Include relevant experience even if it was more than ten years ago.

If, however, your work experience does not match the type of position you are seeking, a functional résumé can showcase your abilities to your advantage. Some examples where a functional résumé would be better:

- ✔ You are seeking a maintenance position but have never held one. You have done the upkeep on your house, added on a room, and completed all the repairs. You helped your neighbor build his garage.
- ✔ You have no experience working in a campground office, but you have worked in customer service. You are familiar with computers and get along with people.

In a functional résumé, the category "Skills" would follow your objective. List your skills in a bullet list or use the skills needed for the position as your categories or headings, such as "Communication Skills" or "Maintenance Skills" and describe how you have used these skills. Perhaps you used them in your hobby or in a community activity. That experience is valid and will be considered, but a chronological résumé will not point this out as effectively. To pick out logical categories, use your knowledge of the job or the job description.

In a functional résumé, skills should be followed by a brief listing of employers for the last ten years.

You can also list relevant skills in a chronological résumé after your work experience. If you have knowledge of certain computer programs or can operate equipment listed in the job description, this would be the place to name them.

## Volunteer or unpaid experience

Volunteer experience and unpaid experience related to the position are valuable and should be included. They will sound more impressive if you state your jobs or skills, rather than "volunteer."
*"Fund-raiser, Non-profit agency, 2002-2004."*

## Remarks or Interests

In the "Remarks" or "Interests" category you can include hobbies, civic activities or other information that might show your good character or relevant experience. For example, if applying to an RV park, "RVer for fifteen years" would show you are familiar with RVs even if you have only recently begun full-time RVing. "Member of the Kiwanis" indicates time spent in community service and implies that you like dealing with people.

## References

For references, you can either list at least three references if you have room  or simply be prepared with a type-written list ready to send off as soon as an employer requests it. If possible, have more than three employers lined up to use as references, especially if you will be applying to many jobs. That way, former employers won't get overwhelmed with telephone calls from potential employers.

> **Always ask permission to use someone as a reference.**

To speed up the process, request letters of reference from each employer and include copies with your résumé. When I left my last job before we began full-time RVing, I requested a letter of reference. My boss even suggested I write it! I wrote two: one detailing the tasks I did in case I wanted a similar position, and a second one stressing my good work habits. My boss happily signed both. I copy and include the appropriate one.

Always get permission to use someone as a reference. Pick references who will speak well of you and remember who you are. Employers have told me they called a reference who had no memory of the applicant.

## One page

Stick to one page, unless you are applying for a technical or professional position and have a lot of relevant experience. For a couple, you can send either both of your individual résumés or write a one-page couple résumé. Often for seasonal work, the employer will have you complete an application even if you have sent a résumé. The résumé is a screening device.

## Electronic résumés

If you are searching for a position in your former industry, you might want to post your electronic résumé at a job search site that has similar listings.

Résumés for the Internet are formatted differently. With literally millions of résumés posted on the Web (Anderson Consulting alone receives four million résumés a year), employers now search databases of résumés by keywords. These terms, including industry terms, buzz words, professional jargon, skill-focused words and commonly used trade terms for that industry are listed in a separate category at the top. Look at the larger job search sites for articles and tips for online résumés. (See **Resources.**)

## Awesome Applicants résumés

WorkamperPlus subscribers to *Workamper News* can post a résumé in the online Awesome Applicants® searchable database. After completing a short form about the type of work you are looking for and availability, you write a short narrative description about yourself. Employers can set search criteria to come up with a list of candidates to contact. You can also e-mail your Awesome Applicants résumé to any potential employer with an e-mail address.

## THE COVER LETTER

When you mail or e-mail your résumé to a prospective employer, always include a cover letter. The cover letter expresses your interest in the position and highlights how your experience and skills match the employer's needs. You also ask for an interview and let the employer know how you can be reached. If you have a gap in employment, such as in the model résumé on page 77, you can explain. For example, "We began full-time RVing in 2009 and, after traveling for a year and one-half, we are now seeking summer employment."

The cover letter should be one page, in business format, typed or word processed, if possible. If you must hand write it, write or print neatly in ink.

## Photos

If you are applying to a private employer, you could also enclose a recent photo of yourselves. Include a photo of your rig too, if your rig will be parked on the premises. Some employers will request them. We took photos of the two of us and our motorhome and made 20 copies of each to include with our applications and résumés. Do not include a photo when applying for a government position. While it is illegal for an employer to ask for a photograph, sending one does beat driving to the location for an interview, especially if it is halfway across the country.

## TELEPHONE RESPONSE

If a telephone number or e-mail address is given in the ad instead of an address, your call or e-mail will be similar to a cover letter. The employer is probably using these to pre-screen potential employees or needs to hire someone fairly quickly. In this situation you want to find out the next step. It may also be an opportunity to get more information to see if the position is a match.

A sample functional résumé and a cover letter follow.

---

### Key points

- ✍ **The purpose of a résumé is to get you an interview or to be considered.**
- ✍ **Résumés can be chronological or functional, depending on your experience.**
- ✍ **The cover letter introduces you, highlights your experience and asks for an interview.**

---

Example of a functional résumé

## JOHN E. WORKER
### PO BOX 321
### ANYWHERE TX 77388
#### 800/609-4892
#### worker5@aol.com

**OBJECTIVE:** Work in an RV park or campground in maintenance

**SKILLS:**

**Maintenance**

Maintained factory equipment and machinery on the job. Used a variety of skills to maintain house and property including plumbing, carpentry, appliances, and simple electrical repairs. Also landscaped yard, mowed one acre of lawn using riding mower, trimmed grass and plants, planted and cared for large vegetable garden and flower gardens. Did all maintenance on own vehicles including cars and motorhome. Added a wooden deck to front of house and remodeled bathroom and bedroom.

**Communication**

Dealt with customers; determined needs as well as problem solving and handling complaints. Supervised and trained eight workers. Organized and oversaw fund-raising event for community service club.

**Operate equipment**
* Forklift
* Backhoe
* Riding mowers

**WORK EXPERIENCE**

**1995-2007** Acme Widgets Factory, San Antonio, TX - Supervisor
* Supervised eight assembly workers.
* Trained new-hires.

**1985-94** Widgets Deluxe, San Antonio, TX  - Factory sales rep.
* Called on industrial clients.
* Planned projects.
* Customer service: troubleshooting, expediting orders, resolving complaints.

**Other:** Worked as plumber's helper, Christmas tree lot worker, sales and customer service.

**REMARKS:** Member, Lions Club, Den leader for Cub Scouts. Full-time RVer since July 2007.

**REFERENCES:** Available on request.

Sample cover letter

**JOHN E. WORKER**
**PO BOX 321**
**ANYWHERE TX 77388**
**408/609-4892**

January 14, 2XXX

Sam Johnson
Happy Valley RV Park
PO Box 431
Happy Valley, CA 92042

Dear Mr. Johnson:

I am responding to your ad in RV Magazine for a maintenance worker to work in your RV park this summer. Enclosed please find my résumé.

My wife and I began full-time RVing in 2007, and after traveling for a year and a half, are now seeking summer employment. I have excellent maintenance skills and have maintained buildings and grounds. I have worked extensively with the public and enjoy people. I am a responsible worker and will do whatever it takes to get the job done.

I would like the opportunity to talk to you about the position. I can be reached on my cell phone at the above number or by e-mail. I check telephone messages once a day and e-mail about every three days.

I look forward to hearing from you.

Sincerely,

John E. Worker

*"Find a job you like and you add*
*five days to every week."*
H. Jackson Brown

# Chapter 8
# How to do a job search

Now that you have your résumé prepared, let's get on with the job search. (This chapter emphasizes print sources, while Chapter 9 focuses on using the Internet.) Follow these three rules for a successful job search. A successful job search will result in two or more job offers.

## THREE RULES FOR JOB FINDING SUCCESS

Rule 1: **The more jobs you apply for, the better chance that you will have choices when you have gone through the job search process. If it all works as planned, you will have two or more job offers to consider that meet your criteria.**

Rule 2: **Each contact is an opportunity to show your good work qualities and professionalism and to sell yourself.**

Rule 3: **Keep your options open.**

## FIVE STEPS TO LOCATING A JOB

1. **Identify** at least twenty employers who meet your criteria for type of work and location(s).
2. **Contact each one.** Send your résumé and cover letter or contact the employer by telephone or e-mail. When you find an employer who is not hiring, you can add another to take its place. For a job that has potential, even if the employer is not currently hiring, ask if you may send your résumé for consideration if an opening occurs in the future.

3. **Follow up** with each employer providing whatever is requested. Also follow up after mailing your résumé to make sure it was received and after the interview to thank the interviewer, keeping in mind Rule 2: *Each contact is an opportunity to sell yourself.*

4. **Use each step of the process** — résumé or application, interview, follow up calls, negotiations — as a screening process to eliminate employers who are not a match, keeping in mind Rule 3: *Keep your options open.*

5. **Choose** the best overall job offer.

> **You do not need to see a help-wanted ad before contacting an employer.**

In this chapter and the next, we will look at the various sources for finding job leads and potential employers. Remember, you do not need to see a help-wanted advertisement before contacting an employer. Some of the best-paying jobs are uncovered by contacting an employer directly. It shows initiative on your part, which many employers value. Follow up on anything that looks promising. If a job offer doesn't result for the upcoming season, add it to your **Job Notebook** for future reference.

## PRINT RESOURCES FOR LOCATING JOBS

**Section III, Job List and More Than 350 Moneymaking Opportunities,** lists dozens of employers and refers you to specific resources for similar employers. A few key sources are listed below.

### Seasonal jobs

✔ ***Workamper News:*** Lists hundreds of jobs for RVers in zip code order, including private and public employers as well as paid and unpaid positions. You'll find listings for positions working for RV parks and resorts, national forest concessionaires, amusement parks, and others, plus volunteer opportunities. Forums, articles on Workamping®, Jobinars and Webinars are excellent resources. Check their bookstore also. A subscription is helpful to keep a finger on what's available and how much employers are willing to pay. WorkamperPlus subscribers can receive the daily Hotline e-mail listing jobs that did not make the print issue or need to be filled quickly.

✔ *Caretaker Gazette*: Lists a variety of site-sitting jobs, from exchange for site to house couple positions that pay as much as $100,000 a year with benefits. It also includes overseas listings.

✔ **RV publications:** General RV magazines occasionally have employment and volunteer listings. Check their classified section.

## Geographic job search

Some useful sources if you are looking for a job in a specific area are:

✔ **Campground directories:** *Woodall's* and *Trailer Life* are two of several available that have listings of RV parks throughout the U.S. and Canada. If an RV park has more than 100 sites, you can be sure they will need extra help during their busy season, but don't rule out smaller parks. Parks with fewer sites but lots of amenities may still be hiring, though they are more likely to offer a site in trade for hours worked. Contact them directly or make an in-person inquiry. Use these directories to supplement print ads for locating other RV parks in the area.

✔ **Classified employment ads in newspapers:** Local newspapers are a source of temporary and seasonal jobs. You will find job fairs listed there too. If you won't stay long enough to work, check the Sunday paper anyway. Some seasonal employers schedule interviews during the winter in southern cities like Phoenix and Los Angeles for summer positions in other areas and advertise in the classifieds.

✔ **Tourist publications:** Annual state and regional travel guides list resorts, RV parks, and major tourist attractions in the area. You can pick these up at information centers along the interstate highways as you enter a state, or call the state's tourist bureau (See **Appendix 1.**) Browse through travel magazines at the library or newsstands for ideas and phone numbers.

✔ **Free employment publications:** Metropolitan areas often have free job or career publications in newspaper dispensers and at public libraries. These weekly magazines have job listings and announce local job fairs.

> **Be creative!**

✔ **Lists of local employers:** State employment service job centers, located in many cities throughout a state, as well as local chambers of commerce, often have print lists of major employers. Look in the government pages of the telephone book or on the Web to locate these centers.

Be creative. A job that requires travel or work at different locations may dovetail with the RV lifestyle. An excellent opportunity may be only a phone call away. Dean and Judy saw an ad in a Phoenix paper for a job installing bathtub liners. They got the job – traveling from hotel to hotel around the country making about $70,000 a year, with benefits and generous time off.

## NETWORKING

The old adage "It's not what you know but WHO you know that counts" applies to working on the road as well. It can mean the difference in finding well-paying, pleasant situations versus getting stuck in a position that seems to last forever and loses money overall. Most situations aren't that black and white, but developing a network saves time and money. In fact, even with the use of the Internet added as a job search tool, making a personal connection is vital. Says JoAnne Smith, consultant with career-management firm Drake Beam Morin of Boston, "... the majority of jobs are still found through networking."

### What is networking?

In her book, *You Shoulda Listened to Your Mother,* Alice Zyetz defines networking as "the development of contacts or exchange of information to help you build, maintain or change your career." Alice advises "Don't overlook any activity that involves people" as a chance to network.

> **360,000 people are only one contact away.**

At a sales conference I attended, the instructor said most people have casual contact with at least 600 people. Each of these knows 600 more people, which means 360,000 people are only one contact away. An astounding 216 million people are only two contacts away. Most anyone in the U.S. is reachable in just a few contacts — but you have to ask.

### Informational interviews

How can we network while traveling from spot to spot? One way to develop your network while learning about jobs on the road is to set up an "informational" interview. You interview an employer with the purpose of finding out more about the job. For example, you are considering working at an RV park, but you don't know that much about it. You make an appointment at the park you are staying in to find out about jobs at RV parks. Most people are delighted to share information.

Interestingly enough, an informational interview often leads to a job offer. "While one out of every 200 résumés — some studies put the number as high as 1,500 résumés — results in a job offer, one out of every 12 informational interviews results in a job offer," says Katharine Hansen, author of *A Foot in the Door: Networking Your Way Into the Hidden Job Market.* "That's why informational interviewing is the ultimate networking technique, especially considering that the purpose of informational interviewing is not to get job offers."

### Others are willing to help

Alice Zyetz continues: "When you network with other people, you find out what jobs are available, what's happening in the industry. When you're new to the job, you want to know what jobs pay, what kind of work people do on the job, where the jobs really are, who has available jobs and names of additional contacts. You shouldn't be ashamed or embarrassed to do this," admonishes Alice. "Others have been in your shoes and are willing to help you as they were helped themselves."

She adds, when you identify someone who might lead to a contact, ask "WHO DO YOU KNOW WHO....? (sells X product, works in Blank City, works for X company or in X industry)."

> **Others are willing to help.**

As I related in our RV work story, before we hit the road, we took a trip from Pennsylvania out west and back. We met a young maintenance worker at Grand Teton National Park and asked her how she got her job. We then stopped at the personnel office and learned we'd need to apply in January for summer jobs. Job announcements are only open for a short time so we might have missed the opportunity to apply without this prior knowledge. Two summers later, we too were working in maintenance at the Grand Tetons with an RV site overlooking Jackson Lake.

By building your network, you'll acquire contacts for both employers and other RV workers willing to give you job leads. Ray and Pat decided to look for a job mid-summer. They posted a note on an RV discussion board on the Internet asking if anyone knew of employers looking for workers to finish the season. Within a few days they had received several possibilities. They called one of the suggested employers and were both offered jobs working for the concessionaire at Mesa Verde National Park.

Forums on working on the road are another way to make contacts and obtain information. Look at Workamper.com, Escapees.com and RV Net.

## Don't give up!

If you don't get a certain position that first season, don't give up. Most sales of products to a business result after a minimum of seven contacts. You are selling yourself, so keep in touch. If at all possible, meet the person who makes the hiring decision, or at least keep in phone contact. When there is an opening, either later in the season or the following year, you will have a decided advantage.

## Find out about moneymaking opportunities

On several occasions, we had talked to RVers about their experiences selling Christmas trees. It didn't sound appealing. One couple had sold trees in the frigid Midwest and had electricity for only an hour a day. Then friends told us about their experience managing a lot in Texas. Kathy had heard about it from "Frenchy," an RVer she met in the laundry room. The word spread through our group of friends. That next winter, six couples who had talked to Kathy and husband Gene sold Christmas trees for the same owner.

From talking to Kathy and Gene we knew this owner followed through on his promises. We also knew questions to ask like, "Will we have hookups?" From talking to others as well, we could evaluate this owner's compensation offer and know that being paid a salary plus $1.00 per tree sold was above average pay.

> **Kathy had heard about selling Christmas trees from "Frenchy," an RVer she met in the laundry room.**

Working for any small business owner has its frustrations. Many RVers have years of business experience and don't always agree with business practices and decisions they see. We've heard of two owners we would not work for through our contacts. Christmas tree selling has some of its own built-in frustrations like delivery trucks from Christmas tree farms that don't arrive on time. With Gene and Kathy as our mentors, we had more realistic expectations.

Each communication with a working RVer can lead to contacts and job ideas. By talking to others you can also learn about both the good and the bad aspects of a job or employer, and thus better evaluate whether a job is a good match for you. Take advantage of this resource.

## Finding the perfect job

Ron and Val are very effective at using networking. They enjoy working in RV parks. They use contacts they make in one RV park to line up jobs in areas they want to work or jobs they'd like to do. They are able to find and check out potential employers through other RV workers they meet on the job. On their off-season, they stop at potential employers if their travels take them nearby.

These meetings give Ron and Val a chance to meet the employer and check out working conditions. More importantly, it gives them an advantage if they decide to apply. If they are not offered a job on the spot, (although they frequently are), they are no longer an unknown quantity to that employer. If Ron and Val can't visit, they might have a mutual acquaintance who would tell the employer about them, raising them above the other unknown applicants. One year Ron and Val spent a month at Silver Dollar City in Branson, Missouri with co-workers from their summer job who were returning to Silver Dollar City for another stint. The biggest perk? Free tickets to all the shows!

> **They stop at potential employers if their travels take them nearby.**

John and Wanda have found that selling a product at fairs and home shows gives them the kind of schedule they like. They have developed contacts with other vendors, and according to Wanda, "There are lots and lots of opportunities out there." These contacts have enabled them to research other products and job possibilities that are more compatible with what they want in a job. They were looking for a vendor willing to ship the product to the shows, rather than having to transport it themselves. Some products like Swedish Back Massage machines were oversaturated at shows, which would limit their income. As a result of talking to others, they found a new product to represent that was a match for their goals.

## Practical networking tips:

✔ **Talk to other RVers about their jobs:** Make it a practice to ask other working RVers about their jobs. Keep your antennea out. If someone is working at a job that looks interesting or has potential, or you overhear someone talking about a job, ask them about it. Most RVers are very willing to help others. And let others you meet know about the places you'd like to work or employers you are considering. You might get good feedback or ideas. Record these in your **Job Notebook.** Be willing to share what you know. Others will be more likely to reciprocate when they learn about something that might interest them.

✔ **Talk to potential employers:** If you stay at an RV park that looks like it has potential, introduce yourself and make an appointment to talk to the owner. If you visit an attraction you'd enjoy working for, go to the hiring official or manager. Introduce yourselves and find out about work opportunities. You may not want a job then, but you'll have an advantage if you decide to apply later.

✔ **Keep in touch:** You never know when you might be able to help each other out. In your **Job Notebook,** keep notes of people you meet, contact information and what you learned.

## YOUR TURN! BEGIN YOUR JOB SEARCH

**Job Search chart:** You have identified the type of work you want to do or are willing to do and the location you want to work for the upcoming season. In your **Job Notebook,** make a chart of the 20 or more employers you plan to contact, along with their contact information. (See sample chart on the next page.)

- Make five columns: initial contact, sent application/résumé, interview. Leave room for notes or comments.
- In the comments, write in the date that it is due or the date completed, so you can see where in the process you are. If you need to make a phone call at a certain time, or have an application in by a certain date, highlight it or do whatever it takes so you don't forget it. You may miss an opportunity with an employer, as well as lose credibility, if you miss a deadline.
- If an employer doesn't pan out this season, cross the name out and focus on the ones still active. As you find other prospective employers, you can add them to your chart.

| Employer | Initial contact | Sent applic/ résumé | Interview | Results/ comments |
|---|---|---|---|---|
| Tom's RV Park | Mar 4 | Mar 5 | April 2 | Call back 4/15 |
| Aramark | Mar 5 | Mar 5 | Mar 28 | offer in Housekeeping |
|  |  |  |  |  |

In the next chapter, we'll look at using the Internet for your job search.

---

**Key Points**
✍ Quantity of possible employers leads to quality of job offers.
✍ Networking is the key to long-term success as a working RVer.
✍ Everyone is a potential contact, either for job information or as a connection to someone who has information.

# Notes

*"Commitment is a line you must cross. It is the*
*difference between dreaming and doing."*
*The Goals Guy at www.goalsguy.com*

# Chapter 9
# How to use the Internet to locate a job

## THE INTERNET

The World Wide Web has a number of resources for working RVers. Websites have job listings, including some sites limited to seasonal work opportunities. Employer websites frequently have employment information and often applications can be completed, printed out or requested online. You can use the Internet for researching an area or type of work. You can also locate information that will help you in your working travels, such as online campground directories. You'll find the Internet is a valuable tool for locating a job.

### Using your own computer

If your computer has a a built-in Wi-Fi card or wireless modem, or you have a telephone hookup and modem, you can access the Internet with your own computer. Many RV parks have either Wi-Fi or a data port available. Truck stops and other retail establishments may have a Wi-Fi signal. Often public libraries have a Wi-Fi signal as well.

If you have your own Internet access, through a broadband modem, satellite Internet, or a provider so you can use a landline, you will have a monthly cost. If you rely on using unsecured Wi-Fi networks, you will not have a consistent, reliable method of getting a signal. (Fair warning: no one method works 100 percent of the time.) Data plans generally run from $29.95 a month to $59.95 a month, or more, depending on the provider and how much data you can trasnmit and recieve.

> **The Internet is a valuable tool for locating a job.**

## Finding Web access on the road

If you don't want the expense of connecting to the Internet for a short period of time, have no way to do that, or you don't even own a computer, you can still access the Web. Grants have enabled public libraries in even very small towns to provide public Internet computers. Even better, this service is free. At public libraries, you can usually sign up for a half-hour to an hour at a time. Rules vary; some libraries allow you to continue working online if no one is waiting while others have a strict time limit.

Also check for access at colleges and even coffee shops, called cyber cafes. We have found public computers in tiny towns at bookstores!

If your computer has Wi-Fi capability you can often be within a few hundred feet and share a high-speed Internet connection. Wi-Fi "hot spots" can often be found at truck stops, Starbucks and other coffee shops, bookstores like Barnes and Noble, and at more and more RV parks. Newer laptops have built-in connections, or you may be able to purchase a PC card for an older one.

> **Check for Internet access at libraries, colleges, and cyber cafes.**

You can sign up for free Web-based e-mail services that you can access from any computer. You'll be able to send and receive e-mail when you are online. Hotmail *(www.hotmail.com),* GMail *(http://mail.google.com/mail)* and Yahoo! *(www.yahoo.com)* are three popular Web-based e-mails. When you are connected to the Internet, go to the site and follow instructions. You will choose a user name and password. Check your e-mail by going to the site when you are online, typing in your user name and password, then going to your "in-box."

If you haven't used a computer to do an Internet search, you can read or purchase a beginners book, such as *The Internet for Dummies,* ask a librarian to get you started (if he or she is willing and not too busy), or ask most any nine or ten year-old child for help! The two charts, "Computer Terms for Internet Searches" and "How to do an Internet Search" can be used to assist or remind you once you have some basics. Further information on using the Internet for job searches can be found at the Job Hunters Bible *(www.jobhuntersbible.com)* and the Riley Guide *(www.rileyguide.com).* Both have useful links too.

## COMPUTER JOB SEARCH

These are important resources and tools for your Internet job search. Take time to browse through these websites when you have computer time. These will also give you ideas of jobs that are available. These websites will be mentioned again when they are good sources for openings for one of the job categories in **Section III** and are listed in **Resources** for easy reference.

### Seasonal job leads

✔ **Coolworks:** *(www.coolworks.com)* Start your online search here. There are more than 60,000 seasonal-type jobs at this one site alone. Employers are divided into categories like national parks, ranches, RV jobs. When you click on an employer, you are often connected right to the employer's website. There you can usually request an application via e-mail, print one out, or in some cases, actually complete your application online.

✔ **Workamper News:** *(www.workamper.com)* Lists featured employers, career opportunities, business and income opportunities, positions in the field of motorsport and subscription information for their print publication. WorkamperPlus subscribers can post their résumés online in a searchable database, rate employers, and participate in the forums, as well as receive the Hotline (last-minute jobs) via e-mail. Subscribers can also list a free "situations wanted" ad.

> **The Internet is useful when you are targeting a specific area.**

✔ **Additional websites:** Other websites that specialize in seasonal work are listed in **Resources.**

### Locating jobs in a specific area

You may be targeting a specific area or be looking for a particular employer. Here is how you can locate that type of information:

✔ **Employers websites:** To find the website of a specific employer in mind, do a search of the employer's name using a search engine like Google *(www.google.com)* or MSN.com *(www.msn.com)*. Scroll down the matches. You will likely find your employer.

# COMPUTER TERMS FOR INTERNET SEARCHES

**Tool bar:**  At the very top of the computer screen is a list of words starting with "file." Below that is the tool bar. Pictures or *icons* stand for the function of each one. If you move the mouse arrow over the icon, hold it there for a few seconds, often what it stands for will appear. The two arrows indicate forward and back. You can start a search by clicking on the "search" icon in the tool bar.

**Search engine:**  It searches through the Web and lists all the matches it finds to the word or words you are looking for.  Google *(www.google.com)* is a popular and effective search engine.

**Search:**  Look up a topic. The search engine searches the Web for matches and returns them in a list of choices called "hits." Ten are displayed at a time. When you click on one, it takes you to that address. Click on the "back" arrow to return to the search results.

**URL or address:** This is found near the top and is the code that tells how to find the website. URLs start with *http://* followed in most but not all addresses by *www*.

**Scroll:** Move up or down the screen or the webpage. You can put the mouse pointer on the the scroll bar along the right side of the screen and hold down the left mouse button, then move your mouse to move the display up or down. Or you can click on the black arrows at each end of the scroll bar. Page Down and Page Up and the arrows on the keyboard do the same thing.

**Links:** Usually these are words that are underlined in a different color. If you click on these using your left mouse button, you will go to a new site. If you want to return to the original, click on the back arrow on the tool bar just above the screen.

**E-zine:** Electronic newsletter.

✔ **State and town websites:** Search for a town, like "Skagway, Alaska," for example. You will find the city visitor bureau site and the Chamber of Commerce. Their lists of tourist attractions, RV parks and major employers will identify potential employers and places to stay. (For a description of how we found jobs in Alaska, see **Appendix 10**.)

✔ **Newspapers:** Many newspapers have their employment ads on the Web. If you know the name of the newspaper, search for that. (See **Resources:** Newspapers on the Web.)

## Other job search sites

There are a number of online job sites where you can search for jobs and/or post your résumé. Monster.com *(www.monster.com)* and Career Builder.com *(www.careerbuilder.com)* have high ratings from job seekers. All fifty states have their local job banks online too. Go to *(www.ajb.org)* and on the home page, find links to state job banks (State Gateways).

If you have a trade or professional skill and are seeking an assignment or project in your field, these are good sources too. There are sites which specialize in computers, technology or engineering, for example. You can also search websites of temporary and placement agencies for your particular field. (See Chapter 20.)

## Help with résumés and interviews

Don't overlook information on obtaining jobs at job search websites. Many have help with résumés and interviews. In **Resources** for this chapter are listed several websites that will be useful. You can find sample résumés to use as templates and "do's and don'ts." See Chapter 7 about posting your résumé online.

---

**Key points**

- **Take advantage of the Internet even if you don't own a computer. Many public libraries and colleges make online computers available to the public.**
- **Find useful information on the Internet about a town or area, or about an employer's job openings.**

---

# HOW TO DO AN INTERNET SEARCH

**Start:** Most libraries start with a page where you can do a "search." (If not, click on the "Search" icon or ask for help from the librarian.) Click the cursor using the left mouse buttton at the line where you can type in your topic, type it, and then hit the "enter" key or click the mouse on the "search" button. The symbol in the top right corner will start moving to indicate it is searching. When the search is completed, the first ten choices will be displayed. Scroll down and pick out the most likely one. Click on the underlined title (often in blue) and it will take you to that site. You will probably find "links" to other related sites. If that choice doesn't look promising, click on the "back" arrow at the top and you will go back to your original list. If none are a match, you can either click the button for the next ten choices at the bottom of the results page or refine your search. Click on the appropriate button at the end of the ten choices.

**Search engine:** If Google is not the default search engine, you can get to that at *www.google.com.*

**The Maze:** Searching the Web is like going through a giant maze. Through the use of "links" and the back button, you can explore many offshoots of your topic. Remember, the blue underlined words or phrases are links. "Back" takes you back one page or address. You can go forward, then backup and go down another path.

**Go to an address:** You may have a site you want to check out. If you have an address like *http://www.coolworks.com,* follow these steps: Above the screen is a place where the address for the page your computer is currently displaying, beginning with http://. Click the mouse there. Delete the current address by using the backspace key and then type in the address *exactly* as written. (You can start with *www.*) Don't add any spaces. Once you've typed in the whole address exactly, hit the enter key and you should go to that address. *Hint:* if that doesn't do the trick, go back to search and type in the name of the website or the key words. More often than not, your site will be listed in the results.

*"A window of opportunity won't open itself."*
*Dave Weinbaum*

# Chapter 10
# How to interview and get results

You've found a listing for a summer job and sent in your résumé. Now you have a message requesting that you call back for an interview. Before you make that callback, review what an interview should accomplish and prepare your questions and key responses.

## GOALS
Your goals in the interview are to

✔ Find out if the job and the employer are a match.
✔ Sell yourself as the best candidate.
✔ Establish the groundwork for a good employee-employer relationship and good communication.

The interview is your chance to sell yourself and make yourself shine. If you are successful the employer will be thinking how fortunate he is that you applied. "I'd better grab that couple before someone else offers them a job. They're just what I am looking for."

> **The interview is a chance to sell yourself.**

You want to find out if this job is a match for you. It may meet your dreams as far as area of the country or type of work. Does it meet your income goals? *Is this an employer you'd like to work for?*

If you ask the right questions, you can learn a lot about what it will be like to work there and for this individual. Besides finding out the basic information, be alert to things he mentions. "Several workers quit in mid-season last summer." This could be a red flag and is certainly worth getting more information. "Oh? What happened?" could be your reply. Be fair, but read between the lines.

Keep in mind, employers have similar goals. They want you to have enough information to determine if you are interested in this position. If the job is a match, then they want to determine if you are the best person they could hire for the job. Making a mistake in hiring is very costly to their business.

## PREPARING FOR THE JOB INTERVIEW

With many seasonal jobs, your interview will take place by telephone. Some companies do require an in-person interview, though perhaps not at the job site. For example, one winter we interviewed with Aramark officials from the Denali National Park location in Phoenix, Arizona. Major companies, like Princess Land Tours, will have two telephone interview sessions: one to tell you about the company and answer any questions you have. If you are still interested at the end of that interview, they will set up a second interview and ask a standard set of questions. For most other companies, the interview is likely to be less structured.

> **Making a mistake in hiring is costly to the employer's business.**

### Find out about the job

If you have certain things you will not do, now is the time to make this clear. I call these *knockout* factors: they would knock this job out of consideration for you. If your refusal disqualifies you, so be it. It is important to clarify these things before you accept the job and drive all the way there. For you too, accepting a job that is not right for you or has unpleasant surprises is costly. The costs are not only the expense of a trip to that location, but the lost wages that you could have made elsewhere.

Have pen and paper handy when interviewed and take notes. These are the questions or categories employers should tell you about, and if they don't, you should ask about each of the following:

✔ **Duties:** What you will be expected to do. If you have a concern about having to clean restrooms and it is not mentioned, for example, you must ask for clarification. If you have a high conviction about doing or not doing something, such as cleaning restrooms or working on Sunday, and it could be a knockout factor — for you or the employer — now is the time to ask.

✔ **Pay:** Are you paid by the hour or by salary? Does part of your work time go to "pay" for your site?

♦ **Hourly:** Though the Fair Labor Standards Act (FLSA) established minimum wage and overtime rules, not all businesses are covered. Certain small seasonal, recreational businesses are exempt. Also be aware that minimum wage varies from state to state and is less than the federal minimum wage in some states.

> **Get an agreement that any extra hours will earn extra pay.**

♦ **Salary:** If you are paid a salary, precisely how many hours are required and will you be paid extra or overtime pay for hours beyond that? If not, beware: Your effective hourly rate will drop.

♦ **Site plus pay:** If you are working for your site, and you work beyond that time, will you get paid? If you are working for pay and a site, clarify how many hours of work are required for the site and get an agreement that any hours beyond that amount will be paid.

♦ **Overtime:** At what point will you get paid overtime pay? Some industries are exempt. If you are on salary, there may be no overtime pay. Note that not all salaried positions are exempted from being paid overtime for hours beyond 40 in a week. In any case, an employer can require reasonable overtime. However, you should be compensated for it.

✔ **Work schedule:** How many hours per week will you work? Is it the same all season? Some employers expect six-day weeks during the busy part of their season with fewer hours at the beginning. If you are depending on a certain income, you need to find this out up front. If you and your spouse want two days off together, get that agreement from the employer during the interview or you may find you only have one day off or different days off. If you plan to explore the area, different work schedules could eliminate this job from consideration.

Find out whether you and your spouse will have the same shifts. If you will be driving to the job site, you may need the same hours to share transportation.

✔ **Length of season:** Make sure you are honest with employers about when you can arrive and when you will leave. Not honoring your commitments makes it hard for other RV workers. Employers are relying on you, particularly if they also hire college kids who leave early for school. In addition, for workers staying their full contract, some employers pay a bonus based on total hours worked, while others may refund rent paid for your RV site. This money could amount to another week or two of pay. Don't blow it.

> Some employers offer a bonus for staying your full contract.

✔ **Tools:** If you will be working in maintenance or mechanics, does the employer provide the tools or do you? If you do, does your compensation reflect that? If you do use your own tools on a routine basis or to supplement the ones provided, put a colorful piece of electrical or duct tape on yours so they don't wander off.

✔ **RV site:** Will an RV site be provided? Are full hookups available and included? It would be inconvenient if the whole season you have to move your rig every week or two to dump. Is your space level? (If you are talking to a non-RVer, get specific. We've been told more than once we had a level site and it was anything but level.) Shaded or in sun? (This can be a factor if it is hot, or if you need to use your solar panels.)

✔ **Cost of RV site:** At what cost to you? It is critical to find out this information. You will need to know a dollar figure before going into negotiation in the next chapter. Find out the number of hours you need to work or the dollar amount you will be paying.

✔ **Required occupancy:** If a site is provided, can you get a written statement stating that your positions require occupancy? If you are required to live onsite, the employer can deduct the expense and you do not have to pay income tax on it. If you are not required to live onsite and an RV site is part of your compensation, you could owe income taxes on the fair market value of that site. (See Chapter 13.)

✔ **Uniforms:** Are uniforms required? If so, who provides them? Will you have to buy new items of clothing? Will you clean your own uniforms or is that provided?

✔ **Other perks:** You might get free or reduced propane and laundry privileges. Some employers offer perks such as a store discount or discounts on purchases at their property; free or discounted use of guest recreational facilities when available; free or reduced-fee tickets for area attractions; or free or low-cost meals. For the land companies associated with cruise ships, like Princess Land Tours, you could be eligible for cruises after a certain amount of hours worked.

✔ **Other concerns:** Where is the nearest grocery shopping? We usually ask if there is a WalMart, since towns that large generally have super-markets and better prices. Is there a hospital nearby? What is the avail-ability of telephone line or cable TV? Satellite dish reception? Cellular phone reception, and is it analog or digital? Wi-Fi or Internet service?

You might also want to clarify to whom you will be reporting to and how many people you'll be working with. Are you covered under Worker's Compensation if you are injured? Will you receive a W-2 form?

> **Make a list of your selling points as an employee.**

## Sell yourself

Besides gaining information about the job, the interview is your chance to sell yourself to the employer as the best candidate for the job. Preparation is key here too.

✔ **Review** your work history to see where you have experience or have used skills that apply in this position. Highlight them on your résumé so you remember to emphasize them.

✔ **List** your selling points as an employee. Think about traits this employer is probably looking for in his type of business. Examples might be

♦ "If I don't have an assigned task, I look to see what needs to be done."

♦ "I have managed a business so I know how important good customer service is."

♦ "My job is to make sure each customer leaves here satisfied."

♦ "I believe in doing whatever is necessary to get the job done."

✔ **Questions:** There are standard questions many interviewers ask, par-ticularly if this is a seasonal job dealing with the public. Think about possible answers ahead of time.

♦ What would you do if you have an unhappy customer? *(Assure the customer they are important, make the situation right if you have the authority, or get your supervisor are possible answers.)*

♦ How do you define good customer service? *(Give the customer you are helping your full attention and finish with one before you start helping another, do whatever it takes to make the customer satisfied are reasonable answers.)*

♦ How do you get along with co-workers? Or, they might describe a situation and ask you how you would handle it. *(I get along well with co-workers. If I have a problem I would talk about it with the person first and try to work it out.)*

♦ What are your weaknesses? *(Notes RV worker Phyllis: State your weaknesses in a positive way. If you can't stand a messy workplace, you could say, "I have been accused of being a neat-nik." Or, if you obsess over minutiae, you might say, "I'm a stickler for details." Phyllis once interviewed someone whose weakness was "I hate to get up early." Hearing this answer, an employer would probably think, "This person may not be on time to work.")*

✔ **Research:** Do your research on the employer and the area. Check on working forums for feedback. Read any brochures you have received. Showing you have read the information or found out something about the company or area elevates you above candidates who have not.

---

### Your turn!

In your **Job Notebook**, make lists for questions you want answered and for points you can use to sell yourself.

✔ **Questions:** List your key concerns and the questions you want answered in the interview. Leave a line or two so you can jot down the answer you get from the employer.

✔ **Knockout factors:** List conditions that would eliminate this job from your consideration. Use this as a checklist during the interview.

✔ **Experience:** List your relevant experience for the position you are seeking in your notebook, or highlight it on a copy of your résumé.

✔ **Selling points:** List your selling points for the kinds of positions you are seeking. Think of the traits that make a valuable employee and list them.

✔ **Likely questions:** Prepare answers to standard questions that could apply to this job. Keep this list in front of you during your telephone interview.

Think about your responses ahead of time, but be honest. There is no "right" answer. If you would not handle a situation the way this employer would, better to find out now than after you have arrived.

## Establish good communication

As you prepare for the interview, remember that a successful interview establishes good communications. You will be laying the groundwork for your future employee-employer relationship. Most problems between employer and employee occur because of poor communications and because expectations weren't clarified. Good questions about what the job entails and what the expectations are let the employer know that you are serious. It also communicates that you intend to live up to these expectations, unless you negotiate something different, and that you expect the employer to do likewise.

## THE INTERVIEW

During the interview, have your résumé, list of questions and concerns, and your selling points with you. Build confidence that you can do the job. As the interviewer goes over the duties of

> **A successful interview establishes good communications.**

the position and his needs, let him know if you have previously done this, even if it is included on your résumé. In reviewing your work history, underscore what you have done that is similar. If he states he is looking for a certain type of person, agree and sell yourself. "Yes, I think customer service is the most important part of the job." You are conveying your interest in the job and helping the employer see that you are a good match.

Work in your positive selling points. One thing Bill, my late husband, always mentioned is that he believed in giving a good day's work for a day's pay. Bill was someone who liked to be busy so this was true for him.

## Other interview tips:

✔ Greet the interviewer with a firm handshake, combined with a smile and direct eye contact.
✔ Be positive and energetic.

✔ Demonstrate your interest by making eye contact, leaning forward and smiling.

✔ Stand or sit straight.

✔ Do not make negative statements about former employers or co-workers. This only makes you look bad. The employer may think you are a complainer, a troublemaker, or can't get along with other people.

## Listen to your gut feelings

Besides getting answers to your list of questions, pay attention to how you feel about this employer and job situation. Ask questions about style of management. Does the employer appreciate initiative or is she a micromanager? May you talk to other Workampers who have worked there? How many employees left midseason? How many repeat employees do they have?

If something in the interview makes you uneasy, either find out more or pay attention to your gut feelings. This is not the only job.

## Telephone interviews:

✔ Use your voice to communicate your interest and enthusiasm.

> **Don't make negative statements about former employers.**

Helen Blankenship, executive director of the Plus 50 Placement Center, Inc., says "Who wants to hire a grump?" She advises, "You want to go in with a good attitude, with an upbeat attitude, with a smile on your face and a real willingness to engage in conversation. You want to act like you really want the job."

## Ending the interview

At the end of the interview, the interviewer should either offer you the job or let you know where the process goes from here. He may have additional candidates to consider. Perhaps the former employee has the job if he is coming back and the employer won't know for a few days.

If you are offered a job, request two or three days to consider it and to discuss it with your spouse. This will give you time to consider the offer and plan your negotiations. Even if you are offered a certain wage that doesn't mean you can't ask for more. You may also have other employers you hope to hear from and this will give you time to contact them again.

Whether offered a job or not, you should make a positive statement saying that this sounds like a company you'd like to work for, and you know you would do an excellent job for them and would like the position. (Of course, say this only if it is true.) If only one of you received an offer and your acceptance is contingent on your spouse getting a position also, make sure you communicate this information to the interviewer.

End the interview with a time frame for either hearing back from the employer or a time for you to follow up.

## Follow up

Follow up an interview with a thank you. Either drop a short note in the mail or send an e-mail, thanking the employer for the opportunity to interview for the position, reiterate that you see this as a match and would like the position. Mention you are looking forward to hearing from him or working with him. This is another way to sell yourself.

Be sure to follow up as you agreed. It is also appropriate to call if an employer does not get back to you as promised. If the employer still hasn't made a decision, find out when you can check back. Take any further contacts as opportunities to sell yourself.

---

### Key points

- ✍ **The interview is for both you and the employer to find out if the job is a good match.**
- ✍ **The second objective for the employer is to find the best person for the job; your second objective is to sell yourself.**
- ✍ **The interview is your chance to establish good communication.**

---

## 10 guidelines for working in RV parks

After their first job working in an RV park, Virginia and Skip and a co-worker couple came up with a list of questions/guidelines to use the next time they apply for campground jobs:

1.  **Don't sell yourself short:** The campground needs someone of your caliber as badly as you need a job. Don't be afraid to tell them what you can do and what you are not willing to do! In the long run, everyone will benefit. The more adamant you are in defining both your requirements and abilities, the more likely you are to find a "good fit" for both the RV park and you.

2.  **Make sure you fully understand the compensation for the job:** We need full-time income. In the future we will only work for parks that pay us for every hour worked, and then we'll pay the monthly rent out of that. We figured that in exchanging 20 hours for a site, we were getting "paid" $2.88/hour for those hours. Be sure to find out the monthly rental for sites. The owners should not value your site as an RV worker for more they value the same site for a camper. Will you get discounts on any amenities they have?

3.  **Make sure you discuss all the work you will be doing:** If you need to work 40 hours a week and all of your job duties center around mowing grass, what happens if you have torrential rains for two solid weeks? Can you do other jobs to get in your 40 hours?

4.  **Does the campground carry Worker's Compensation** for its employees? Requirements vary from state to state. Better to know your position before you need it.

5.  **Are uniforms required?** If so, who pays for them? Will you have to go buy anything?

6.  **Are the tools provided** to do the work they are asking you to do?

7.  **Are you required to use your own vehicle?** In one campground, the office was over one-half mile from our site. The trips added up.

8.  **Is phone, cable TV or modem hook-up important to you?** Now is the time to check out availability.

9.  **What size site will you have?** Some campgrounds don't want to waste their premium sites on workers. Do you have ample room to open your front door and get in and out, or put your awning out?

10. **Ask about the distance to shopping and medical facilities:** If you are unfamiliar with the area, call the Chamber of Commerce. The more you know, the less likely you are to be disappointed.

*"A pessimist sees the difficulty in every opportunity, an optimist sees the opportunity in every difficulty."*
*Winston Churchill*

# Chapter 11
# How to negotiate for better compensation

Like interviewing, to get what you want, you need to be prepared going into negotiation.

## PREPARATION

You have been offered a job paying $7.50 an hour plus a site. You need $8.50. Do you throw this job out? Not before you negotiate for better pay. In larger corporations, there is often a standard pay rate for each position, though individual managers may have some latitude. In smaller companies, particularly where you are talking to the owner, you can often negotiate better pay and perhaps additional perks.

> **Before you start negotiating, be prepared.**

If this offer comes during the job interview, ask for a few days to consider it and talk it over with your spouse. That will give you time to evaluate the job offer and compare it to other offers or jobs in the works.

### Negotiation hints

Before you start negotiating for better compensation, consider these:

✔ **Be prepared:** Know what you want and need in terms of pay and perks. Know the going rate for this position. If you have figures from similar employers in the area, all the better.

✔ **Compute what you will be paying for your RV site:** In the interview, you should have found out what you will be paying for your RV site. It may be a dollar amount or you may be required to work a certain number of hours to "pay" for your site. Before you accept an offer or negotiate further, make sure you clearly understand exactly how much you are paying. Several ways to value your RV site are explained in the chart titled "What is a site worth?" on page 112.

As an example, if each of you will be working ten hours a week for your site (20 hours/week) and the monthly rate for the site is $250, you are being paid an equivalent of $2.89/hour for those hours. Figuring an

> **Know what is non-negotiable for you.**

average of 4.33 weeks per month, your computation would be as follows: Work 20 hours/week x 4.33 weeks = 86.6 hours a month for your site. $250 ÷ 86.6 = $2.89/ hour. Check additional ways to "compute" the value of your site or your "hourly rate" in "What is a site worth?" Is this a fair value for your time? Unless your duties are minimal, you are working too many hours for this site. (Of course, only you can decide this, weighing all factors.)

✔ **Know what you are worth:** If you bring added value to the job in terms of experience, energy or job skills, you should be compensated for that. If this employer doesn't need or isn't willing to pay for your skills, then you have to weigh the offer in terms of the benefits to you. For example, you really want to be in that area, so it may be worth taking less pay. Remember there are many jobs available. If you want higher than average pay, it is going to take you a little longer to find a match than for the person who is willing to take the first offer.

✔ **Know what is nonnegotiable for you:** Think about your bottom line. What is nonnegotiable? For example, Bill and I worked only for hourly wages, not on salary. We wanted to be paid for all the time we work. An attractive salary can work out to a low hourly rate when you put in lots of hours beyond the 40-week. For someone else, cleaning restrooms might be unacceptable. For other working RVers, a campsite with full hookups, or being near medical facilities could be a necessity. You probably have a bottom line as far as pay goes.

✔ **Postpone discussing actual dollar compensation until later in the process:** While you want to find out what the usual pay is for the position, you don't need to discuss the amount until later in the process. Operate on the assumption that this is the starting offer and there is room to bargain. (If the amount is ridiculously low or clearly not a match, you probably will eliminate this job in the interview.)

By postponing discussions of salary, you will be in a stronger position after the employer is sold on your skills and wants *you* to fill the position. In addition, you need time to evaluate the job offer. It is difficult to do that during discussions. If necessary, postpone discussions of pay with something like, "I'm sure we can work out a fair compensation package."

> **"There's a slight problem... money."**

## THE PROCESS

We are assuming that you sold yourself during the interview and underscored your ability to do the work and that you are a good worker. Before you make any additional demands, assure the employer that this sounds like just the kind of company you would like to work for and that you would do an excellent job for them. You really want this job. This puts you in a position to ask for more.

### Asking for more

"There's a slight problem...money." You can use various reasons: "I really want to work here but I have been offered $8.00 an hour at another RV park. Can you do any better?" One statement Bill successfully used was "I know you are used to hiring older, retired folks, but my wife and I are still prime workers. We're not retired." (If you are retired, you can say you "aren't typical.") We got $2 an hour more than he initially offered. Even if the offer sounds fair to you, ask "Is this the best you can do?" Maybe the employer has more in his budget for your compensation.

Another approach is suggested by Jack Chapman, a career consultant specializing in salary coaching and the author of *Negotiating Your Salary: How to Make $1,000 a Minute*. When you hear the dollar offer, he advises, "You say 'Hmm.'" He adds, "Repeat the figure with a contemplative tone in your voice — like it's the start of a multinational summit meeting. Count to 30 and think. When you're done thinking — and this time the interviewer will be the one squirming in his seat — respond with the truth based on what you know you're worth in the marketplace: 'sounds great' or 'sounds fair' or 'sounds disappointing.'"*

---

* *(Jack Chapman quoted from Marcia Passos Duffy's "Essential tips to help you get the salary you deserve," at* WetFeet.com. *Posted: 01/03/2001).*

If what you are "paying" for your RV site is not equitable in your analysis, you can use this as a bargaining point to reduce your charge for the site, increase your hourly rate, or obtain additional perks. Many park owners have not done a similar analysis. In the example above, where you worked 20 hours/week for your site at $2.89/hour, you would be better off earning your regular hourly rate for all hours worked and then pay the space rent out of your pocket.

If the salary you want isn't possible, perhaps the owner will give you free propane and laundry, meals, or some other perks. If your expenses are less, this can add a little to your paycheck indirectly. For example, a free lunch every work day can reduce your grocery bills. Maybe the employer could expand the job responsibilities or combine this job with another position, making it worth paying more.

> **Terry supplemented her salary by doing waitressing for pay plus tips.**

If you want or need to make this job work, you might find a way on the job to earn more money. Terry was able to supplement her salary by doing waitressing at the resort for pay plus tips. Meanwhile she was learning about fine dining, a skill that could pay off someday. Perhaps you could sell craft items in the store or hang a sign outside your RV advertising your service like sewing or sharpening scissors.

## Keep your options open

You are trying to get the best job; the employer wants the best employee. Each of you is trying to get things lined up for the season. If you have followed the job strategy in Chapter 8, you are juggling more than one possible employer and may already have a job offer or two.

How do you keep your options open and be fair to these employers? How do you decline a job offer yet keep the door open for another season?

If you truly don't think this job is a good match, of course, gracefully bow out. "As much as I think this would be an excellent place to work, I'm afraid I need to earn more money than you can offer," or "This summer we've decided to work closer to our grandchildren." I recommend you keep your options open for the possibility that you might want this job another season. "I hope you will consider us again in the future."

If you are considering several employers, you need to send strong, positive messages to each even if the particular job isn't your first choice. It is much like asking a gal to marry you. If she gets any vibes she is second choice, she'll be looking for another man, especially if there is another waiting on the sidelines.

## JUGGLING JOB OFFERS

If an employer offers you a job, you can, of course, request a few days to consider the offer. You and your spouse need to talk it over. You could let the employer know that you are waiting to hear back

> **If she gets any vibes she is second choice, she'll be looking for another man!**

from another employer whom you are also considering and should hear something within a few days. If you set a firm date to call back, most employers will allow the extra time to make a decision.

At this point, in fact, you have ammunition to call back the employer you really want to work for, tell him you have another offer but really want to work here. Will he be making his hiring decision soon? The fact that you may slip out of consideration may prompt positive action on his part. At least he may share with you why he is waiting. It could be that a former employee hasn't let him know if he is returning and you are his first choice if he has an opening. With this information, you can decide if you want to accept the first offer or take your chances and wait for the better position. If you stall the other employer too long, she may very well hire her second choice.

If you decide on a job you would really like to have and a hiring decision hasn't been made, be persistent without being a pest. So many employers and hiring officials have told us that when there was a candidate who kept in touch — called them, dropped them notes — they *had* to hire them. Anyone who wanted the job that badly just had to be given a chance.

### You've accepted a job and you get a better offer

You have made a commitment to one employer but then get another offer. The second job pays more money or is exactly what you want to do. Congratulations! You are in an enviable position. But what do you do?

Some people feel strongly that they should honor the first commitment. You should never violate your principles. But you also have to look out for yourselves and remember this is a bidding process on both sides. If a second job offers you each a dollar more per hour, this can amount to an extra two-thousand dollars over the course of a six-month season. If you do it in a way that is fair to the employer, it can be done honorably.

First of all, begin your job search early. Then you have a good chance of lining up good offers well before start dates. It would be one thing to leave an employer in the lurch the week before he is expecting you to be there, or just not show up. It is another to give a warning a month or more in advance. If you get the better offer within a few days of accepting, the employer probably has a number of other candidates still available.

> **Finding a job is a bidding process on both sides.**

Some employers have told me they start their job search for summer positions in November so they can get the pick of the candidates. They know some will get better offers, but they also count on the fact that many people will stop looking once they have a firm job lined up. When we told one national park we had gotten a better job offer at another park with better pay and a much longer season, he understood. He said it happens all the time. Plus we had given him plenty of notice so he could still fill those positions.

One time we told an employer we could not be there until a certain date because of a prior work commitment even though he wanted us there right away. We took our chances that he would wait. Sometimes an employer will wait in that case; other times they need someone right away and can't wait. But for us, that was the honorable action and we still got the jobs.

## Turning down a job offer

If you do decide to decline a position that you have accepted, please let the employer know as soon as possible. This is a common courtesy, but one a few RV workers fail to follow. It gives all of us a bad name and may come back to haunt you. Remember, Rule #3 for job-finding success: *Keep your options open.* This may be a place you want to work during another season.

**Your turn!**

✔ **Figure what perks are worth to you:** To have an idea how much a given perk is worth, look at how much you are spending on items typically offered as perks such as site, laundry and propane.

✔ **Research area equivalents:** Find out monthly rates for RV sites in the park you are interested in as well as surrounding parks. Talk to RV workers doing similar jobs and check *Workamper News* to research the going rate. Since this may be difficult to do right at the time you need it, record this information in your **Job Notebook** whenever you come across it so you have a range of what is being paid. Don't be afraid to ask for more; just ground your request in reality and what you have to offer.

✔ **Compute what you will be paying for the RV site:** If an RV site is involved, use the examples in "What is a site worth?" (See next page) to determine what you are "paying" for the site or what you are "earning" per hour. Use area equivalents to get a ballpark figure if you don't have actual figures.

---

**Key points**

✍ **Get prepared  before going into negotiation for compensation.**

✍ **Negotiating better compensation than what is initially offered is often possible.**

## What is a site worth?

There are different ways of looking at what a site is worth in terms of compensation.

◆ What would you be paying for a site if you weren't working? If you normally boondock, then this campsite, while convenient, is actually a cost.

◆ What is the normal seasonal or long-term rate per month? The employer should not value your site at more than this amount.

◆ Fred was told by the employer that his site was valued at $700/month but regular campers paid only $300/month. Fred would be better off paying the $300/month in rent and getting the extra $400 in increased wages, or an extra $2.50/hour. ($100 week divided by 40 hours)

◆ You are working 20 hours per week for a site. You get paid $5.00 per hour for work after that. You are effectively paying $100 per week for your site ($5 x 20). Is this a fair value, both in terms of what other campers are paying and what the site is worth to you?

◆ Value it this way too. The monthly rate for your site is $200/month and you work ten hours/week in exchange for your site. You will work about 40 hours for your site in a month so 40 divided into $200 is $5.00/hour. That's not minimum wage, unless other amenities bring the value up.

◆ Consider your duties. If your duties consist of being on the premises "in case you are needed" or to "keep an eye on things," your RV site with no monetary pay may be a fair exchange.

◆ If the site is in a resort and thus valued quite high, will you actually use these extra amenities? If not, this site may be worth considerably less to you than to the employer.

◆ **Note:** If you anticipate leaving for any length of time during your season (or if an emergency comes up), will you be charged rent? If so, how much? If this situation happens, you could offer to move your RV to a non-income producing space while you are gone. This information will also give you a monetary value for your site.

# Chapter 12
# How to succeed on the job

In the preceding chapters, we have taken a number of steps in the job-search process to find an employer who meets your goals for working and an employer who is a match for you. You've asked plenty of questions so you have realistic expectations. Those who have the best success finding good work situations also talk to the employer several times over the intervening months, getting a better feel for the employer and confirming that the work situation is still the same.

Once you are on the job, how you handle situations on the job will, in large part, determine the sort of season you'll have. There are also factors out of your control.

## GET OFF ON THE RIGHT FOOT

Principal factors in your success on the job are good communications and fulfilling your promises. Using these two keys, you will avoid many work-related problems. You have been doing both throughout your job search — from your first contact in response to the ad, then with each subsequent contact through the interview and negotiation process. There is one more step you should take before starting your new position.

### Employment agreement

When you accept a job, particularly if it is a small business, ask the employer if he has a written contract or agreement spelling out what was discussed. If an employer

> **An employment agreement lets employers know you expect them to live up to what was negotiated.**

does not, we ask, "If we send a letter confirming what we discussed, will you sign and return it to us?" We haven't been turned down. Some RVers are either uncomfortable with this or don't feel it is necessary. We feel it is a protection and lets employers know you expect them to live up to what was negotiated. See Workamper.com for a sample work agreement.

The government and larger corporations usually have employment handbooks and forms they send to new employees. In this case, it wouldn't hurt, however, to send a thank-you letter that mentions any new items your new supervisor agreed to that are out of the ordinary, such as days off together, 40 hours of work each week guaranteed, etc.

## ON THE JOB

Once on the job, if problems or questions arise, discuss them right away. If things are hectic, wait until the end of the day, but address the issue as soon as practical.

Depending on the position and how closely your supervisor works with you, keep her informed of problems and accomplishments. If a customer is furious over something that happened, let your supervisor know right away so if she has to deal with the problem, she is prepared for it. When Bill was working on a building project, he kept the foreman informed of his progress and checked to make sure that he was doing what was wanted along the way. You'll get a feel for how much to do this, but better to err on the side of too much communication than too little.

> **It is better to err on the side of too much communication rather than too little.**

### Be adaptable

Take time on the job to observe how things are done before making suggestions or telling the boss "how we did it at such-and-such company." In fact, expect that this owner or manager will do things differently than you might have done them elsewhere. If you do suggest a change, include any monetary benefit and be diplomatic!

### Good work habits

It goes without saying that you should be on time, do your work, and if you're not busy, look for something to do. Employers appreciate employees who are flexible. If an employer needs help in another area and an employee is willing to pitch in, that goes a long way. You may want an extra day off, or to change your schedule to accommodate an event or visiting relative. If you have pitched in where needed, your employer is going to bend over backwards to help you out if possible.

## Difficult people

In any job, you can be stuck working with difficult people. It may be a co-worker, or perhaps even the boss. Some people are abrasive and even abusive. In most cases, you shouldn't take it personally. They probably treat other people much the same. This is not to say you should let it pass. Later in the day and in private, you should let this person know that this is not appropriate. If you can, state it diplomatically, "When you said '___,' I felt (distressed/uncomfortable) because I need to be treated with respect." You're more likely to get a positive response.

Some people are not even aware of how they sound to others. You will likely get much different treatment on the job if you speak up and call it to their attention.

As in your jobs or career before you hit the road, you need to set limits. You'll find a few owners or supervisors will take advantage of workers and expect them to work extra hours or on their days off. Depending on the situation, and whether or not this is a one-time thing, you may want to help them out. But if you sense that this could become a pattern, you must check this behavior immediately.

> **"Start the way you mean to go."**
> *Age-old advice to daughters*

"Start the way you mean to go," mothers advise their daughters when getting married. If you wait on your husband hand and foot, that is what he will expect from then on. You may want to tell the owner that you are sorry but that wasn't your agreement. You have plans and are unavailable this evening or weekend.

Bill and I accepted a job at a houseboat company. At the time we interviewed, the owner wanted us to go on salary, but we rejected that and were hired at an hourly wage. We were also guaranteed 40 hours a week and overtime for work exceeding 40 hours. We followed up with a letter clarifying our agreement, which the owner signed and returned to us. It became clear almost immediately that we were the only hourly workers. Everyone else was working on salary and was working far in excess of 40 hours a week. Pressure was put on us to change to salary at the equivalent of our hourly rate of pay. We then could be required to work a "reasonable" amount of overtime at no extra pay. We declined.

Then Bill was asked to work on his day off. He said no. We left for the day to reinforce the fact that we would not tolerate changing the rules. As it turned out, we left that job; there were a number of agreements the owners did not live up to and they continued to pressure us into working on salary. We at least had a written agreement the owners had signed, so they could not come back and say they never agreed to that. Know your limits and draw your lines. Otherwise, you may have a miserable season.

> **If you have a problem, try to work it out with that person first.**

Remember, if you have a problem with a supervisor or a co-worker, you should always try to work it out with that person first before going to the owner or manager.

## You are only there for a short time

If you have been an owner of a business or in a supervisory or management position, it may be difficult to watch the owners of a company run their business. Some people seem to be successful in spite of themselves! Take a deep breath. You hit the road to get rid of stress. You are not there to run the business, only to do the best job you can in the position for which you were hired. Remember, it is their business. They make the decisions. Let it go.

On occasion, it turns out a situation isn't ideal, but you have made a commitment. It may be too late to get an equivalent job somewhere else. Then it's time to remember that you are only here for six months, or whatever time you agreed upon. Remember that this job is a means to an end. Even if it isn't what you wanted, it is serving a purpose. This job is allowing you to live a lifestyle of freedom and choice plus the opportunity to explore an area. Sticking with this job may help you get a more desirable job next season. "This too shall pass."

Bill and I had government jobs with co-workers who were extremely lazy. In short, they weren't doing the job they were paid for. Bill and I had a choice in these situations. We could make ourselves miserable by concentrating on how unfair and wrong this was. Instead we decided to concentrate on ourselves. We did the best job we could, a job we could be proud of. If someone else chose not to do a good job, it was out of our control. We had clear consciences and were always proud of the quality of work we did. We chose the second way of reacting, avoiding ulcers.

## CHOOSING TO LEAVE

What do you do when you cannot work in the situation you are in? You have tried talking to the employer and it just isn't what you want or had expected. You have other options and don't need to stay in a situation you dislike. Be sure to give your two weeks' notice unless it is impossible to do so. Every once in a while we hear of a Workamper who has left in the middle of the night or taken their rig for an errand and not returned rather than give proper notice. Unless you are in imminent danger, this is a dishonorable way to handle the situation. Employers talk to one another, so for the sake of your own reputation and that of other working RVers, follow this simple courtesy.

### Health and safety

You may have to make a judgement about staying or leaving if your health or safety is jeopardized. For example, as hurricanes in Florida approached, RV workers had to decide whether or not to get their rigs out of the path of the hurricane. One RV couple had to decide whether to stay in a park where there were frequent break-ins. And still another worked at a lodge with vermin in the living quarters and restaurant kitchen. Each had to make a decision. While keeping your commitment is important, your own health and safety have precedence.

> **Be sure to give your two weeks' notice unless it is impossible to do so.**

### Unethical situations

What if you find yourself asked to do something that violates your principles or violates the law? Sue worked in accounting for a company. Her boss did not account for petty cash properly. She discussed it with the next level of management and was not backed up. This put her in an awkward position and could have made her answerable for discrepancies. She decided to quit rather than compromise her integrity.

You need to follow your conscience and do what is right according to your principles. It is not worth the stress it will cause. You also need to obey the law, as well as follow safety and building codes or accepted procedures, as in the case of accounting. Otherwise you could be the "fall guy" if a problem ever arises. Do not take a chance with your work or personal reputation.

## EVALUATE EACH EXPERIENCE

Analyze your situation after each job. Are there questions you should have asked? If you had known more about the actual situation, would you have accepted the job? Don't beat yourself up. Record these new questions in your **Job Notebook** for the next time.

### Ask for a reference letter

When you leave a job or a volunteer experience on good terms, ask your employer if you can use her as a reference and also obtain a letter of reference on company letterhead. Duplicate positive letters and include them with your applications to similar employers. Many prospective employers will be satisfied with a reference letter and this will avoid having your former employer called repeatedly if you are applying to numerous positions.

Many employers appreciate it if you write a letter as a model. Include your duties and accomplishments and your excellent worker characteristics. Make it easy for them and you'll get a nice letter to show prospective employers down the road.

---

**Key Points**

- ✍ **Good communication and accurate expectations are essential for job success.**
- ✍ **Always do a little more than is expected of you and follow through on commitments.**
- ✍ **Set limits with both owners and co-workers.**
- ✍ **If the job goes sour, remember: this too shall pass.**
- ✍ **If all else fails, your house has wheels.**

---

*"A goal is nothing more than a dream*
*with a time limit."*
*Joe L. Griffith*

# Chapter 13
# Legal and tax considerations

*Disclaimer: This chapter is provided for informational purposes only so that you are aware of issues that may impact your finances. Nothing written here should be construed as legal or financial advice. Remember, the burden for compliance with these laws rests with you and not your tax preparer, IRS employees, or authors of any books or articles you might read. Since these issues can have considerable ramifications, if you are in doubt, see your legal and tax advisors to determine the effect on your individual situation.*

There are legal and tax considerations that could affect your income and expenses.

## DOMICILE AND STATE OF RESIDENCY

Domicile and residency are often confused. For people living year-round in a house, they are, for all intents and purposes, the same. They do not, however, have the same legal meaning. For an RVer, your domicile and residence will coincide, at least part of the year, but as you travel and work in other states, the two will differ.

> **As a full-time RVer, you can choose your state of domicile.**

### Domicile

As a full-time RVer with mobility, you have the opportunity to choose your legal domicile. This is your "home" state or where you are domiciled the majority of the time. Your domicile is the place where you intend to remain permanently. It is your true and principal establishment, to which whenever you are absent, you "intend to return." You have only one domicile. If you are domiciled in a state, you must establish this by your subjective intent as well as by actual residence.

## Establishing your domicile

Some states make it easy for full-timers to get a driver's license, motor vehicle registration and tags, as well as to register to vote. RVers have reported that South Dakota, Texas and Florida have reasonable costs and are easy to work with to establish your domicile.

Just because you drive your RV to a new state, register it there, and establish an address does not mean you establish a new domicile, even if you declare it so. If you don't clearly establish one state as your domicile, more than one state may conclude they are your domicile at tax time or at the time of your death. Some states—California, New Hampshire and Ohio in particular—are very aggressive about claiming you have tax-liability even when you thought you were a casual visitor.

> **A number of actions help establish your domicile.**

In an article, "How to Change Your Domicile from New Hampshire to Florida," attorneys from the New Hampshire firm of Cleveland, Waters and Bass, P.A. list a number of actions that help establish your new domicile. *(www.mckan.com/pubs.htm)* As an RVer, you should consider doing as many of the following as are feasible in establishing your new domicile. This is especially true if you own property in a second state. Remember, if you are challenged, the government has the presumption of correctness and it will be up to you to prove that you are right.

✔ Remove trailers, mobile homes and boats from your old state and re-register in the new.
✔ Spend at least half the year in your new state.
✔ Do not store furniture or heirlooms in your old state.
✔ Change your driver's license to your new state. Any fishing or hunting licenses in your old state should reflect your non-resident status.
✔ File a declaration of domicile with the town clerk.
✔ Change your voting registration.
✔ File a new will in your new state.
✔ File your federal tax returns at the Service Center for your new state.
✔ File state income tax returns (if applicable).

✔ Transfer any club memberships to your new state.
✔ Change your address on your passport and any accounts to your new state.
✔ Subscribe to the local newspaper.
✔ Consider moving the remains of close deceased relatives to your new state.
✔ Make major purchases in your new state.

## Impact for working RVers

Your choice of domicile will have a financial impact. Taxes, license and registration fees, and insurance rates vary by state. Working RVers often choose a no-income tax state (Alaska, Florida, Nevada, South Dakota, Texas, Washington or Wyoming) to minimize state income tax obligation. (New Hampshire and Tennessee do not tax earned income, but do tax interest and dividend income.) Besides income taxes, other taxes like sales tax (especially important when buying an RV), inheritance taxes, real estate taxes, and personal property taxes differ. Vehicle insurance and health insurance costs vary between states and sometimes even by region within the state.

> **It is worth the research to weigh all the factors in choosing your domicile.**

Research, then weigh all the factors in choosing your domicile. To get some background information, you can compare rates at *(www.taxadmin.org/fta/rate/ind_inc.pdf )*. Another state income tax comparison chart is at the Federation of Tax Administrators website or check at the individual states' websites. See **Resources** and **Appendix 5.** *Choosing your RV Home Base,* from Roundabout Publications is also a good resource.

## Residency

When you are physically present in a state, that is where you are currently residing — even if only a day as you travel through. In the course of a year, you can, and probably will, reside in more than one state. You may own an RV lot or property. You could reside there part of the time, but maintain your domicile elsewhere.

States want their residents to do certain things: pay taxes, register their vehicles, and obtain a driver's license, to name a few. States will consider you a resident after a certain number of days; requirements vary by state. (Taking a job in a state may be evidence that you are a resident.) If you have spent time in a state, and you did not earn money in that state or from a source in the state, you will not have to file an income tax return there.

## INCOME TAXES

No matter where you earn income, you will be subject to federal income taxes. State tax is different. If you work in a state for part of the year, you must pay state income taxes on the income earned in that state. If you work in two

> **No matter where you earn income, you will be subject to federal income taxes.**

different states, you will pay each state income taxes on the income earned in that state (or while in that state). For example, you worked in Colorado for four months and earned $8,000. Then you worked in Arizona for four months and earned $7,000. You pay income taxes to Colorado on the $8,000 and income taxes to Arizona on the $7,000, filing non-resident or part-year resident forms in each state. (If you make under a certain amount, you may not have to pay state income taxes; however, you will have to file a state tax return in order to get a refund of any money that was withheld for state income taxes.)

Your state of domicile also wants tax on your income, however you will get credit for income taxes paid to other states.

✔ In the above example, if you are domiciled in a state where you must file tax return, you will get a credit for the income taxes paid to Arizona and Colorado, and pay taxes on any other income to your state of domicile.

✔ If your state of domicile is an income tax state and you work in a no–income tax state, your domicile will collect taxes on the amount earned in the no–income tax state. For example, if you are domiciled in Oregon and work in Wyoming, a no-income tax state, Oregon will tax your Wyoming income.

✔ If you are domiciled in a state where no filings or income tax is required, you only need to be concerned about filing in the states where you worked.

To minimize state income taxes, you should establish your domicile in one state. You then have temporary assignments in the other states and are non-resident. Otherwise, if you have income from a pension or interest and dividends, and you work six months in Utah, for example, you could have to pay income tax on six months of your pension or interest income earned while working and living in Utah.

If you do have a home base and travel to work at a temporary job lasting less than one year, you may be able to deduct travel expenses and a per diem allowance for meals. Check with your tax preparer to see if you qualify.

Each person's financial situation is a little different, tax law is complex and varies from state to state, so check with your tax preparer beforehand so you aren't surprised at tax time.

## RV SITES TAXABLE?

If you receive a free RV site when you work, is the value treated as income for tax purposes? It might be considered federal income unless your employer requires that you live there. According to IRS Code Section 119, (see IRS Publication 15B) if you are required as a condition of your employment to stay at the premises, the value of the lodging which you receive qualifies as "excludable income," meaning you don't need to report it on your return. You must, however, docu-

> **Your free RV site could be "excludable income."**

ment the value of lodging you received, in case you are challenged. Keep a brochure which lists the rates, plus the manager's name, phone number and dates. Request a statement from the employer to the effect that you are required to live onsite as part of your employment conditions. The employer can also take a deduction so both parties actually benefit. Furnished meals in some cases are also excluded from taxation. Note: You may not be able to exclude this "income" for either RV site and meals when computing your income for state tax purposes.

## EMPLOYEE VS. INDEPENDENT CONTRACTOR

What are the differences and the financial implications of working as an employee versus working as an independent contractor?

Employees:

✔ Employer pays half the social security tax.

✔ Employer pays unemployment insurance.

✔ Employer controls how work results are achieved.

✔ Employer sets your schedule.

✔ Employer issues regular paychecks for hours worked.

✔ Employer must pay overtime according to state law.

✔ Employer must pay for Worker's Compensation to cover you in case of injury.

✔ Employer may require that you incur expenses that you may claim on your income tax return; however, these are usually limited.

Independent contractors:

✔ Pay their own expenses.

✔ Can deduct many of the costs of doing business, such as travel, telephone, equipment and tools, business supplies and a home office.

✔ Set their own schedules and have little or no supervision.

✔ Are responsible for the final product and may be sued for improper performance.

✔ Pay the full social security tax (15.3%) and must pay quarterly estimated taxes.

✔ Are not covered by Worker's Compensation nor eligible for unemployment compensation.

✔ Often do work of a "professional" nature.

## IRS factors

In most cases it is clear which category you fall under. In the case of sales positions, it may not be so clear since a salesperson can work either as an employee or an independent contractor. Occasionally there is abuse where employers have contracted with someone to provide services when in fact that person was actually an employee. Hiring an independent contractor saves the employer money (Payroll taxes, assessments for unemployment and Worker's Compensation coverage, etc.), but the employee will not be covered if injured on the job or unemployed. If you

> **An independent contractor can deduct many of the costs of doing business.**

have any questions about a particular job situation, you may view IRS publication 15-A at their website *(www.irs.gov)*, or order a copy from the IRS (800/829-3676).

## DRIVER'S LICENSE AND REGISTERING YOUR VEHICLES

States require that anyone working as an employee in their state, who has a vehicle or existing driver's license, obtain a new driver's license and register their vehicles in that state within a certain number of days. If you are working temporarily there as an independent contractor or have your own business, you may be exempt.

In a few states you can obtain temporary licenses and plates if you will be employed a short time. See **Appendix 6** for contact information for state agencies handling vehicle registration.

> **States require people working in their state to obtain a driver's license.**

Re-registering your vehicles could be quite costly. Not only do you have registration fees that are often based on the value of your vehicle, but you will probably have to change your insurance to the new state at different rates, possibly more. After your job is finished, you will probably want to re-register in your domicile, an additional expense.

Most workers on the road we have talked to do not get a new license or change registration in each state; however, you are risking fines and penalties in addition to these fees if you do not switch in the time period allowed. If you choose not to re-register your vehicle, obey all traffic laws and don't get stopped. If a vehicle with an out-of-state license plate is sitting in an employer's parking lot day after day, it may be noticed. In a resort town with lots of out-of-state visitors, your vehicle with an out-of-state tag is less likely to be noticed; you're probably just a tourist.

You must make your own decision on this one.

The key to these factors is to do your homework ahead of time. Protect yourself and avoid costly surprises. Remember, when it comes to choosing a domicile or where to work, one size does not fit all. The best choices for one RVer may be different than ones for another RVer.

**Key Points**

🖐  **Your choice of domicile can impact your income.**

🖐  **States have different laws and regulations regarding income taxes, driver's licenses and vehicle registration.**

🖐  **Check the ramifications for you before taking a job.**

# Section III
# Job list

## CHAPTER 14
### Jobs at RV parks and resorts

1. Manager and assistant manager
2. Reservations clerk or guest service worker — day and night shifts
3. Registration and reservations worker— computerized system
4. Gatekeeper
5. Office workers like secretary, bookkeeper or accountant
6. Maintenance worker
7. Construction — carpenter, plumber, electrician
8. Propane service technician
9. Janitor or housekeeper
10. Mechanic
11. Groundskeeper
12. Food service staff
13. Recreation or activity director
14. Craft or activity instructor
15. Golf marshal
16. Entertainer
17. Security personnel
18. Marina worker
19. Canoe rental clerk and livery driver
20. Shuttle van driver
21. Bike rental clerk, mechanic
22. Pool operations — lifeguard, pool cleaner
23. Retail stores operations — sales clerk, inventory and pricing clerks
24. Tour guide or salesperson for lots in membership parks
25. Offer services to other campers, i.e., haircuts, massages, sewing
26. Worker for contractor-offered services at RV parks and resorts - food, marina, etc.

## Site-sitting jobs

27. Construction sites: mainly providing a presence
28. Construction sites: paid to provide 24-hour security
29. Storage units: management, night security, or provide vacation relief
30. Gate guard at an oil field for a security company
31. House-sitter
32. House-sitter, providing also pet or plant care
33. Caretaker of ranches or other property
34. Caretaker or work in exchange for site, extra hours for money
35. Manager of a household - house couple
36. Child care provider—nanny
37. Gun club or shooting range—caretaker

## Sales of Christmas trees and pumpkins

38. Christmas tree lot manager or helper
39. Pumpkin lot manager or helper

# CHAPTER 15

## Jobs traveling in your RV

40. Gas pipeline inspector
41. Wagon master/tail gunner for RV caravans
42. Mechanic for RV caravans
43. Deliver RVs
44. Salesperson of advertising at campgrounds- maps or directories
45. Salesperson or manufacturer's rep
46. Inspector of RV parks for directories
47. Door-to-door sales for Air Photo
48. Mystery shopper
49. Judge at dog shows
50. Circus worker
51. Booking agent for a circus
52. Groom for a circus
53. Travel with a carnival: rides, setup, welders, office, mechanics, CDL drivers
54. NASCAR circuit help
55. Salesperson of products to businesses (open territories)
56. Product installer with changing job locations

## CHAPTER 16
### Jobs in RV sales and service
57. RV salesperson
58. Retail salesperson: supplies or parts department
59. Quality control inspector
60. Technician: walk-throughs with new buyers
61. Detailer
62. Mechanic
63. Service technician
64. Service writer
65. Lot attendant
66. Inside office worker: receptionist, clerk, accountant or bookkeeper, computer workers such as operator, programmer, data input clerk

### Camping World/RV supplies
67. Retail sales clerk/cashier
68. Stocker
69. Service writer
70. Mechanic
71. RV technician
72. Janitor
73. Bookkeeper
74. Parts advisor
75. Merchandiser
76. Shop attendant
77. Goodwill Ambassador

### Working for RV clubs and organizations
78. Paid staff for office work and club functions
79. Editorial or graphic designer
80. Webmaster or computer programmer
81. Manager and assistant manager for club RV parks
82. Activity director for club RV parks
83. RV safe driving instructor

130 *Support Your RV Lifestyle!*

# CHAPTER 17
## Seasonal jobs with the National Park Service
84. Fee collector
85. Ranger: law enforcement, interpretation, general
86. Visitor Use Assistant
87. Park guide
88. Maintenance: laborer, maintenance worker, motor vehicle operator
89. Positions in biology, archeology and other fields

## Seasonal USDA Forest Service jobs
90. Forestry aid and technician
91. Aids or technicians in archaeology, biological, hydrological, lands, range, real estate and surveying
92. Fire suppression and fire support workers
93. Fire tower lookout

## Seasonal BLM jobs
94. Forestry and range (fire positions) aid and technician
95. Material handler
96. Motor vehicle operator
97. Cartography aid or technician
98. Engine operator
99. Fire suppression and fire support workers
100. Horse or mule wrangler

## Army Corps of Engineers
101. Park or gate attendant at COE projects (bid)
102. Hired worker for bid-winner at project

## Other federal seasonal work
103. Post office help at Christmas
104. IRS tax season worker
105. Census taker

# CHAPTER 18
## Working for a concessionaire in a national park
106. Hotel jobs like front desk clerk, housekeeper, back office worker
107. Restaurant jobs like cook, waiter/waitress, hostess, cashier
108. Retail store jobs like cashier, stocker
109. Warehouse workers
110. Tour or recreational activity jobs like tour guide, boat or raft operator, boat rental agent, boat instructor, golf course-related
111. Gas station jobs like cashier, mechanic, attendant
112. Medical clinic jobs like receptionist, nurse, physician's assistant
113. Campground host
114. Maintenance worker
115. Rodent and pest control worker
116. Shuttle driver
117. Helicopter pilot or worker for flight-seeing operations

## Nonprofit associations
118. Clerk or cashier selling books and other items at an NPS visitor center
119. Warehouse worker
120. Bookkeeper — place orders, keep books

## National forest concessionaires
121. Campground host
122. Maintenance worker
123. Manager of several campgrounds
124. Holder of concession rights to run a FS campground
125. Forest fire support worker

## State parks
126. Ranger — present programs, enforce rules, give tours
127. Maintenance worker
128. Fee collector
129. Visitor center worker
130. Campground host
131. Park aide
132. Operator of a hunting check station

## County and city parks

133. Maintenance worker
134. Fee collector
135. Visitor contact personnel
136. Operator of a concessionairc activity

## CHAPTER 19

### Resorts

137. Hotel and motel jobs like front desk clerk, housekeeper, child care provider, maintenance worker, waiter/waitress, chef, hostess, back office worker, security person, bellman, cashier, retail clerk, bartender
138. Activity director or recreation leader
139. Restaurant jobs like wait staff, hostess, chef or cook, busboy, bartender
140. Gas station jobs like cashier, mechanic, attendant
141. Retail jobs like cashier, salesperson, stocker or warehouse worker
142. Grocery stores like cashier, bagger, stocker
143. RV parks jobs like registration and reservation staff, cashier, maintenance, groundskeeper, store clerk
144. Adventure/recreation tours: jobs like raft guide, stable hand, tour leader, reservations staff, cashier, mechanic, maintenance worker, driver, loader or packer
145. Golf course jobs like golf pro, shop staff, groundskeeper, ranger/ starter, mechanic or helper for care of golf carts, snack bar attendant or food preparer, customer service representative
146. Marina jobs like boat rental agent, boat instructor, mechanic, fuel attendant, cashier
147. Personal services like hairdresser, nanny or childcare provider, computer programmer, handyman
148. Shows: usher, ticket sales staff
149. Flight-seeing or helicopter tour operation workers
150. Costumed character at amusement park or clown
151. Dog musher/guide, dog caretaker

## Dude ranches

152. Wrangler
153. Wait staff
154. Cook
155. Housekeeper
156. Maintenance worker
157. Child care provider or worker
158. Office worker
159. Airport driver
160. Laundry worker

## Bed & Breakfasts (B&Bs)

161. Housekeeper
162. Breakfast preparation like cook, wait staff
163. Guest check-in and greeting
164. Vacation relief staff or manager

## Ski resorts

165. Lift ticket seller
166. Ski instructor
167. Child care provider or worker
168. Driver
169. Retail clerk
170. Food related jobs like cook, wait staff, busboy, bartender
171. Weather reporter for area radio stations

## Amusement and theme parks

172. Food service worker
173. Ride operator and mechanic
174. Game operator
175. Retail sales clerk
176. Campground worker
177. Tram driver
178. Costumed character
179. Maintenance and repair worker
180. Interpreter
181. Tour guide
182. Warehouse worker

## Cruises and land tours

183. Housekeeper
184. Food preparation and wait staff, bartender
185. Lecturer or performer
186. Dance host (also ambassador or gentlemen host)
187. Recreational leader for gym, golf, dance, exercise, children's activities
188. Bus driver/guide
189. Customer service or shore representative
190. Bus maintenance and cleaning worker

## Casinos

191. Blackjack dealer
192. Food preparation and wait staff
193. Bartender
194. Security
195. Porter/porterette and change person

## Wall Drug and similar

196. Retail clerk
197. Maintenance worker
198. Cook
199. Cafeteria worker
200. RV park-related worker
201. Usher
202. Stocking and inventory clerk
203. Demonstrator of old-time crafts like blacksmithing, weaving
204. Driver of a horse-drawn buggy or wagon

## Disney World

205. Merchandise host/hostess, cashier, roving vendor, display merchandiser
206. Attractions host/hostess, tickets host/hostess
207. Culinary: wait help, bussing, steward, cashier host/hostess, cook
208. Housekeeping: custodial host/hostess, room attendant, houseman, laundry worker, 3rd shift custodial worker
209. Life guard host/hostess, pool maintenance worker
210. Transportation: parking lot guides, boat pilot, tram driver

211. Seating host/hostess
212. Character performer
213. Hotel-related jobs: front desk, bell services, housekeeper
214. Office, technical and reservations: front office receptionist, reservationist
215. Wardrobe: costume assistant

## Working/volunteering overseas

216. Teacher overseas
217. Support worker at Antarctica
218. Short-term laborer
219. Manager for RV park in Mexico
220. Property caretaker

## CHAPTER 20

## Temporary jobs

221. Office work: clerical, accounting, computers
222. Factory or assembly work
223. Professional
224. Construction work: carpentry, plumbing, electrical, sheet rock, block work
225. Product demonstration
226. Tax season work: accounting
227. Tax season work: clerical
228. Substitute teacher
229. Temporary medical jobs: nurse, therapist or physician
230. Fruit or vegetable picker
231. Work during a grape harvest: grape sampler, weigh master
232. Worker for wheat harvest
233. Corn detasseler
234. Agent in reservation center for campgrounds
235. Flagger for highway construction projects
236. Deliver telephone books
237. CDL driver, long or short haul

## Holiday-season work

238. UPS driver or warehouse worker
239. Christmas retail salesperson or giftwrapper

240. Mall sales for See's Candy or Hickory Farms
241. Santa Claus at a mall or department store
242. Bell ringer collecting donations
243. Fireworks sales
244. Post office temporary worker
245. Post office contract worker
246. Baggage hander for cargo aircraft
247. Sign twirlers
248. Usher at holiday cultural events
249. Flower shop drivers, designers, salespeople.
250. Phone workers at call centers for catalog orders & surveys
251. Worker at Renaissance festival

## Contract work and temporary work for professionals

252. Computer project consultant
253. Technical writer
254. Engineer
255. Medical short-term assignment: nurse, therapist, physician
256. RN or LPN at family or children's camp
257. Teacher

## Special events

258. County or state fairs
259. Sports events
260. NASCAR events in a support capacity: security, parking, cleanup, souvenirs, food service, admissions, tickets
261. Home and garden shows
262. Shows in Quartzsite, Arizona
263. Golf tournaments
264. Events at stadiums or convention centers
265. Race tracks: horse, dog races
266. Swap meets: booth sales, parking

## CHAPTER 21
## Sales of RV-related products and services

267. Solar panels
268. Upholstery and carpet cleaning
269. Solar ovens

270. Laptop computers and related equipment
271. GPS devices
272. Brake assists and other RV accessories
273. Windshield repair
274. RV repair or handyman work
275. Hair cutting, sewing, massages
276. Badges
277. Redwood signs
278. Satellite dishes and antennas
279. Satellite Internet equipment or Wi-Fi cards
280. Pet grooming
281. Sharpening knives and scissors
282. Locksmithing
283. RV detailing

## Other RV-based businesses

284. Engraving
285. Selling advertising and producing RV park maps (own business)
286. Carving
287. Artist or craftsperson: painting, beading, photography, weaving, jewelry etc.
288. Offering guided tours
289. Teaching classes in exercise, dance or crafts
290. Photographer— digital photo imaging
291. Word processing or medical transcription
292. Desktop publishing
293. RV book publishing and sales
294. Newsletter publication
295. Musician or performer
296. Giving massages

## Internet-related services

297. Sales of products on the Web through eBay or other online auction sites for yourself or others
298. Website sales
299. Produce an electronic magazine (e-zine)

## Consulting/professional

300. Innsitting business
301. Business consultant
302. Seminar speaker
303. Computer consultant, webpage designer
304. Computer "debugging" and repair
305. Freelance writer
306. Freelance photographer
307. Investor in stock market
308. Tax preparation
309. Performer at school assemblies
310. Instructor — exercise programs
311. Academic instructor — online courses

## CHAPTER 22

### National parks, forests and other federal agencies

312. Campground host
313. Environmental educator
314. Videographer or photographer
315. Construction worker
316. Grant writer
317. Visitor center attendant or naturalist
318. Interpreter (of resources)
319. Law enforcement desk officer
320. Search and rescue (SAR)
321. River patrol
322. Ranger in the back country permit office
323. Assistant on archaeological digs
324. Fire tower lookout
325. Worker on the Trash Tracker houseboat
326. Worker on the GRIT houseboat
327. Lighthouse tour guide
328. Carpenter and other tradesmen
329. Special project worker
330. Campground host at military Fam camps

## State parks
331. Campground hosting, which can include a variety of tasks
332. Clerical, computer and fiscal help at headquarters
333. Maintenance projects
334. Off-season park surveillance, minor maintenance projects, weekend campground hosting and interpretive hosting
335. Fee collector
336. Staff at visitor center or naturalist
337. Tour guide or docent
338. Period-costume guide or interpreter
339. Retail salesperson in a gift shop
340. Photographer, update slide collection
341. Teacher of Off Highway Vehicle (OHV) and Personal Water Craft (PWC) safety classes
342. Golf course worker
343. Campsite construction worker
344. Archaeological assistantant or helper
345. Backcountry patrol
346. Lighthouse tour guide or caretaker

## Nonprofit volunteers
347. Construction of a Habitat for Humanity build
348. Office or computer work for a Habitat for Humanity affiliate
349. Disaster relief work
350. Maintenance or office work at a church camp
351. Maintenace, office work, tour guide, programs at YMCA camp
352. Volunteer overseas — environmental, construction, health and education projects

## Exchange of services
353. Exchange work for space in an RV park
354. Work out an exchange with a private individual
355. Park at a business in exchange for night security
356. Help friends or relatives in exchange for a place to park and hookups

# SECTION III.
# MORE THAN 350 MONEYMAKING
# OPPORTUNITIES

*"I flunked retirement…"*
*Lee Iacocca*

*Jobs 1-39*

# Chapter 14
# How to find jobs with a campsite

You may be parked along a stream with a view of snow-capped mountains in summer. You could be nestled among the palm trees or exploring miles of lush Sonoran desert in the winter. You could be part of the excitement of Christmas or enjoying the solitude of a remote ranch or estate. You pick the spot. A job awaits.

Fortunately, not only can you choose your desired location, you will also find employers for some types of positions prefer to hire employees who bring their houses along with them and will even provide an RV site.

## JOBS AT RV PARKS AND RESORTS

1. *Manager and assistant manager*
2. *Reservations clerk or guest service worker - day and night shifts*
3. *Registration and reservations worker- computerized system*
4. *Gatekeeper*
5. *Office workers like secretary, bookkeeper or accountant*
6. *Maintenance worker*
7. *Construction - carpenter, plumber, electrician*
8. *Propane service technician*
9. *Janitor or housekeeper*
10. *Mechanic*
11. *Groundskeeper*
12. *Food service staff*
13. *Recreation or activity director*

14. *Craft or activity instructor*
15. *Golf marshal*
16. *Entertainer*
17. *Security personnel*
18. *Marina worker*
19. *Canoe rental clerk and livery driver*
20. *Shuttle van driver*
21. *Bike rental clerk, mechanic*
22. *Pool operations - lifeguard, pool cleaner*
23. *Retail stores operations - sales clerk, inventory and pricing clerk*
24. *Tour guide or salesperson for lots in membership parks*
25. *Offer services to other campers, i.e., haircuts, massages, sewing*
26. *Worker for contractor-offered services at RV parks and resorts - food, marina, etc.*

RV parks and resorts hire employees during their busy season to help cover the increased workload. You'll find more jobs available during the summer, but don't overlook winters where the "snowbirds" are — the southwest, Texas, Florida — or parks in ski resort areas. You could work all year around.

While the owners frequently act as managers, you'll find that many parks hire manager couples, assistant managers and staff to register campers, sell items in the store, or provide meals in a restaurant. Maintenance staff takes care of grounds, fills propane tanks, cleans restrooms and makes repairs. Larger parks may hire activity directors as well.

> **Beautiful Lakeside Resort! Couple needed to work in store and marina. Work 15 hours for site, $ for extra hours. Many perks.**

Some of the jobs listed above are found only in the larger, resort-type RV parks. If you have skills or experience in more areas, you increase your value. You might be able to create a position combining several different jobs in a smaller RV park. A smaller park may hire someone to work part-time at a particular task, such as activity director, or to work in exchange for an RV site if the park can't afford a whole position.

## Where you find these jobs

A number of RV parks and resorts advertise in *Workamper News*. You may also find advertisements in other RV publications or on RV-related websites and discussion groups related to working on the road.

You can also identify RV parks and resorts that are potential employers in an area using campground directories or by contacting the local Chamber of Commerce. Contact them directly. For resorts and larger parks, you may find listings in the Help Wanted section of local newspapers.

> RV workers Ron and Val: "Normally I would say 100 sites is a good measure of whether a campground would need some extra help or not. A lot depends on what amenities they have. A smaller campground with a pool and Jacuzzi, etc., probably could use the extra help but not 40 hours per week."

## Compensation

The compensation for working in an RV park or resort can range from a simple exchange (with no money changing hands) to good working wages, along with an RV site.

In an exchange, you work a certain number of hours per week and in return are given a site. Hours worked may be per person or per couple. The park may or may not add an hourly wage for hours exceeding that minimum.

For paid positions, you can receive an hourly wage or monthly salary. Your RV site is generally part of your compensation. Perks — such as free or reduced-cost propane, laundry, store items, meals or other amenities —

> **Golfers!**
> **RV resort and golf course needs you. Work for site, $$ and golf privileges.**

may also be included as part of your compensation. Complimentary tickets to area attractions could even be part of the deal.

Compensation can vary tremendously. We have met RV workers working almost full-time for just a site. Others volunteer a few hours for a site to reduce their expenses. Still others have negotiated excellent wages or salaries as well as perks and been very well compensated; for example, one couple who worked in Colorado several years ago negotiated their site, one free meal a day, propane and laundry plus $8/hour each.

So you are clear on what you are being offered and what your RV site "costs," review Chapter 10, "Find out about the Job" and Chapter 11, "What is a site worth?" (page 112) before taking a job.

As Greg Robus, former editor and publisher of *Workamper News*, stated, "The employer's idea of what his or her exchange package is worth is irrelevant. It's up to each Workamper to be selective and to only accept jobs that offer a compensation package that suits their individual needs."

## Finding better paying jobs

To find (or create) higher paying jobs, do your research. Know what other RV parks in the area are offering so you have an idea of what is realistic. Know your own worth. Your skills are probably worth more than a bare minimum wage, especially if you are willing to work and not just doing something to keep busy. Sell yourself and ask for more during the interview and negotiation process, especially as you accumulate experience. Look for opportunities that aren't listed in the usual publications, as well.

✔ **Develop your RV worker network.** See Chapter 8.

✔ **Talk to the owners** when you stay at an RV park. Conduct an informational interview. See Chapter 8.

✔ **Increase your value** by taking a training and certification program for campground managers or learn a computerized reservation system. ARVC and National RV Park Institute offer courses and certification programs. The Escapees RV Club's program trains members desiring to work in RV park management at member parks. Obtain a training CD for a reservation system. See **Resources.**

## Related possibilities:

$ **Contract services:** Some RV parks and resorts contract out services like operating the restaurant, a marina, or other activities. You might be able to bid on these positions. Watch for advertisements in the previously mentioned sources, but also keep your eyes and ears open.

$ **Membership parks:** If you belong to a membership campground, there may be opportunities for paid work or for an exchange of services for your site. Talk to management.

$ **Specialized parks or camps:** Church, Scout and YMCA camps may need summer maintenance and office help or caretaking during the off-season. Military RV and fam camps for families of active and retired military personnel may also hire, as do some clothing-optional resorts.

**$ Offer services:** Stay in an RV park for a period of time and then offer services to park residents. One fellow was resident handyman during his winters in an Arizona RV park that catered to winter snowbirds. He did repairs to the inside of rigs for more elderly residents. Another RVer, to raise money for unexpected truck repairs, offered to repack wheel bearings while in an RV park. Just a few jobs and he was on his way. Sewing and haircuts could be offered to other residents without disruption to park activities. The management, of course, should approve these activities, and you may also need certain licensing. (See Chapter 21 for more information on operating your own business.)

**$ Working specific locations: Ron & Val** are exceptionally good at finding positions in RV parks and campgrounds. Ron usually works in maintenance, Val in the office or fee collection. They have been working every other year in a state park in Colorado to spend time with grandchildren. The other years, they target an area and line up positions before heading to that location. Ron and Val check with all sources. They use *Workamper News*, other job sources (Chapter 8), and network with other RVers, talking to co-workers and RVers about RV parks that are good employers. Besides considering the salary, they weigh the perks: free site, free laundry, discounts and tickets to attractions.

**$ Ski resorts: Gabby & Janice** managed an RV park in Ketchum, Idaho, one winter. They are ski buffs and this job gave them the opportunity to be near Sun Valley and get discounted ski passes. Expecting to have just a few winter visitors at any given time, the owners left them in charge. More visitors kept showing up, and it turned out to be a bigger job than they expected, but they got in a lot of skiing.

**$ Church camps: Rich and Fran** found employment at a church camp and conference center Fran had attended as a child. Pay was better than average plus they got three excellent meals each day. Fran worked in the office handling the phone and computer input as well as registration and check-in for attendees. Rich supervised a crew of four eighteen-year olds as Head Housekeeper. With free site and meals, they could bank most of their paychecks all summer.

$ **Clothing-optional resorts: Al and DeAnna** have worked at several clothing-optional resorts. They visited the first resort and liked it. They called a couple of years later and, after a telephone interview, ended up being the first couple hired. Says DeAnna, "Nudist and clothing-optional resorts are expensive to live in so working there is an opportunity to live the lifestyle. It's really inexpensive because you tend to do your recreational activities like swimming pool, parties, and other activities there rather than spending money out. So it was a good thing for our budget to be there." Most clubs want their employees to have experience with the lifestyle prior to working there. DeAnna advises visiting a resort before taking a job to see if you are comfortable there. Some resorts are more family oriented. They can be either privately owned or run by a board.

## SITE-SITTING JOBS

27.  *Construction sites: mainly providing a presence*
28.  *Construction sites: paid to provide 24-hour security*
29.  *Storage units: management, night security, or provide vacation relief*
30.  *Gate guard at an oil field for a security company*
31.  *House-sitter*
32.  *House-sitter, providing also pet or plant care*
33.  *Caretaker of ranches or other property*
34.  *Caretaker or work in exchange for site*
35.  *Managing a household— house couple*
36.  *Child careprovider — nanny*
37.  *Gun club or shooting range — caretaker*

Construction companies and individuals hire people to watch their property when no one is there. We've often noticed ranches seeking this kind of help. Some jobs require simply a presence on the site for a certain number of hours per day. In other cases, you may have certain tasks to do. People seek others to help them with projects like gardening, restoring old buildings, and new construction in exchange for a site.

Often money is paid for extra hours in these cases. Nonprofit and government agencies may also seek RVers who are willing to work in exchange for their sites. Quite a variety of tasks can be involved and you can likely find one that appeals to you.

Caretaking property requires more duties than simply site-sitting, and is generally longer-term. Duties could include care of animals, garden, fencing, house repair or inside duties.

## Where you find these jobs:

*The Caretaker Gazette* lists these types of situations in their publication, varying in location, duties and compensation. *Workamper News* and other RV publications may also have ads of this type. You can find agencies online that provide house-sitting opportunities. You will probably be charged a fee to join and may need to be bonded. Research the company and check to see if they provide liability insurance.

Word of mouth, local classified ads, large construction companies, real estate agents, security firms — all are potential sources. Self-storage units often hire couples to manage the property and live onsite. Look for ads in the classified section of the local newspaper, or use the Yellow Pages and contact a storage place directly.

## Potential compensation:

Rather than offer pay, many housesitting arrangements and caretaking assignments are an exchange of services. You get full or partial hookups or a place to stay, perhaps use of amenities, in exchange for specified duties. If your duties go much beyond bringing in the mail and watering plants, you can probably expect some compensation. If you work for a construction site or storage place, you should get compensation in addition to your site. All this is negotiable, of course.

## Related opportunities:

**$ Housekeeping couples (and singles)** are sought in *Caretaker Gazette* and by agencies for duties as cook, gardener, chauffeur, child care or housekeeping. Household managers oversee other household and groundskeeping staff. Some positions offer lucrative compensation; $100,000 a year plus benefits is possible. Most employers require excellent references and previous experience or training plus require a commitment of at least a year. Most positions come with housing; you would need to negotiate a spot to park your RV.

**$ Gun clubs** hire RVers to park onsite and keep an eye on things. *Workamper News* is one source.

**$** **House couple: Bill and Marna** decided several years ago they wanted to work as a house couple since those positions paid almost $40,000 year. Not having any direct experience, but feeling confident in their knowledge and abilities, they asked friends to write letters of reference and went to an agency. They were placed at an estate where they worked for one year. They were later interviewed for a position working with a celebrity.

**$** **Site watchers: Mike and Nancy** were referred by summer job co-workers to a company that constructs microwave towers and hires RVers to watch the site. On some assignments one person was required to be onsite 24-hours a day. At others they had to be present only at night. Compensation was more when they provided 24-hour a day security. For either type of job, when workers were there, they could leave to explore the area or do their shopping. Says Nancy, "It was a pretty easy way to earn money, though on one job we got stuck out in the desert after it got very hot."

**$** **RV homesitters: Al and DeAnna** have obtained housesitting assignments through friends. Most recently they were able to visit Hawaii. Explains DeAnna, "We paid for our airplane flight; they supplied the house, a car, and insider's information about what they liked best about Honolulu. I fed the dogs and took them out on two walks a day. We kept in contact with the owners via e-mail and were able to let them know about an urgent call from their credit union." They could easily have extended their stay. Al was at a garage sale nearby, and told the lady he was pet sitting and was offered another job. Word of mouth and meeting other pet owners can also lead to assignments.

## SALES OF CHRISTMAS TREES AND PUMPKINS

38. *Christmas tree lot manager or helper*
39. *Pumpkin lot manager or helper*

The smell of pines, children excited about Christmas — part and parcel of selling Christmas trees. Managing a Christmas tree lot is a short but intense way to earn some cash. As the managers, you may be able to hire local workers to unload, display, water, trim, sell and load trees onto customers' cars or you could find yourselves doing all or part of these tasks. It depends on the owner and how busy the lot is. Lots usually open the day after Thanksgiving and stay open until all the trees are sold or Christmas Eve, whichever comes first.

The negatives of this job are several. Long hours and the weather can be a challenge. Many Christmas tree lots are on dirt. If it rains, you'll work extra hard at keeping your rig clean. In some cases, dealing with the owners can be a challenge. The biggest headache we had was finding and hiring reliable helpers.

## Potential compensation

In the three to four weeks the lot is open, you can earn a nice chunk of money. At this writing, average compensation for managing a Christmas tree lot is around $3,500. Additionally many owners offer some sort of bonus. We earned a bonus of $1.00 or so for each tree sold; other owners give an unannounced bonus or one based on how well the managers do overall. Still other owners pay on a percentage basis. Don and Cynthia earned 18% of the after-tax sales at their lot.

## Related opportunity

Pumpkin lots work in a similar way, though aren't as intense. Often a pumpkin lot reopens as a Christmas tree lot so you can work both. Compensation isn't as good because pumpkins sell for a lot less. But you might earn an additional $1,000 or more, depending on the situation.

## Questions to ask

Some questions to ask if you are considering this type of work, gleaned from the experience of other RVers:

✔ **What sort of site and hookups will I have?** Are there provisions to empty my holding tanks or use a portable toilet? Do I have electricity? How many amps? Is my lot paved or dirt?

✔ **How is my pay figured?** Most have a set fee for the time period. Some have a base pay and then an amount per tree sold. Others pay a percentage of sales. Make sure nothing can be subtracted for any reason. Can we earn a bonus? How is that computed?

✔ **What duties do we have?** These vary by owner. Duties may include setting up and preparing the lot, trimming trees and putting them in stands, watering, flocking trees, loading and unloading the truck, loading trees on customers' cars, etc.

✔ **What responsibilities do I have for money?** Do I have to reconcile receipts against cash or complete any forms? *(These duties can add an hour or more to an already long day)* Are tree prices firm or can I offer a discount to make a sale? *(Depending on how your compensation is figured, this could make a difference in your total income.)* How often will cash be picked up? *(Are you in a safe area if you have to keep cash overnight? Or at least in a fenced, locked yard?)*

✔ **Who will hire workers?** If I do the hiring, do I have a budget, or will this come out of or affect my compensation? If not, will there be a helper here at all times or only during certain hours? What will happen if a worker doesn't show up? Who pays them? *(The owner should take care of this, otherwise you could have a nightmare of taxes and forms to complete.)*

### Where you find these jobs

Sources for jobs include *Workamper News* and word of mouth. A good way to line up a job is to stop by a Christmas tree lot or pumpkin lot in the area you might like to work the following year. Find out from this year's manager what the situation is. Get the contact name and follow up after Christmas. Most owners like to firm up their managers by September.

Also check the National Christmas Tree Association website for retail lots in the area you are interested. If you have targeted an area, check with the local Chamber of Commerce as well. They may also be able to tell you lot locations and owners for their area.

From our experience, before taking a job selling Christmas trees, we would definitely recommend talking to someone who has previously worked for this owner. Your expectations will be more realistic and you may avoid some potential problems. In the right circumstances, we would do it again. It was fun being part of the magic of Christmas and a challenge to sell more trees and increase our bonus.

**$ Christmas tree workers: John and Susan** relate, "The first time we sold trees, we didn't know the questions to ask but we needed money so we hired on with a company in Missouri. Temperatures were as low as 20 degrees below zero, plus wind-chill factor, with frozen water for five days in a row." Electricity was only available for a few hours a day. Another disadvantage was that this was a new lot. Whereas an established lot would have clientele that would return year after year, a new lot depends on people driving by and noticing it." John and Susan were getting paid by the number of trees they sold. They only made $1,700. "Our second experience was better. There was a base of $2,500 plus an additional amount for each tree sold." They could hire employees to help out, whom the owner paid for. "We enjoyed helping people pick out their Christmas trees."

A job with a campsite is ideal for the RV worker. You will need to ask questions to make sure the position is a match. The employer has certain needs and a budget. If one situation is not right, there are plenty more in this category to investigate, so don't get discouraged.

These types of jobs can work for RV workers needing to make a living and those for whom income is not a strong consideration. If you need to make a living, you will have to look harder to find a job that pays well. All the job-finding skills you developed in **Section II** will come into play. Others have found good jobs. So can you.

# Notes

*"Don't say you don't have enough tine. You have exactly the
same number of hours per day that were given to Helen Keller,
Pasteur, Michelangelo, Mother Teresa, Leonardo da Vinci,
Thomas Jefferson, and Albert Einstein."*
*H. Jackson Brown*

# Chapter 15
# How to get traveling jobs in your RV

An RV is a great way to take advantage of jobs where you move from location to location. These include jobs like checking gas pipe lines, working on RV caravans, selling advertising or other products to RV parks and selling a product in different locations.

## JOBS TRAVELING IN YOUR RV

40.  *Gas pipe line inspector*
41.  *Wagon master/tail gunner for RV caravans*
42.  *Mechanic for RV caravans*
43.  *Deliver RVs*
44.  *Salesperson of advertising at campgrounds*
45.  *Salesperson or manufacturer's rep*
46.  *Inspector of RV parks for directories*
47.  *Door-to-door sales for Air Photo*
48.  *Mystery shopper*
49.  *Judge at dog shows*
50.  *Circus worker*
51.  *Booking agent for a circus*
52.  *Groom for a circus*
53.  *Travel with a carnival: rides, setup, welders, office, mechanics, CDL drivers*
54.  *NASCAR circuit help*
55.  *Salesperson of products to businesses (open territories)*
56.  *Product installer with changing job locations*

## CHECKING PIPELINES

At least one employer who contracts to check pipelines for gas leaks advertises in RV publications. Companies in this industry offer paid training and then you are assigned an area in which to work. Many contracts are in metropolitan areas. You could work in one area for several months and then move to another site, depending on what contracts the company has available. In the case where the gas lines are located in rural areas, you generally work in teams instead of by yourself. You receive an hourly wage and some travel expense money.

$ **Gas detection worker: Stuart** began work in San Antonio, Texas, after being trained to use gas-detection equipment. Some of the jobs were only about three weeks long. Says Stuart, "It worked out to about $400/week." Since most jobs were of short duration and they only had one car, it was difficult for his wife, **Theresa,** to get a job.

## RV CARAVANS

A number of companies put together RV caravans, guiding people traveling in their own RVs to destinations like Mexico in the winter and Alaska in the summer. The caravan companies hire wagon masters to lead the trip and tail gunners to bring up the rear. Compensation depends on the size of the group and your experience. The wagon master (a single or a couple) is like the activity director and tour guide. The wagon master arrives first at each stop to verify arrangements for the RV park and any activities at the location. Being good with people, knowing the area you are traveling (most caravan companies require that you take one of their caravans as a customer first), and being able to handle the unexpected and make it look planned are all desirable traits.

> **Wagon masters and mechanics wanted.**
> **Lead caravans to Mexico or Alaska and travel free!**

The tail gunner brings up the rear and makes sure everyone gets safely to the day's stop. If one of the rigs has a mechanical breakdown, he stays with the rig until help arrives. Some caravans include paid mechanics as well.

Fantasy RV Tours is one company that sponsors caravan trips and hires people to lead them. You must attend their training, plus have been a paying customer on at least one of their caravans. Pay is $100–$150/day and your fees for RV parks, admissions, etc. are covered.

## DELIVER RVS

RVs have to be transported from the manufacturer to the dealer. Transport companies provide this service and contract drivers with CDLs who work as independent contractors. Owners of trucks capable of hauling 5th wheels and trailers are paid so much per mile from factory to dealer (one-way) to deliver the rig. Drivers are also needed to deliver motorhomes. The earning potential is more than $50K/year if you are willing to hustle. A couple can increase earnings if one drives a truck hauling a rig and the other delivers a motorhome. To maximize earnings, you need to line up a "back haul"on the return trip. If you can contract with an RV manufacturer directly, you can also increase your earnings.

> **Drive your own pickup. Deliver travel trailers and 5th wheels to dealers. Earn $1200/week and more.**
> *RV Transport*

If you don't want to work full-time, transport companies also use RVers who want to make occasional deliveries, want time in between deliveries to sightsee, or prefer to deliver only occasionally. Delivering an RV, for example, could be a way to get up to Alaska in the spring to see the area.

There are a number of costs that go against that income, however. Out of this figure comes your gas, insurance, as well as wear and tear and depreciation on your own vehicle. Your earnings may pay for your truck in a year, but you will also have to buy a new one more frequently.

*How to Get Paid $50,000 a Year to Travel Without Selling Anything* is written about this line of work. It's a good guide to understanding the industry and getting started.

$ **Deliver RVs- long haul: Bob & Caren** delivered trailers and 5th wheels for a company. They got paid per loaded mile, meaning one way. Since they had to drive home, that meant the actual pay per mile was half that. In their case, they did not find delivering RVs very profitable once they had paid all the expenses associated with the delivery. Bob and Caren were charged for the first $1,000 worth of damage to the rig, including stone chips, that happened during the trip. If the weather was bad, they would often sit it out because of possible damage. They could stay in the trailer or 5$^{th}$ wheel at night, but couldn't use the facilities.

**$ Deliver RVs-short haul: Bob and Andi** fell into an RV delivery deal by being at the right place at the right time. The dealer from whom they had purchased three rigs was short on drivers to drive motorhomes back from an RV show. They offered, were hired and that has led to other assignments for this dealer.

### Questions to ask

✔ **Driver's license:** Do you need a Commercial Drivers License (CDL)?

✔ **Pay:** Are you paid per mile or per loaded mile of travel (both ways, or only one-way)? Can you take a side trip on the way? Are you an independent contractor or employee?

✔ **Expenses:** What expenses are you responsible for? Can you use the RV to sleep in or cook in?

✔ **Responsibilities:** What damage will you be responsible for?

✔ **Time frame:** Will you be traveling on a deadline?

Figure how much money you will really make after you pay your expenses, including wear and tear and depreciation on your tow vehicle.

## SELL ADVERTISING IN RV PARKS

Several companies produce site maps for RV parks. The production of the map is financed by the sales of ads in the map to local vendors. While the couple or person is working on the map for the RV park, they have a complimentary site. The RV park gets free maps of their park and nearby area to hand out to their visitors. Management of the RV park is asked to give you a list of potential advertisers; businesses that their customers would be likely to patronize

> **Travel the areas of your choice selling advertising. Lucrative commission. Leads and full training provided.**

during their stay. This makes the salesperson's job easier because you have targeted businesses, a name and a referral from the park. Once you've sold all the spots, you send camera-ready materials to the main office.

You get paid based on the dollar value of the ads you sell. You generally do not get paid until the advertiser pays.

The company may provide you with leads or names of RV parks where a former employee sold ads, or you may have to find some or all prospects on your own. You work as an independent contractor, which gives you some deductions for expenses but you must pay full social security taxes at 15.3% rather than the 50% employee rate. (Obtain Publication 533 from the IRS for an explanation at *www.irs.gov.*)

You can do very well at this type of work if you are good at sales. Like any sales job, it takes a while to develop good clients and to zero in on the parks that are lucrative. Over time, sales people usually winnow out the low-producing parks and concentrate on a few high-producing parks. One couple worked for a company, then started their own business and now produce the maps from start to finish. Doing the site maps for just a few parks they have developed as clients they make around $40,000 a year and work only a few months. Similar companies print menus with local advertising for small restaurants.

## Related opportunities

$ **Sales or manufacturer's rep:** selling things to RV parks for their use or to sell in their stores.

$ **Campground inspector** for a campground directory.

$ **Represent products** to other types of businesses as well.

$ **Sell advertising** for a campground guides, like Wheelers Resort and Campground Guide.

*$* **Advertising sales: Stuart and Theresa** worked for one of the companies that produces site maps at RV parks. After a training period at headquarters, they were given several leads, parks for which former representatives had done maps. How successful they were in a park had a lot to do with the support that the park owner gave businesses in town. If the owner encouraged campers to visit them, it was a much easier sell for Stuart and Theresa. Stuart noted that successful reps have a few lucrative parks in locations they enjoy. He also pointed out that to figure true income you must figure telephone calls, mileage and other expenses against the amount you gross. Since you are an independent contractor you have some additional deductions, but you also must pay expenses with that income.

## OTHER SALES

Sales of other products not RV-related can work well for RVers. Some companies, like Air Photo, actively recruit RVers. In fact, Air Photo is a good match for RV workers who want to be their own boss and want the flexibility to travel while they see the country. In business since 1985, Air Photo does speculative aerial photography of homes, estates and farms throughout the United States. Salespeople then call on the owners with a 11" x 14" photo of their house, fully matted in studio-quality frames. Besides this product the homeowner can purchase other products and packages; CD-Roms and a larger canvas-mount picture are most popular. Out of 100 photos, a salesperson typically sells 25-30, earning 30 percent commission. Bonus commissions are paid after sales goals are reached.

A new salesperson—single or couple—receives a manual and supplies. Training is provided, and most salespeople are ready to go within one week. With inventory in 38 states, they usually have a job for most places you'd like to travel. When you request an area, you receive a printout of photos and addresses so you can locate a convenient RV park. Once you decide, Air Photo ships the photos and a box of frames. All shipping is paid for by the company. Salespeople can take cash, check or credit card.

**Air Photo: Hap** sold part-time for Air Photo for more than ten years He is one of several successful solo salespeople. (Hap's wife, **June,** did work with him selling for a number of years.) Says Hap, "They are the greatest people in the world to work for. They treat all their employees like each one is special." Hap notes that the biggest challenge is finding people at home. If you can contact them, you usually make a sale.

### Questions to ask about commission sales

✔ **Pay:** Ask how and when you will be paid. What, if anything, could cause a deduction? Can you earn bonuses? Make sure you know what needs to be filled out in order to get paid and if there are deadlines or requirements you must meet in order to get paid on time and the full amount.

✔ **Territories and leads:** Are there defined territories? Could another salesperson call on one of your clients? How do you get leads? Does the company supply any?

✔ **Training:** What sort of sales training and support is provided?

✔ **Supplies and facilities:** In the case of selling an item (see Chapter 23), do you have to transport product or displays in your rig? Will the company ship them to you? Will you be selling indoors?

✔ **Expenses:** What expenses are you responsible for? Do you pay for your own RV site or does the company?

Be sure to check out the company and its reputation before working for them. Check the Better Business Bureau in their home state and with other sales people who work for the company. Also, if you have no sales experience, do a self-evaluation. Do you have the personality to sell? See **Resources** for articles to help you decide.

## MYSTERY SHOPPERS

A number of businesses contract with companies that provide "mystery shoppers" to rate their customer service. The mystery shopper goes to the store to buy a product or use the service and then rates the business on their experience. Sometimes a pre-visit phone call is required.

According to Dawn Lindsey of Genesis Group, Inc., the average shopping assignment pays $15,

> **Shoppers needed for financial institution in southern CA. Takes about 20 minutes to complete. Requires an interaction with a teller, a new account counselor and a phone call.**

but some pay $25 or $40. One job paid $190 for two-day's work. Some companies provide this service only in their own area; others like Genesis have national clients and assignments in many states. Lindsey says that a shopper can do only one assignment in a particular store and location once every six months. Notes Lindsey, "Many of our schedulers work only with shoppers who have e-mail. Assignments and reporting is all done using e-mail." Shoppers can let schedulers know their travel plans and can pick up assignments in that area. Most agree that this work helps pick up extra money but is not a way to support yourself.

## OTHER OPPORTUNITIES

$ **Judging dog shows** is one of the ways Judy helps subsidize her travel. While she only gets a small fee to judge, the clubs putting on the shows do pay expenses. Prior to hitting the road full-time she often had to fly to an assignment. Now that she is a full-time RVer, she is able to travel in her RV and enjoy the sights along the way.

$ **Sell products at shows:** Work opportunities exist selling products at various shows: RV shows, state and county fairs, home and garden shows and many more. You can sell your own products or work for another vendor. See Chapters 20 and 21, Working for Special Events and Working for Yourself for complete information.

$ **Circuses and carnivals:** Working in a circus may be your dream. Perhaps you'd rather work on the midway of a carnival. Both move from location to location on their circuits. Most stay in one section of the United States. *Workamper News* often carries an ad for at least one circus; we've seen ads for booking agent and horse groom. Check the Internet for websites of circuses and carnivals. Check to see whether you'll be able to park your RV with their trucks, or if you'll have to find a nearby RV park.

$ **Motorsport tracks and circuits:** NASCAR and other motorsport circuits provide employment opportunities. You can get a job going from race to race. The tracks themselves hire workers and race teams. In addition, vendors who sell products at these events may need employees. See Chapter 21, Special Events, for working at individual tracks. Check the Motorsport page at *Workamper News (www.workamper.com)* for potential employers. You will need to check on an individual basis about an RV site at the event and if you will be charged.

$ **Products and services with changing job locations:** Two couples (below) who wanted to make more money and were willing to work most of the year found other opportunities. The first couple answered an ad in the help wanted section of the Phoenix newspaper and found a high-paying job with benefits that fit their RV lifestyle. Don't overlook "real jobs" that could lend themselves to RV travel.

$ **Installers: Dean and Judy** answered an ad in the *Arizona Republic* for workers to install bathtub liners in hotels. The company obtains a contract to replace the liners in a hotel and sends a team to do the job. Dean and Judy were the first RVers they hired. They were provided a room, but usually brought their RV and parked it on the hotel parking lot. If they had a job in New York City or another crowded metropolitan area, they might leave their rig temporarily at a park or in storage. This full-time job had benefits and allowed for time off when needed.

*$* **Field inspector: Nick's** experience site-sitting construction sites with wife Joanne, led to a job for Nick as a field inspector. In this position he traveled to construction sites making sure company standards were met. The sites ranged from California to Florida. They were in one location from a couple of weeks to several months, depending on the project. Nick's background as an electronics technician and business degree graduate, along with what he learned from site-sitting, served to make him valuable to this company.

Working at a job where you can travel from place to place in your RV combines the best of both worlds: travel and making money. More companies with non-RV-related products that are seeking sales reps are willing to hire RVers for these positions. To evaluate whether or not these positions are moneymakers, you must factor in your travel expenses to judge your true income and remember that for most commission sales positions, it will take you a few years to build your client base so you have a dependable income.

# Notes

*"Integrity is the single biggest character trait needed for
success. Never compromise your integrity."*
*The Goals Guy at www.goalsguy.com*

*Jobs 57-83*

# Chapter 16
# How to get jobs within the RV industry

The RV industry itself provides opportunities for seasonal as well as full-time employment. Sales and repair of RVs, related equipment, plus working for RV clubs and organizations are a few of the ways you could earn money.

## JOBS IN RV SALES AND SERVICE

57. *RV salesperson*
58. *Retail salesperson: supplies or parts department*
59. *Quality control inspector*
60. *Technician: walk-throughs with new buyers*
61. *Detailer*
62. *Mechanic*
63. *Service technician*
64. *Service writer*
65. *Lot attendant*
66. *Inside office worker: receptionist, clerk, accountant or bookkeeper, computer workers such as operator, programmer, data input clerk*

RV dealers need many types of workers to sell and service RVs. In areas that attract RVers, the dealership may hire workers to supplement their year-round staff during the busy season. In the sales area, you might find positions both selling new and used RVs as well as selling parts and writing up service orders.

Before the new buyer takes possession, the RV is inspected to make sure all systems are working properly. Then someone conducts a walk-through to demonstrate the systems to the buyer. Larger dealerships may have an individual for each of these duties, while smaller dealerships often combine these tasks with another.

> **Attention—Mechanics and Service Technicians — Seasonal or year-round positions available with large dealership in the Southwest.**

Dealers also have parts and service areas. In the service area, mechanics work on the engine, service technicians work on other systems like refrigerators, water heaters, etc. Good certified mechanics are always in demand, as are qualified service technicians.

The Recreational Vehicle Industry Association (RVIA) offers a Recreational Vehicle Service Technician course at several locations around the country for training in this field. Camping World RV Institute offers similar training. (See **Resources.**)

### Where to find positions

To locate RV dealers in tourist or snowbird areas, check in the help-wanted section of the local classifieds or stop by RV dealers with a copy of your résumé and speak to the appropriate manager.

### RV sales and service:

**Page and Ardith** worked in Anchorage, Alaska. Their first summer, Ardith got a job at the largest RV dealer in the city, while Page worked construction. Ardith gave walk-throughs to buyers of RVs, explaining how everything worked inside and out. When she wasn't busy with that, she would do detailing or other tasks. Salesmen would often request she perform the walk-through on her days off, paying her $25 out of their pockets for doing so. Their second summer, Page also got a job there moving RVs around the dealership, and they were permitted to park their RV right on the dealership lot as well.

**Sylvia and Jack** have worked at Camping World and for a large RV dealer. Jack is an "Automotive Service Excellence" (ASE) certified mechanic and can also work on repairs to inside systems and structure, making him more versatile. Sylvia enjoys people. She worked as a cashier and as a quality control inspector. As inspector, she gave rigs their pre-delivery inspection, listing what needed to be fixed before delivery. She would also note the condition of rigs before they were worked on to make sure mechanics and technicians cleaned it up properly. The dealer paid for their site at an RV park, a big savings.

**Charlie** attended a nine-month RV Repair and Maintenance School at Mt. San Antonio College, Walnut, California. Classes covered the basics of repairing and maintaining an RV. Charlie would be able to get jobs part time with this skill and also repair his own rig. **Norma** worked for a temporary agency while he attended school. Later they both worked for a company in Glendale, Arizona, Charlie installing solar equipment on RVs and Norma working in the office.

## CAMPING WORLD/RV SUPPLIES

67. *Retail sales clerk/cashier*
68. *Stocker*
69. *Service writer*
70. *Mechanic*
71. *RV technician*
72. *Janitor*
73. *Bookkeeper*
74. *Parts advisor*
75. *Merchandiser*
76. *Shop attendant*
77. *Goodwill Ambassador*

Camping World, with more than 75 locations in 27 states, hires seasonal workers. They hire Multi Location Crew members (MLC) who can transfer on a seasonal basis from location to location. There are several options: work four to six months a year and return each year, work only nine months, or work year round with only one to two weeks between assignments. Positions include retail positions

**A world of opportunity! Work for the largest retailer of aftermarket accessories for RVs. Many locations, competitive benefits.**

like cashier and stocker, service writer, installer, service technician, janitor, and bookkeeper. Goodwill ambassadors work as independent contractors.

Apply at the nearest retail location, or obtain an employment package and mail to their headquarters.

Camping World operates the Camping World RV Institute in Bowling Green, Kentucky. It offers a nine-week Service Technician course. Camping World's own employees attend this course, but it is open to others. The course is designed to train qualified RV service technicians. Students can take the entire program or individual units.

Other large RV supply stores may also hire seasonal workers. An area like Phoenix, Arizona, which has lots of winter snowbirds, is a good candidate for openings in this area.

## WORKING FOR RV CLUBS AND ORGANIZATIONS

78. *Paid staff for office work and club functions*
79. *Editorial or graphic designer*
80. *Webmaster or computer programmer*
81. *Manager and assistant manager for club RV parks*
82. *Activity director for club RV parks*
83. *RV safe driving instructor*

An organization with a sizable membership will need help. Often volunteers help with rallies, events and activities. If you find you enjoy working with a club, there might be a paid position. Most paid positions are offered to volunteers who are willing and able to do the job. For example, Pat and Dennis, members of the Escapees RV Club, worked as volunteers at the club's semiannual Escapade, a five-day educational rally. They were tapped for another club task, then were asked to be directors of the Western Escapade, making all the arrangements, getting volunteer staff and handling details.

> **Exp. manager and asst. manager couples needed. Club-affiliated RV park. Full hookup site plus salary.**

To get a paid position, become involved with an RV club or organization as a volunteer. You will probably get noticed if you work hard, but make your desires known to the manager or the person who would do the hiring. These positions are usually not advertised formally.

## OTHER RV INDUSTRY MONEYMAKERS:

$ **Selling RV related products:** solar panels, auxiliary brakes. See Chapter 26.

$ **Providing services to RVers** like carpet cleaning, windshield repair. See Chapter 21.

$ **Selling maps** to RV parks or advertising in RV park directories. See Chapter 15.

$ **Writing articles or taking photographs** for RV magazines. See Chapter 21.

$ **Working as a park manager** or worker at a club or membership RV park. See Chapter 14.

$ **Teaching RV safe driving:** Instructors are hired to conduct safety courses for RVers at RV rallies.

You may be able to use skills from your former life that fit some aspect of the industry. You could also get specialized training to qualify for higher-paying jobs in the RV industry. Seasonal work opportunities exist, or you could work full-time if you are looking for a new career!

# Notes

*"If you want to be happy for a year, win the lottery. If you*
*want to be happy for life, love what you do."*
Mary Higgins Clark *in* On the Street Where You Live

*Jobs 84-105*

# Chapter 17
# How to get seasonal federal jobs

## SEASONAL JOBS WITH THE NATIONAL PARK SERVICE

84. *Fee collector*
85. *Ranger: law enforcement, interpretation, general*
86. *Visitor Use Assistant*
87. *Park guide*
88. *Maintenance: laborer, maintenance worker, motor vehicle operator*
89. *Positions in biology, archeology and other fields*

## SEASONAL USDA FOREST SERVICE JOBS

90. *Forestry aid and technician*
91. *Aids or technicians in archaeology, biological, hydrological, lands, range, real estate and surveying*
92. *Fire suppression and fire support workers*
93. *Fire tower lookout*

## SEASONAL BLM JOBS

94. *Forestry and range (fire positions) aid and technician*
95. *Material handler*
96. *Motor vehicle operator*
97. *Cartography aid or technician*
98. *Engine operator*
99. *Fire suppression and fire support workers*
100. *Horse or mule wrangler*

## THE JOB PROCESS: APPLYING THROUGH *USAJOBS*

Our first job on the road was working at Grand Teton National Park. After that Bill and I worked at six other national parks. We explored ghost towns and hiked colorful canyons in Death Valley. We parked our RV with a view of glaciers and the Lynn Canal in Alaska. Working in Glen Canyon, we had time to explore little visited ruins of the ancestral Pueblo people. People pay a lot of money to vacation in these places and we were being paid to be there.

Working in the beautiful outdoors and making good money — that combination is made possible by working for the National Park Service (NPS) and other agencies that care for our public lands. More seasonal jobs are found with NPS than with other federal agencies, but seasonal positions can also be found with the U.S. Forest Service (USFS) and Bureau of Land Management (BLM).

> **USAJOBS**
> **The U.S. Government's official site for jobs and employment information provided by the United States Office of Personnel Management.**
> *www.usajobs.opm.gov*

Seasonal work can include law enforcement, interpretation, biology, forestry (usually fire suppression), and maintenance. Some clerical, archeology, history, and specialty positions may be hired on a temporary basis, depending on the needs of the agency and the specific location.

For government positions, note that each job title is assigned two letters (GS or WG) and a four-digit number for the particular job series. Jobs are either General Service positions (GS) or Wage Grade positions (WG). Wage grade positions are maintenance positions, General Service positions are all the others except supervisory-type positions. The main difference is that the salary scale is different for the two types of positions; WG positions pay more per hour than GS postions for the same grade level.

The government process can be confusing due to laws that Congress has passed and regulations of the U.S. Office of Personnel Management (OPM). It can seem harder to complete the application process than do the job. But don't let that discourage you. It is well worth wading through the process. If you don't get jobs the first time around, be persistent.

Many parks, as well as other agencies, have been given authority to hire their own employees. Hiring for each position includes these steps:

✔ Jobs are announced publicly.

✔ Applications or résumés must be postmarked and received on time, following all instructions. Incomplete applications, or applications received after deadlines are not considered.

✔ Eligible applications are determined to be qualified or unqualified, that is, they meet or don't meet the basic qualifications.

✔ Qualified applications are rated by category as highly qualified or qualified. Some jobs will also include the category "best qualified."

✔ A register of the best qualified applicants ranked with highest listed first is given to the hiring official. In the actual hiring process for seasonal workers, veterans get preferential points or consideration.

✔ The hiring official can consider anyone in this pool.

---

### Hiring reform

**Reforms to the federal job application and hiring process make the process easier. As of November 1, 2011, occupational assessment questionnaires will replace the essay questions (KSAs) that agencies used in the past. Applicants will be kept informed about the process and their applications will be acknowledged. The goal is to simplify the process and attract good candidates to fill positions.**

---

## Obtaining job announcements

Job announcements can be obtained from OPM's online website *(www.usajobs.opm.gov)* through their automated telephone system, touch screen kiosks and by contacting the individual agency location directly. Some positions are "local hire," where job announcements are posted locally and/or through local state employment job service locations. This is done when there is a critical need that is not being met.

Though listed at USAJOBS, USDA Forest Service jobs are listed also at *(www.avuedigitalservices.com/)*. You can search for jobs with the Forest Service at this site or find announcements at USAJOBS, where you'll be directed to apply at the related site, *(www.avuecentral.com)*.

Jobs are announced all year long. Usually summer seasonal positions are announced any time from October to the beginning of summer. Check USAJOBS frequently. If you are interested in a particular park or location, call them in October or November to find out when they expect to announce their seasonal jobs.

Most seasonal jobs are grades 3, 4 or 5. Some are as high as grades 6 and 7. When searching through announcements, look particularly at positions with those grade levels. You will probably have to open (click on) the actual announcement to determine if this is a seasonal position. (See next page for a "partial" job announcement.)

> **USDA Forest Service Laborer positions WG 3502-02/03 (5). These are full-time (40 hrs/week) temporary positions, not to exceed 1030 hours. Salary $10.45 to $11.45 hourly.**

When you get a copy of the announcement read it very carefully. Critical information may be located anywhere in the announcement. If this looks like a position for which you are qualified that interests you, then you usually have two to three weeks to mail your paperwork to them. You are encouraged to apply online, however if you fax it note that it takes two to three days to process. Follow directions carefully. If you miss a deadline, your application won't be considered.

### The application process

In the meantime, prepare your résumé on your computer or online at the USAJOBS website. Take time to read through appropriate sections at the Information Center at USAJOBS for valuable information about the hiring process and suggestions for making your résumé more effective. See *(www.usajobs.gov/infocenter/).*

The Federal Government now requires a résumé, which can be completed online in the Résumé Builder or uploaded to the USAJOBS site. The USAJOBS Résumé Builder allows you to create one uniform résumé that provides all of the information required by government agencies. Instead of creating multiple résumés in different formats, you can build your résumé once and be ready for all job opportunities. However, you can create five résumés in the Résumé Builder plus upload two additional

---

**PARTIAL NPS JOB ANNOUNCEMENT**
MAINTENANCE WORKER  ✳ *Position*
OPEN PERIOD 09/20/2010 - 10/07/2010  ✳ *Submit*
*application between these dates*
SERIES/GRADE: WG-4749-05/  ✳ *Job series and grade*
SALARY: $ 14.00 HOURLY
ANNOUNCEMENT NUMBER: ROMO-11-17
HIRING AGENCY: INTERIOR, NATIONAL PARK SERVICE
DUTY LOCATIONS: 0026 vacancies ESTES PARK, CO
                0005  vacancies GRAND LAKE, CO

REMARKS: TOTAL WORK UNDER THESE TEMPORARY
POSITIONS IS EXPECTED TO LAST NOT MORE THAN 6
MONTHS (**NTE 1039 WORKING HRS IN SERVICE YEAR**)
INCUMBENTS MAY ALSO BE TERMINATED AT ANY TIME
PRIOR TO THE END OF THE PROJECTED SEASON.
WEEKEND & HOLIDAY WORK MAY BE REQUIRED. SOME
WORK IS OUTSIDE IN EXTREME TEMPS & AT
ELEVATIONS UP TO 13,000 FEET. *1039 hrs indicates it is a*
*seasonal position, lasting no more than six months.*

CONTACT:    Kathy Edward  ✳ *Call for more information*
            Rocky Mountain National Park
Applications will be accepted from: Open to all qualified persons.
✳ *Permanent positions are generally open only to current*
*government employees. This is another indicator of a*
*seasonal position.*

---

résumés. If you apply to different categories of jobs, this would make application easier. You need to make sure you include the required information to evaluate your qualifications if you upload your own résumé. The required information is listed on the job announcement.

If you prefer, you can access the OF-612, Optional Application for Federal Appointment, at *(www.usajobs.gov/infocenter/forms.asp#icc)*. You can complete it online as well as save it and print it out.

After completing some basic information, you fill out your work experience. You are asked for employer name, address, dates and salary, then you have 3000 characters to include your duties, accomplishments and related skills. On the announcement you'll see the list of all the items that need to be included in your résumé.

For some job announcements you may be taken to a different site, *(https://applicationmanager.gov)*. This requires a separate user name and password. In all cases, you have the option of faxing your résumé, occupational assessment questionnaire and other documents. A required form for your answers and the cover sheet—Form 1203-FX—must be used when using the faxing option. An alternative cover sheet may sometimes be used. It takes two to three days to process a fax. To avoid disqualification, be sure to follow directions!

Do not confine yourself to paid experience, such as three months clerical or office work. Include any volunteer, community and "life" experiences that apply to the job. For example, in getting a maintenance job, Bill included an experience block about adding onto and remodeling our house.

## Occupational Assessment Questionnaires

The Occupational Assessment Questionnaire replaces the KSAs or Knowledges, Skills, and Abilities that used to be required. Instead of essay questions, now you are asked to rate your compentency in various skills or answer whether or not you have that skill or experience.

> **Maintenance Worker WG 4749-05**
> **Rocky Mountain National Park**
> **3 positions in Estes Park**
> **Maximum 1039 hours**

Since the answers to these questions are either Yes or No or multiple choice, you cannot elaborate in the questionnaire. You will, as noted elsewhere, need to document this experience or skill in your résumé to receive credit.

## Examples of questions on an Occupational Assessment Questionnaire:

1. For a Visitor Use Assistant: Collect money on a job (e.g. sales, toll collection, etc.).

## OCCUPATIONAL ASSESSMENT QUESTIONNAIRE

This questionnaire consists of completing some basic information about yourself and then answering a number of Occupational Assessment questions by marking the circle that corresponds with your answer for each question. A typical queston asks you to pick A through E for your experience in each area they name:

A- I have not had experience, education, or training in performing this task.

B- I have had education or training in how to perform this task, but have not yet performed it on the job.

C- I have performed this task on the job. My work on this task was monitored closely by my supervisor or senior employee to ensure compliance with proper procedures.

D- I have performed this task as a regular part of a job. I have performed it independently and normally without review by a supervisor or senior employee.

E- I am considered an expert in performing this task; or I have supervised performance of this task or am normally an individual who is consulted by other workers to assist them in doing this task because of my expertise.

**An important note:** Even thought it is a multiple choice questionnaire, for each question below, you must document your skill level in your résumé. This means, for example, that it you rate yourself at the expert level (E) for a skill or task, you must document when you have supervised or trained others doing that skill or task. If you rate yourself at the independent level (D), you must show that you did the task as a regular and recurring part of a job. Your skills will be verified in your résumé and your score will be lowered for skills that are not documented.

In this case, you pick A, B, C, D or E as specified in the accompanying box above to indicate how much experience you have had in this area and fill in that circle on the questionnaire.

In your résumé for a Grade 04 position, you need to show one year of specialized experience, including but not limited to, fee collection, disseminating visitor information, and assisting with employee orientation/training; or four-years of education beyond high school; or a combination of the two. If you worked in retail for three years and collected money 75 percent of the time, you would want to give the start and end date and that percentage to document your experience.

2. For a Maintenance Worker: Prepare surface for painting by scraping, sanding, and brushing.

The choices are slightly modified for this question to reflect this type of job, but similiar in nature to the ones in the box on the previous page. As noted, you must document your ability and experience in your résumé in order to receive credit for your answer.

In maintenance, you do not need to include stop and start dates or percentages. It is enough to demonstrate that you have done it, though showing you have more experience makes your résumé more credible. You could put something like this in your résumé:

**Remodeled home:** *Added a two-room addition. Covered with wood siding to match existing structure. Painted existing structure. Prepared surface for painting by scraping, sanding and brushing, then applying exterior latex paint.*

You will want to read and print out, if possible, the questionnaire while completing or modifying your résumé to make sure you do include this experience in at least one experience block. Always save copies in case you need to use the information again.

### Tips for your application or résumé

- ✔ **Use active verbs:** Use active verbs to describe your work and be specific. Do not use "help" or "assist" without explaining exactly what you did. "Helping" could mean handing the hammer to your husband.
- ✔ **Keep sentences short and clear:** Short sentences that are to the point are easier to read and are more powerful.
- ✔ **Break experience into paragraphs:** Several shorter paragraphs make your message stand out more so than one long one.

✔ **Include key requirements:** Key requirements will be spelled out in the announcement, which will help you target your résumé. The announcement may also include a listing of the knowledges, skills and abilities you will be rated on during the proces. If you are near a federal agency or employment office, ask to look at Handbook X118C in the personnnel office for details on this and other positions of interest.

✔ **Study announcement directions:** Read the announcement carefully and modify your résumé if necessary to address all the elements mentioned in the position's duties. For General Service (GS) positions, there will probably be a minimum time requirement for certain work experience so be sure to put the percentage of time for each type of job you did. For example, the position you are applying for requires six months of experience in bookkeeping. You were receptionist and bookkeeper for a year, doing each job 50 percent of the

> **Bureau of Land Management**
> **Visitor Use Assistant**
> **Series/grade: GS 0303-03/04**
> **Six months position**

time. If you put down 50 percent you will qualify with six months experience. If you do not put down a percentage, personnel MUST give you 1 percent. You'd only get a day or two credit.

✔ **Complete résumé:** Make sure your application package is complete and all directions followed for submitting it.

✔ **Be accurate:** Put your birth year, not this year's date. If you put down this year, your application will be rated unqualified. You must be at least 18 to work in a government position.

✔ **Select grade level:** Fill in the lowest grade you will accept if the position is for more than one grade, such as grades 4 and 5. Always write in the lowest one on the announcement. If you put a 5 down but don't get a good score for that level, you will not be considered for the grade 4 position, even if you have a top score. Remember, you can always turn an offer down.

✔ **Claim veteran points:** Claim any veteran points you are eligible for and fax copies of the correct forms.

✔ **Include backup documents:** Note the requirements of the position. If college is required for this particular position, send copies of your college transcript or list of college courses according to the directions supplied.

## Tips to help the rating panel give you a high score

✔ **Use key words:** Use the same terms in your résumé that were used in the Occupational Assessment Questionnaire. If the questionnaire says, "Prepare surface for painting,"then use the same phrase in your résumé.

✔ **Résumé and questionnaire must match:** When you indicate that you have experience in a certain task in the Occupational Assessment Questionnaire, the rater must find reference to it in your résumé or you get no credit.

## Then what?

Double-check your résumé and Occupational Assessment Questionnaire to make sure you have not omitted anything. Compare your responses to the requirements listed in the announcment. Make sure any other necessary forms or attachments are included. Be sure to allow the additional two to three days if you are faxing your documents.

## The process

Your application will go through the process of being determined qualified or non-qualified and then rated on a point score of 100 possible points if it was qualified. Veterans can earn extra points for being in the military, and additional points if they were injured or disabled. These points are added to their score. Theoretically a veteran could get as many as 110 points, if he or she is a 30 percent-compensable vet.

> **Internal Reveue Service Order Entry Clerk GS 0303-03 Full-time, seasonal position. Primary work season is November through April.**

Once the hiring official has the register, she may contact you first to find out if you are still interested and available before taking the time to do reference checks. On the other hand, you may be contacted for the first time with a job offer. It can be anywhere from 30 to 60 days or even more before an agency makes a decision.

## Should you contact the supervisor who may hire you?

Under the new process, you should receive information after your résumé is received and at other points in the process. In that case, contacting the supervisor won't be necessary.

Some supervisors don't mind being contacted and take that as an indication of interest. Others will let you know where they are in the hiring process, but won't discuss the matter further. Still others feel any contact is improper. If you can obtain the supervisor's name, it doesn't hurt to call and at least find out when he expects to make a decision. If the supervisor seems receptive, you can express more interest and offer information, but play it by ear. If, for some reason, you do not hear anything, after 30 days, you could contact Personnel and find out

> **Park Ranger (General and Interpretation) GS 0025-05/07 These will be filled year-round as needed. Go to *www.usajobs.opm.gov/* for current vacancies and to apply online.**

whether or not your application was qualified and what category you are in—best qualified, highly qualified or qualified. That will give you some idea of your chances.

**$** **National park maintenance worker: Jim** works seasonally for two national parks. Summers he works in maintenance at Glen Canyon National Recreation Area, helping the permanent maintenance workers take care of one of the uplake marina/campground areas. Winters he heads in his motorhome to Death Valley National Park where he takes care of restrooms and lookout points on a 100-mile route.

**$** **Forest Service workers: Jack and Sylvia** worked for the U.S. Forest Service at Mt. St. Helens National Park. They were both offered jobs in maintenance. This is a national park, administered by the U.S. Forest Service.

## SEASONAL JOBS WITH BLM AND USFS

Finding seasonal work for the Bureau of Land Management (BLM) and the USDA National Forest Service (USFS) is similar. Sort for those agencies at USAJOBS to find job announcements.

BLM has a description of their seasonal positions on their website. Those could include aid and/or technician positions in cartography, engine operator, fire suppression, forestry and range (fire positions), horse wrangler, material handling, and motorvehicle operation. Most of the seasonal jobs with BLM are wildland fire jobs. These are descibed on a separate web page (*www.blm.gov/wo/st/en/res/blm_jobs/how_to_apply/wildland_fire_positions.html*). You can then read about the hiring process and find wildland fire positions. If you go to the web page that lists jobs, you can find the wildland fire jobs pre-sorted at USAJOBS. (*www.firejobs.doi.gov/index.php?action=search_jobs*). Not all wildland fire jobs involve fighting fires directly on the line. We know RVers who work in public relations and in dispatch during fires.

The USDA National Forest Service (USFS) lists nationwide seasonal positions on USAJOBS. These jobs will then refer you to another website, (*www.avuecentral.com*) which OPM has authorized the Forest Service to use to make Temporary Appointments under the USDA Demonstration Project for Temporary Employment. If you locate a seasonal job at USAJOBS, you will be referred to this site where you can apply. You can search for jobs at either website.

To find out more about jobs with the Forest Service, visit their website. (*www.fs.fed.us/fsjobs*) Positions included at this time are archaeology, biological, forestry, engineering, electronics, hydrological, lands, range, real estate and surveying aids or technicians. See Chapter 18 for information on working for Forest Service concessionaires.

The U.S. Forest Service can hire low-income workers 55-years of age and older for a work experience and job training program through the Senior Community Service Employment Program (SCSEP). Wages are at least minimum wage. Training is available in research, clerical, archaeology, maintenance, computers, forestry, and information, as well as other fields. Contact Personnel in individual Forests.

## Watching fire towers

Most positions for manning fire towers are through the U.S. Forest Service. Positions are both paid and volunteer. If looking for paid positions, look at the USAJOBS site under Forest Service (Department of Agriculture) for forestry technician positions. Check also the "Fire Hire" section of the USFS website. You can also contact Personnel at individual forests who will usually put you on a mailing list to receive their job packets. In some cases they may only have one paid position at a particular fire tower, but the spouse could work as a volunteer. Contact the forest you are interested in directly for volunteer positions.

*$* **Fire tower lookout: John** mans Mount Cooledge Fire Lookout summers at Custer State Park in South Dakota. Every 15 minutes, from 7:30 a.m. to 8:00 p.m., he makes a 360-degree sweep with binoculars, looking for fires. If there are lightening storms, he stays up past his shift in case there is a hit, plus searches carefully the next morning. Smokes can appear immediately, or delay for several days. John has had lightening hit the tower when he was in it. "A tremendous flash and then the crash. Not so good for the eardrums. We can stand on a wooden stool with glass insulators if we want."

If John spots smoke, he uses an Osborne Fire Finder to locate the azimuth direction line of the fire and then guesses the distance from the tower. He tries to locate it to the quarter section of a quarter section. Once the fire is located, he contacts the agency responsible and uses his radio to direct the crew to the scene. During the fire, crews use the tower to relay communications, coordinate helicopter or tanker air drops, order meals

> **Forestry Technician**
> **GS 0462-05 Man fire tower. Spot, report fires, and direct firefighters to location.**

and for other communications. When nothing is going on, he acts as the communication center for Custer State Park (where the tower is located), answering visitor calls, helping staff and directing 911 emergency traffic.

## GETTING THAT FIRST JOB

Breaking into a federal agency can be challenging. Once you have some experience and have supervisors within the agency, getting other positions becomes easier. We are assuming, of course, that you did a good job. If your experience does not lend itself to the position you want, you might want to consider volunteering for the agency. Through volunteering you get agency experience that is as valuable and counts as much as paid experience; in addition, you'll have valuable contacts and references.

*$* **SCA volunteer: Tammy** was a Student Conservation Association (SCA) volunteer at Glen Canyon National Recreation Area. She received a small stipend and her housing while working as a volunteer and did basically the same job as the other interpretative rangers. The following summer, Tammy was hired as a paid ranger at Glen Canyon.

You might also apply for the entry-level positions, even if you would prefer a higher position. If your goal is interpretative ranger, for example, you might apply first as a Visitor Use Assistant. You may be collecting fees or strictly working an information desk, but it is a stepping stone to the position you want. Likewise in maintenance, the lower grade positions or laborer positions can give you an entry to jobs requiring more skill.

Once you have a job or two under your belt, you will find that the agency is like a fraternity. Invariably as you move to a new location, you will find that you and the other workers know some of the same people. Often a hiring official will see a supervisor or reference that she personally worked with and give that person a call first. If you have done a good job, this reference will go a long way with the hiring official.

## BENEFITS OF FEDERAL SEASONAL WORK

In addition to higher wages, there are other benefits to working for the federal government. You receive four hours of sick leave biweekly, which can be carried from one seasonal position to the next, and four hours of annual leave. Annual leave for seasonal workers is paid as a lump sum payment about a month after your last day. There are paid holidays and a Sunday differential. The government must pay overtime for hours worked over eight hours per day (unless you are on a nine- or ten-hour per day schedule) or for hours worked over forty in a week. If your position requires wearing a uniform, you will receive a uniform allowance to help pay for it.

In maintenance, you do not drive your own vehicle or use your own tools. Those are provided. Interpretative rangers may have to drive their own vehicles to a job site, but if they have a job-related assignment, they are usually provided a government vehicle to drive.

If you successfully complete your season and have worked under six months (1040 hours), you will likely get "rehire" status. This means that next year, if you want to come back and the position is still there, you can be rehired without having to re-compete. In other words, you do not have to go through the whole application process again; instead you'll complete a short rehire form. Since there is no guarantee you will be rehired, to be on the safe side, you may want to send in another application anyway. (That way you must be considered.)

## ARMY CORPS OF ENGINEERS.
*101. Park or gate attendant at COE projects (bid)*
*102. Hired worker for bid-winner at project*

The Army Corps of Engineers (COE) obtains park and gate attendants through a bid system to perform much of the day-to-day operations at its more than 460 water resource projects and more than 4,000 parks. When a contract comes up for bid, you must write or call for a bid package, which contains the scope of the job and prior successful bids. The package is comprehensive, detailing what the job entails, hours, what you must provide and what the agency will provide. If the successful bid is not included, you can call the contact number for that information. If you are the lowest qualified bidder and win the contract, you work as an independent contractor, not an employee. Contracts vary tremendously so you need to read them quite carefully. The successful bidder usually has the option to renew without competition for a second and third year, at the government's option.

Each year, *Workamper News*, in its September/October issue, lists projects that will solicit bids as well as those seeking volunteers. The annual issue also explains how the bidding system works in more detail, as well as things to consider before placing a bid. They recommend you visit the park manager at the project(s) where you would like to work.

### Things to consider:
✔ **Number of days and hours of coverage:**  Some contracts require 6-7 days of coverage.
✔ **Tasks:** Some contracts mix maintenance and gatekeeper work.
✔ **Shared or solo:** Will you be sharing duties with another couple?
✔ **RV Site:** Does the contract come with a full hookup site?
✔ **Previous bids:** Check the previous bids for what the hourly rate actually was. To underbid or match that bid, will you be working at less than minimum wage?
✔ **Taxes:** As an independent contractor, you must pay estimated taxes and full social security tax.
✔ **Visit first:** If at all possible, visit the site first so you can better assess what the position requires.

Since 1998, Department of Defense regulations require that contractors register with the Central Contractor Registration and obtain SIC, CAGE Code and DUNS numbers. These numbers are explained and can be obtained over the Internet. Instructions are included in the bid package.

## $ Gate attendants:

**Dave and Linda** successfully bid on a Corps of Engineer contract at Lake Shelbyville, Illinois. The request for bids was listed in *Workamper News*. As gate attendants, they were required to be bonded. They bid the jobs at around $6.00/hour each but know people who have gotten more and some who have gotten less. Their particular position did not require any maintenance, nor enforcing any of the rules, which they prefer. Says Dave, "We worked in a nice, spacious fee booth that's equipped with air conditioning, computer, TV, phone and radio communications with the rangers."

**Richard and Juli** bid successfully for gate attendant positions at the Greers Ferry Lake Project in Arkansas and worked there for two summers. He would rate his experience an "8" on a scale of 1 to 10. Advises Richard, "Read the scope of work very carefully in order that you fully understand what you are agreeing to do. Contract requirements, as well as successful bid prices, can and do vary dramatically between and even within districts." He strongly recommends visiting the parks where you are considering submitting bids on a weekend during the busy season. Amenities can vary considerably even within a project area.

## OTHER FEDERAL SEASONAL WORK
*103. Post office help at Christmas*
*104. IRS tax season worker*
*105. Census taker*

Other federal agencies may also have temporary work. The Post Office hires additional workers at Christmas. The Internal Revenue Service (IRS) hires more clerks, mail clerks and tax examining technicians to process tax returns in some locations. At census time, thousands of workers are hired to prepare for and administer the census.

## VOLUNTEERS

Most federal agency sites are searching for volunteers. Usually a specified number of hours per week are required for your free site. At some locations, particularly if amenities are limited, you might get a stipend in addition to your site. For more information, see Chapter 22.

When you work in a national park or forest for a government agency, you are paid well and work in a beautiful or interesting location. More effort is required in the application process than for other seasonal jobs, something not every RV worker is willing to do. For us the payoffs are worth the extra effort.

# Notes

*"Attention is like a searchlight; when its beam is spread over a vast
area, its power to focus becomes weak, but focused on one thing at a
time, it becomes powerful. Great men [and women] are men [and
women] of concentration. They put their whole mind on one thing at a
time." Paramahansa Yogananda*

# Chapter 18
# How to get jobs working in the outdoors

For many RVers, getting to spend time in the beautiful, less crowded areas of our country is high on their list of RVing goals. In addition to seasonal opportunities with the federal government, there are many other ways to work in the outdoors. Main employers are concessionaires and state and local agencies. Second only to working in RV parks, this type of employment is most likely to have RV sites available for their workers. If not included, sites are usually at a very low cost compared to staying in a private RV park.

## WORKING FOR A NATIONAL PARK CONCESSIONAIRE

106. *Hotel jobs like front desk clerk, housekeeper, back office*
107. *Restaurant jobs like cook, waiter/waitress, hostess, cashier*
108. *Retail store jobs like cashier, stocker*
109. *Warehouse workers*
110. *Tour or recreational activity jobs like tour guide, boat or raft operator, boat rental agent, boat instructor, golf course-related worker*
111. *Gas station jobs like cashier, mechanic, attendant*
111. *Medical clinic jobs like receptionist, nurse, physician's assistant*
113. *Campground host*
114. *Maintenance worker*
115. *Rodent and pest control worker*
116. *Shuttle driver*
117. *Helicopter pilot or worker for flight-seeing operations*

## WHAT IS A CONCESSIONAIRE?

Concessionaires are private companies that have been granted the right by a government agency to provide visitor services on government land. Many larger national parks have concessionaires. The Forest Service has turned over many of its campgrounds in many forests to concessionaires. And state and local agencies may also have private industry provide visitor services at their parks.

### National parks

In large parks such as Yellowstone, concessionaires provide visitor services like hotels, stores, gas stations, and recreation within its boundaries. Private companies bid on the rights to offer services and in return are regulated by the National Park Service and pay a percentage of their profits to the government. These concessionaires hire many more people than the government agency. Some concessionaires like Aramark and Xanterra Parks and Resorts operate in more than one national park, making it possible for employees to transfer easily to another location.

Concessionaires generally begin hiring for summer work in January and February. A number of concessionaires are listed on the Coolworks seasonal work website. You can find out the types of jobs available and often download or complete an application. Contact information is listed there too. Several concessionaires advertise in *Workamper News*.

> **Earn a free house-boat vacation! Work at beautiful Lake Powell.**

If you don't have access to a computer, you can contact the national park where you'd like to work and ask them for contact information for the concessionaires in their park. Call or write for an employment package.

### Mind-boggling job possibilities!

To give you an idea of job possibilities, think of all the jobs associated with hotels and retail operations like gift shops, grocery stores, gas stations. Then remember that in some parks you can raft down a river, rent a boat and go fishing, or ride horseback. At many recreation areas, the emphasis is on water activities. At Glen Canyon National Recreation Area on Lake Powell, for instance, houseboat rentals are popular. So are jet skis and motorboats. Seasonal workers are hired to clean, maintain, and rent out houseboats, instruct customers, and sell fuel. At the Grand

Tetons as well as Lake Powell, tour boats offer scenic boat rides. At Death Valley, there is a golf course. All these activities require workers.

## Advantages and disadvantages

Concessionaires generally do not pay top wages but instead offer a number of benefits to employees. These might include:

✔ **Low-cost housing,** dormitory or RV site.

✔ **A low-cost meal plan** is often available. At Death Valley, at this writing, employees get two free meals a day, paying only for dinner.

✔ **Employee discounts** may be given on purchases. Often use of recreational facilities is permitted either at no charge or for minimal cost when available. Employees who work the entire season at Lake Powell get a one-week houseboat vacation, paying only for fuel and insurance. Boats can be rented during the season when available for the cost of fuel and insurance. At other locations, raft trips, horseback riding and other activities would work the same.

✔ **Spend time** in a place that tourists spend big dollars to visit is the *real* benefit that most concessionaires tout.

Wages are the big drawback. Most pay around minimum wage, though skilled jobs like mechanics could pay higher. Supply and demand affects wages. I've seen housekeeping pay $8/hour and up in some locations because they had a difficult time getting enough workers.

> **Golf in beautiful Death Valley! Furnace Creek Resort now hiring for winter positions.**

## Ask questions

Be sure to check when and how you will earn overtime pay. Certain seasonal businesses do not fall under the Fair Labor Standards Act, and therefore regulation is up to the state. Arizona is a state that does not have a minimum wage or overtime law; certain Arizona employers may not have to pay any overtime. Some states don't require seasonal employers to pay overtime until an employee has worked more than 48 or even 52 hours. ou can bet they will work you right up to that limit.

As with every employer, it is important to clarify conditions of employment, your site, how much you pay for (utilities or other) and how much, days off, etc. At Lake Powell, they changed the meal plan so now a nonworking spouse could not eat in the dining room. Some, like Flagg Ranch between Yellowstone and Grand Teton, expect you to work six days a week. Is that acceptable? Will you and your spouse have the same days off? The time to negotiate is *before* you accept the job, not after you arrive and find conditions not to your liking.

$ **Tour boat: Chuck** worked on the tour boat going to Rainbow Bridge for Aramark at Lake Powell, Utah. He usually worked four long days with three days off. Each morning, he cleaned the windows, then cleaned and vacuumed the inside. Next he picked up the lunches. The tour lasted most of the day. They would gas up and then, if enough people had signed up, get ready for the evening tour. "If we had an evening tour, we turned right around again. The crew did get a free box lunch, and if we went out again at night, we'd get another box lunch for dinner! It cut down on the food bills. If we went out at night it could be a 14-hour day." One captain let him pilot the boat occasionally.

$ **Concessionaire employees: Jim and Barb** have worked for several national park concessionaires doing a variety of jobs. These have included gas station attendant, housekeeper, gift shop cashier, houseboat instructor and boat rental agent, reservationist, bookkeeper, tour guide and bus driver, and front desk clerks. Some of these positions have been more enjoyable than others, often depending on the quality of management. They note, "Sometimes even the good places will have a bad season if there is a lot of turnover in key concession and park management staff." They also advise not taking a supervisory position before working as an entry-level employee. This gives you a chance to look at how the company works and the problems faced by first-level supervisors.

$ **Boat instructors: Bob and Michelle** also worked at Lake Powell for Aramark. They corresponded with their manager and were offered a position via e-mail. The perks were a real attraction. They were able to raft down the Colorado south of the dam at no cost. They joined the Fishing Club and could rent a speedboat for the day for a total of $20, including a full tank of gas. (With a 40-gallon tank and gas at $2.40/gallon, this was a great deal.) The employer set up trips for employees to neighboring parks such as the Grand Canyon and Bryce Canyon. At the end of the season, they were eligible for a houseboat rental for a week for the cost of insurance and fuel. Aramark's cafeteria offered discount meals cards purchased with pre-tax dollars, another savings.

## Mixed reviews

Experiences working for concessionaires are mixed. If the company has trouble filling positions or has high turnover, you may be asked or even expected to work more hours than you want. You may be expected to work in another department if needed. If you were not interviewed by your supervisor at the time of hiring, you should insist on talking to him or her since the supervisor may have different ideas on how to run the department than what you thought had been agreed upon with the interviewer. On the bright side, in many cases employees of concessionaires come back year after year and their co-workers are their summer families.

In working here, as elsewhere, you need to know your limits, make sure you and your employer are clear on them, and then stick to them. Be realistic. Concessionaires are in business to make a profit and most cut costs to the bone. Then sometimes you need to remember why you are working here — to be in a beautiful place and earn enough money so you can live this great life on the road. As Jim and Barb say, "Remember, it ain't a career, and your home is on wheels!"

> **Work in Sequoia Nat'l Park! Cheerful, outgoing couples with RV needed, April-Oct.**

## NONPROFIT ASSOCIATIONS

118. *Clerk or cashier selling books and other items at an NPS visitor center*
119. *Warehouse worker*
120. *Bookkeeper — place orders, keep books*

In most national park visitor centers and national forest offices, books and other educational items are offered for sale by a nonprofit association in the visitor center. Congress established these nonprofit association guidelines to support education, research, and other programs for the benefit of the park or agency. They often publish books and literature for visitors, using the profits to support programs in the Park. For example, since its inception in 1932, the Grand Canyon Association has provided the Park with over $15 million in aid.

**Work at the Grand Canyon! Sell educational items at visitor centers. Must have own RV.**

Most associations hire seasonal help. They usually pay more than entry-level concessionaire jobs. Contact the national park or forest to get contact information for its nonprofit association and apply to them directly. They may have an arrangement with the agency or concessionaire for an RV site or other housing.

$ **Nonprofit association managers and sellers: Jim and Alida** have worked three summers for the Grand Canyon Association. Answering an ad in *Workamper News,* they sold books and other items at one of the five locations in the Park. Their second season they were promoted to managers of the store at the north rim. "We share space with the Park Service so we help answer visitor questions and assist rangers in administering the Junior Ranger program to young visitors ages four to fourteen. We have enjoyed this part of the job too." They are asked all sorts of questions about lodging, hiking trails, scenic drives and about other parks and attractions in the greater Four Corners region. As managers their duties have expanded to include inventory management, the daily remittance of funds, ordering, and more. An RV site is included, as well as free membership in the association, which entitles them to discounts on books and merchandise here and in many other national parks. They are also eligible for a sales and end-of-season bonus.

## NATIONAL FOREST CONCESSIONAIRES

121.  *Campground host*
122.  *Maintenance worker*
123.  *Manager of several campgrounds*
124.  *Holder of concession rights to run a FS campground*
125.  *Forest fire support worker*

The U.S. Forest Service has contracted the running of many of their campgrounds to private individuals or companies. These concessionaires in turn hire personnel to manage and maintain their campgrounds. A concessionaire might have one or more campgrounds, in one or more national forests.

If you work for one of these contractors, you will have a site (not all have hookups) for a salary or hourly wage in return for performing certain duties. The company may provide uniforms and tools, but in many cases you provide your own vehicle and tools. The concessionaire will provide supplies like toilet paper if your duties entail stocking and/or cleaning restrooms.

Concessionaires advertise for employees in *Workamper News*. I have seen at least one concessionaire in Quartzsite, Arizona, recruiting employees during the big shows in January and February. They do hire solo workers as well as couples. Contact a U.S. Forest where you'd like to work to find out if they have a concessionaire running their campgrounds.

Experiences of RVers working for forest service concessionaires have ranged from "wonderful" to "the pits." Again, it is important to clarify just what will be expected of you and what the company will provide. As an employee, you may have to draw some lines so they do not take advantage of you. Since you will likely be parked right in a campground, visitors think you are available 24 hours a day. You might feel that if you don't do something, it won't get done. However, you could end up spending a number of hours working for no pay.

## $ Paid campground hosts:

**Laurel and Dave** worked as campground hosts in the Stanislaus National Forest in California. The woman who hired them was the concessionaire for two campgrounds. Laurel collected the fees, making three rounds during the day, and another just after sundown. When the campground filled, she hung up the "Campground Full" sign. In between, she raked out campsites, cleaned fire pits, stocked the pit toilets with toilet paper, and kept it litter-free. The hardest was reminding people about the rules, particularly that dogs must be on leash. Says Laurel, "I would have to remind people more than once, especially if it was a tiny dog that everyone thought was cute and, of course, would never bite anyone." Once a week she cleaned the pit toilets. Dave's primary job was picking up the garbage from the Dumpsters twice a week (in a real garbage truck), and taking it to the landfill. He also maintained the water pumps, ran the backhoe, and did odd jobs as they occurred. Between them they earned $1,500/month plus propane and a site with sewer and water but no power. They worked 8–10 hours/day and had two days off a week.

**Ellie and Weldon** worked for the concessionaire as campground hosts at Odell Lake in Oregon. Their campground had twenty-two campsites, a five-slip boat dock with ramp, a fish cleaning station and eight pit toilets. Each day they opened the pay envelopes at the self-pay station, then later went to each site, collecting from anyone who had not paid. They also cleaned the restrooms and the fish station. The day after a camper vacated a site, they cleaned out the firepit. Weekends were busier. They were on duty by 5:00 a.m. to control the parking of boat trailers and turning people back when the lot was full. Twice a week they picked up trash around the sites, picnic areas, and parking lots as well as the boat dock area and along the roads.

They were issued a golf cart, buckets and litter sticks and had plenty of cleaning supplies, toilet paper, paper towels, etc. Says Ellie, "Our supervisors were great, bringing our supplies each week when they picked up our accounting sheets."

They were paid $500 a month and received a full-hookup site and propane. Since there were only two full-hookup sites in the district, it was on a first-come, first-served basis. The other campground hosts had to use the public toilets or drive to the RV dump in town every couple of weeks.

"It was a good experience, totally stress-free and fun," recounts Ellie.

## Other Forest Service concessionaires

The Forest Service also contracts other tasks such as firefighting support services. Some provide firefighters and airplane or helicopter support.

> **Fire support workers needed for fire season.**

Other companies provide water trucks, mobile laundry units, shower trailers and other miscellaneous items and services. Pay for fire camp work usually starts at about $100 a day with more for workers having advanced skills like a Commercial Drivers License (CDL) or pilot's license. You need to be flexible and available on short notice. How much you work depends on how busy the fire season is that summer. Contact either a regional or local Forest Service office to find out contact information for the contractor. *Workamper News* occasionally has ads.

Companies also contract with the Forest Service to supply commissaries at the base camp for fires. Firefighters can buy items like toothpaste. One enterprising fellow printed 50 t-shirts of the fire and set up a stand outside the firefighters' base camp. He was sold out in a matter of hours.

*$* **Helicopter tour pilot: Terry** flew helicopters in Vietnam and had his helicopter pilot's license. He had also gotten his commercial rating, which is necessary to transport passengers. Ultimately he wanted to fly for one of the companies that contracts with the Forest Service to fight forest fires. To get some current flying hours, he worked for one of the helicopter tour companies at the Grand Canyon. A website *(www.justhelicopters.com)* lists jobs for helicopter pilots and mechanics. In talking to a company with a listing, he heard about this job. Pay was very good and Terry was paid for his shift whether he flew customers or not. Terry was later able to get on with a contract service fighting fires. **Heidi** worked for a stable that rented horses. She was able to ride, which she enjoys, and earned tips from riders she took out on trail rides.

### Become a U.S. Forest Service Concessionaire
If you are interested in bidding on campgrounds yourself, ask to be put on the mailing list for requests for bids so you are notified the next time campgrounds come up for bid.

> Intermountain Region USDA Forest Service: *Concessionaires are selected from competitive solicitations that are offered from time to time. Most concessionaires operate under a special use permit from the Forest Service for one to five year periods. To obtain such solicitations (commonly called a prospectus) when they are offered, one needs to get in direct contact with the specific National Forest in which one is interested.*

## STATE PARKS
126. *Ranger- present programs, enforce rules, give tours*
127. *Maintenance worker*
128. *Fee collector*
129. *Visitor center worker*
130. *Campground host*
131. *Park aide*
132. *Operator of a hunting check station*

Don't confine your search for an outdoor job to the federal level. State parks also hire seasonal workers. These positions could be in fee collection, maintenance, and visitor contact positions like a visitor center or interpretive activities.

> **Washington State Parks hiring Park Aides.**
> **3-5 month temporary positions.**

Pay at state parks may be less than at federal parks but is usually above minimum wage. Contact a state or district office, or a state park directly for more information. You may also find information at a local job service. (See **Appendix 4** for state park contact information or check government pages of local phone books.)

### $ State park workers:

**Ron & Val** have worked several summers at Cherry Creek State Park in Colorado. Ron worked in maintenance and Val worked most recently supervising fee collection. Working here let them spend time off with their grandchildren. Since they want to see other parts of the country, they worked here alternate summers for several years. They do such a good job, they can come back anytime they want.

**John & Ginger** have worked at Custer State Park in South Dakota several summers and also at Anza Borrego State Park in California. At Custer State Park, John manned one of the fire tower lookouts, sweeping the skies regularly for any sign of fire or lightening strikes. When there were fires, John worked at the communications center, helping staff and visitors and directing emergency traffic. Ginger worked at one of the entrance stations as a crew leader. Housing is provided at $3/day for RV site or other housing, if available. As an added benefit, the park provides a pass good to all area attractions like Crazy Horse Memorial and Black Hill Playhouse stage productions.

**Nick and Joanne** also worked at Custer State Park one summer. Joanne worked at the entrance stations and Nick worked with another man heading up the seasonal campground attendant staff. The highlight for Joanne was helping out with the annual buffalo roundup. She got to play cowgirl, driving buffalo into the chutes for their inoculations. Yeehaw!

## COUNTY AND CITY PARKS

*133.    Maintenance worker*
*134.    Fee collector*
*135.    Visitor contact personnel*
*136.    Operator of a concessionaire activity*

Local agencies at the county or city level are also potential employers. Sharon & Ron ran a concessionaire operation for a county park in San Diego County.

**$** **County park concessionaire: Ron and Sharon** worked at Lake Miramar in San Diego, California for the concessionaire. They worked four days a week, with three days off to explore area attractions. They had a variety of duties: selling bait, tackle, and lake permits; operating the snack shop and renting boats. They ran it like it was their own business, doing the ordering, completing paperwork, and making the deposits. They were provided a shaded, fenced enclosure, close to the stand for their rig.

## GATEWAY TOWNS

Many businesses locate just outside national parks in gateway towns, providing tourist services and activities. Rocky Mountain National Park in Colorado, for example, provides no housing and very limited food services within the park. Visitors obtain these at Estes Park and Grand Lake. See Chapter 19 for job ideas in these towns.

When Bill got a job at Rocky Mountain National Park I needed to find a job. We arrived the first of June and nearly every business had a Help Wanted sign in the window. If you wanted to work in retail, you could have had a position that day! I worked first for Safeway and then gave tours at the Stanley Hotel.

This category of jobs is huge and usually comes with either a free or low-cost RV site. Many job sites are in beautiful places where you can enjoy outdoor activities like hiking, boating and fishing. While pay tends to be lower, you may have a skill that is worth more (or in demand due to short supply) or be willing to take on management responsibilities.

# Notes

*"It's only work if you'd rather be doing something else."*
*Flagstaff Tea Party newspaper*

*Jobs 137-220*

# Chapter 19
# How to get jobs at resorts and travel destinations

Where tourists go, there are jobs! Resorts, amusement parks, and tourist destinations hire workers during busy seasons for their operations. Whatever your skill or desired type of work, you can likely find a position. It's fun being behind the scenes and paid to work at a place where vacationers spend big bucks to be. Often you can take advantage of perks or local discounts.

## *RESORTS*

137. *Hotel and motel jobs like front desk clerk, housekeeper, child care provider, maintenance worker, waiter/waitress, chef, hostess, back office worker, security person, bellman, cashier, retail clerk, bartender*
138. *Activity director or recreation leader*
139. *Restaurant jobs like wait staff, hostess, chef or cook, busboy, bartender*
140. *Gas station jobs like cashier, mechanic, attendant*
141. *Retail jobs like cashier, salesperson, stocker or warehouse worker*
142. *Grocery stores jobs like cashier, bagger, stocker*
143. *RV parks jobs like registration and reservation staff, cashier, maintenance, groundskeeper, store clerk*
144. *Adventure/recreation tours: jobs like raft guide, stable hand, tour leader, reservations staff, cashier, mechanic, maintenance worker, driver, loader or packer*

145.    *Golf course jobs like golf pro, shop staff, groundskeeper, ranger/starter, mechanic or helper for care of golf carts, snack bar attendant or food preparer, customer service representative*

146.    *Marina jobs like boat rental agent, boat instructor, mechanic, fuel attendant, cashier*

147.    *Personal services like hairdresser, nanny or childcare provider, computer programmer, handyman*

148.    *Shows: usher, ticket sales staff*

149.    *Flight-seeing or helicopter tour operation worker*

150.    *Costumed character at amusement park or clown*

151.    *Dog musher/guide, dog caretaker*

Towns that attract a heavy tourist population during a season often need workers to supplement the year-round work force. You may or may not be provided housing by the employer; it depends on the type of work and how scarce housing is. In some towns, like Jackson Hole, Wyoming, and Skagway, Alaska, housing is in such short supply, or so expensive, that some employers must provide a place for employees to live if they want to have enough workers. Resort towns are similar to concessionaires in a national park (Chapter 18), only on a larger scale; think of all the services that are required — hotels, shops, gasoline, restaurants, and activities — to name a few.

> **Resort in Cody, WY Send photo of self and RV. Bonus for working full season.**

If a resort area interests you, call, write or e-mail the local tourist information center for a trip planner or brochure. Find other potential employers by calling or writing the Chamber of Commerce or check its website for a listing of members.

## Housing

It is important early in the application process to find out about housing or RV sites. You may be on your own. If that is the case, ask the employer if he has contacts in town or is able to get you a discounted site. The earlier you make arrangements, the better your chance of lining up something. Obtain a list of RV and mobile home parks (often cheaper) from the Chamber of Commerce or visitor information center.

You might also be able to find an RV spot if the employer has none available. Here's what some working RVers have done:

✔ **Employer:** One couple, working for a bed and breakfast in Moose, Wyoming, helped put in hookups next to the garage so they could park onsite.

✔ **Mobile home park:** Another working RVer couple in Ft. Meyers, Florida, found a low-cost site close to work in an older mobile home park. Resort RV parks were charging up to $800/month.

✔ **Friend or relative:** If you have a friend or relative in the area, you might be able to work out something with them. Be polite guests and pay your expenses.

✔ **Campground host:** Still another couple camp-hosted at a small nearby park, working ten hours/week on their own schedule, leaving time for jobs in town.

✔ **Membership park:** A couple, working at Disney World, worked out an arrangement at their membership park to work in exchange for their site.

✔ **Elks Lodges:** Members of Elks Lodges can park their RVs at a reasonable rate at lodges all across the United States.

✔ **Talk to locals:** Get to know the locals and ask around. If there is a park that already has a campground host but is a good prospect, express your interest and keep in touch. We did just that in Alaska and half-way through the summer took over the position at a National Park Service campground and received free propane and a stipend.

*$* **Tourist town: Jay and Sandy** were headed west when they stopped in Tombstone, Arizona, for a few days. They loved it. Says Jay, "You can watch Wyatt Earp and the boys shoot it out three times a day. You can have a drink in an authentic and haunted saloon, and sit and talk to anyone from a tourist from Ohio to a Hell's Angel from Liechtenstein. We were going to stay three days and it turned into months, perhaps the most fun we've ever had." Sandy quickly got a retail job and negotiated higher pay and benefits too. Jay happened to mention at the local corral that he was from Montana. They assumed he knew a lot about horses (he knew a little) and after an informal chat with the boss, he was hired on by the Tombstone Stage Lines. He got people to ride the stage, giving them a history lesson. Soon he was driving the stage too. Reminisces Jay, "One of the men I met had the distinction of

being the only man in the U.S. convicted of a DUI on horseback. It made the national news!"

To escape the summer heat, Jay and Sandy found jobs on *Coolworks.com* as Jeep tour drivers in the Grand Canyon area. They negotiated a free RV space, an increasing pay scale, and received tips. They worked here for two seasons. "Good money, good people, but Tusayan is a small town that hosts five million people a year. Not the best living conditions but we were able to save money."

## DUDE RANCHES

152.  *Wrangler*
153.  *Wait staff*
154.  *Cook*
155.  *Housekeeper*
156.  *Maintenance worker*
157.  *Child care provider or worker*
158.  *Office worker*
159.  *Airport driver*
160.  *Laundry worker*

People who want a western experience on a ranch can visit a dude ranch. According to The Dude Rancher's Association, their 100-plus member ranches hire seasonal employees for positions such as wranglers, cooks, wait staff, housekeepers, maintenance workers, child care providers, and office workers. Northern ranches do their hiring for summer positions from November to April. Southern ranches do their hiring for winter positions from August to October.

> **Dude Ranch**
> **One couple from May-Sept.**
> **Positions in housekeeping, cooking, maintenance.**

Jobs on dude ranches typically involve hard work, long hours and participation in evening guest activities such as line dancing, hayrides and staff talent shows. They also require good people skills, and an ability to live and work well with others. Employee housing is provided, but you would need to check on an individual basis whether they would have a space for and would permit an RV parked on the premises. Some dude ranches do have RV parking.

$ **Dude ranch workers: Rich and Fran** found a summer job at a family-owned dude ranch in Colorado. They saw a brochure about the ranch, looked it up on the Internet, and then contacted the owners directly. Rich worked as head of maintenance doing everything from painting to feeding the pigs. Fran worked in the office handling the phone and registration, as well as marketing and writing ad copy. They were asked to stay through a Colorado winter and work the following summer, so were given a two-room cabin to stay in for the winter. Their compensation also included three meals a day, a good salary and their RV site for summer. Notes Fran, "Most dude ranches house employees in cabins. Our employer put in an RV site, and after having a positive experience with RV workers, has added two more RV sites for employees."

## BED & BREAKFASTS (B&BS)

161. *Housekeeper*
162. *Breakfast preparation like cook , wait staff*
163. *Guest check-in and greeting*
164. *Vacation relief staff or manager*

B&Bs may hire help during their busy seasons. Duties could range from food preparation, housekeeping, checking in guests to any and all of the above.

Owners may hire people to run the B&B on a temporary or full-time basis. Some people make a living as innkeepers, taking over for owners when they want to get away for a while. You can take classes and obtain a free "aspiring Innkeepers" kit through the Professional Association of Innkeepers International (PAII). As a member, you can be listed at their site as available for short-term or substitute assignments. (See **Resources.**)

$ **Bed and breakfast workers: John and Kay** spent two summers working at a B&B near Grand Teton National Park. They assisted the owner in all aspects of running it. They were able to park their RV right by the garage after John put in the connections. They had actually applied to an ad in *Workamper News* to work at a nearby RV park. The park owner passed their résumé on to the B&B owner and they were hired.

## SKI RESORTS

165. *Lift ticket seller*
166. *Ski instructor*
167. *Child care provider or worker*
168. *Driver*
169. *Retail clerk*
170. *Food related jobs like cook, wait staff, busboy, bartender*
171. *Weather reporter for area radio stations*

Don't rule out ski resorts. They too provide plenty of jobs if you don't mind the cold. For ski buffs, these jobs could get you a free season lift ticket or at least a discounted one. Janice and Gabby have worked in a number of winter resorts so they could ski. See their story in **Appendix 10.**

$ **Ski shuttle drivers: Joe and Terry** worked for two winters in the Aspen/Vail area for Colorado Mountain Express. They drove ten-passenger vans between Aspen and the Denver airport after a one-week training period. They worked four-day weeks, usually 10-15 hours/day. The job averaged $10/hour plus tips, which could be quite good. The second season they averaged between $12-14/hour with tips. Says Terry, "The job had minimal supervision, which appealed to us." Loading luggage on the van was hard work, but they enjoyed playing tour guide. They received uniforms, discounted seasonal ski pass and a 10% bonus for staying the whole season. They found their job at a job fair held by Hamilton Stores, their summer employers, in Yellowstone National Park. One benefit is free ski passes.

## AMUSEMENT AND THEME PARKS

172. *Food service worker*
173. *Ride operator and mechanic*
174. *Game operator*
175. *Retail sales clerk*
176. *Campground worker*
177. *Tram driver*
178. *Costumed character*
179. *Maintenance and repair worker*
180. *Interpreter*
181. *Tour guide*
182. *Warehouse worker*

Like resort areas, amusement parks hire many seasonal workers. They may also contract out services and that person or company then hires employees. Find some ads in *Workamper News* or contact the park you are interested in directly. The park may not have an RV site, so clarify that first. If you have to pay resort prices for a site in town and commute to the park, you may not reach your money goals. On the other hand, if this is something you have always wanted to do and it is worth the cost to you, go for it!

$ **Amusement park workers: Ray and Pat** worked at Adventureland in Iowa after responding to an ad in *Workamper News*. They both started out in food service. When an opening occurred in maintenance in the campground, Ray transferred there. The RV park provided for employees for a fee was one of the nicest they have stayed in while working, with large blacktop sites and trees. Wi-Fi, a heated pool and a clubhouse were available. They enjoyed their jobs and found Iowa an interesting state to explore.

## CRUISES AND LAND TOURS

183.  Housekeeper
184.  Food preparation and wait staff, bartender
185.  Lecturer or performer
186.  Dance host (also ambassador or gentlemen host)
187.  Recreational leader for gym, golf, dance, exercise, children's activities
188.  Bus driver/guide
188.  Customer service or shore representative
190.  Bus maintenance and cleaning worker

Cruises transport hordes of visitors to Alaska in the summer and to warmer destinations in the winter. They hire many workers, particularly in housekeeping and food service. From talking to those who have tried it, cruise work is not the glamour job portrayed on the *Love Boat*. Unless you are part of the professional staff, you are not allowed to be on deck during off-duty times. One cruise line we contacted told us they did not allow husband-wife teams to work on the same ship. A nice benefit, however, is that seasonal cruise employees are eligible for free cruises after a certain number of hours worked.

If you do have an area of expertise and could provide educational talks, you could offer to exchange your services for passage. One of my former supervisors who works for the National Park Service does this each year. Single men are in demand as dance partners on cruise ships and at least nine cruise ship lines seek them out for employment. Another RVer is a golf pro and found that cruise lines hire golf pros on their Caribbean cruises. One line has an artist-in-residence on board their cruises. If you have something to offer and you enjoy cruises, check it out.

> **Work for the leader in the Alaska cruise industry! More than 1500 summer seasonal workers needed.**

A better way to earn a cruise might be to work for a cruise line's land-based operations. Both Princess Land Tours and Gray Lines of Alaska offer free cruises after working approximately two summer seasons.

In Alaska during the summer, Princess Cruises and Holland America/ Gray Lines operate hotels and provide many tours for their passengers at each port. Seasonal workers are hired to greet the ships and load passengers on their buses. Bus drivers transport cruise passengers to their local tours or between Anchorage and Skagway by bus to continue their tour package. Both companies hire hotel staff and have a domed train running between Anchorage and Fairbanks via Denali National Park. Training and testing to get your Commercial Drivers License (CDL) is provided for bus driver trainees before starting work. Some work locations do have RV sites for employees for a fee.

 **Cruise line land tours: Bill,** my late husband, briefly worked part-time for both Princess Land Tours and Gray Line in Skagway, Alaska, before finding a full-time job he liked. At Princess he greeted passengers getting off Princess cruise ships and directed them to the proper bus for their tour. He and the other customer service reps collected paperwork from the drivers used for paying tour vendors. Bill enjoyed working with the mostly college-age kids and talking to visitors. Had the position been full-time, he might have stayed on the whole summer. "Princess bus drivers made excellent tips," observed Bill. His very brief stint with Gray Line was prepping buses for the day's tours.

## CASINOS
191. *Blackjack dealer*
192. *Food preparation and wait staff*
193. *Bartender*
194. *Security*
195. *Porter/porterette and change person*

Every once in a while, bells clang and the one-arm-bandit pays or someone hits big at black jack. To be part of that excitement may be on your wish list. In the long run, you'll probably end up with more money working as a dealer than being on the other side of the table.

In gambling towns like Las Vegas and Laughlin, nearby community colleges offer courses in becoming a dealer. Most courses last 4–6 weeks and cost from $300–500. Weldon, who completed a dealer's course in Bullhead City, across the river from Laughlin, Nevada, explains what happens:

*The only casinos in Laughlin that would take break-in (new) dealers were Circus Circus, Edgewater and Riverside. When your instructor feels you are ready, you go to casinos and "audition," or try out. They will either hire you or tell you that your game needs more practice. When you are hired you go on the Extra Board, which means that you work at their whim, maybe only one day a week or every two weeks as needed. At certain times of the year they need more Extra Board than others. The time on the Extra Board can be anywhere from three months to a year. Once you get off the Extra Board, you will probably be working five days a week and will know what your days off are, though they'll vary from week to week.*

*You are observed constantly and rules are very stringent. Explains Weldon, "You can't be self-conscious because you have floor people watching the dealer, you have pit bosses watching the floor people, you've got the "eye in the sky" watching the floor people and the pit bosses and the dealers, you've got floor surveillance that is watching everyone, so it's very security-conscious."*

Pay is minimum wage plus tips. At some casinos you are eligible for health insurance after three months.

To earn more, you need to learn more games. First are usually the "circus games." These include Pai Gow, Let it Ride, War, Caribbean Poker, and Baccarat. To learn Roulette you can go back to school or learn on your breaks and after hours. Weldon learned on his breaks. After a while, they pulled off the regular Roulette dealer and gave Weldon a try.

Weldon also notes that going to other states from Nevada is easier than the other way around. In Nevada you "toss cards," or deal hand-held games and also deal from a four to six-deck shoe. In most other states dealers use only the shoe. Weldon remembers first learning to toss cards: "You hold the cards in your left hand, then flick a card with your finger to get it to spin. I had cards going through the Venetian blinds, underneath the table, everywhere."

Advises Weldon, "If you want to deal and travel around the country, go to Nevada, learn to do the hand-held games as well as the shoe. Get that Nevada gaming card, because with that you can get in anywhere."

Casinos also hire workers as change people, cashiers, in food service, security and housekeeping.

## A FEW RESORTS THAT HIRE RV WORKERS

### WALL DRUG AND SIMILAR
196. *Retail clerk*
197. *Maintenance worker*
198. *Cook*
199. *Cafeteria worker*
200. *RV park-related worker*
201. *Usher*
202. *Stocking and inventory clerk*
203. *Demonstrator of old-time crafts like blacksmithing, weaving*
204. *Driver of a horse-drawn buggy or wagon*

Drive west on I-90 through South Dakota and see sign after sign announcing Wall Drug. In the 1930's the owners put signs out on the highway advertising free ice water, which brought in the customers. Now on peak summer days, Wall Drug can have 15,000 to 20,000 visitors a day and is a tourist destination in its own right. They hire a number of RVers and students to work in the cafeteria, retail sales and maintenance. Pay is a little above minimum wage; overtime

> **Portray a character of the historic gold rush! Work in the beautiful Black Hills of South Dakota.**

is paid after 40 hours. In addition Wall Drug provides uniforms, gives an employee discount and has low-cost RV parking in their trailer park. Half of the trailer park fee is returned if you stay the whole season. Other resorts like this also hire workers but may have a different focus or theme such as history. RVers with the ability to do old-time crafts like blacksmithing or weaving may find work dressed in period costumes.

## DISNEY WORLD

205.  *Merchandise host/hostess, cashier, roving vendor, display merchandiser*
206.  *Attractions host/hostess, tickets host/hostess*
207.  *Culinary: wait help, bussing, steward, cashier, host/ hostess, cook*
208.  *Housekeeping: custodial host/hostess, room attendant, houseman, laundry worker, 3rd shift custodial worker*
209.  *Life guard host/hostess, pool maintenance worker*
210.  *Transportation: parking lot guide, boat pilot, tram driver*
211.  *Seating host/hostess*
212.  *Character performer*
213.  *Hotel-related jobs: front desk, bell services, housekeeper*
214.  *Office, technical and reservations: front office receptionist, reservationist*
215.  *Wardrobe: costume assistant*

Disney World recruits full-time RVers. They appreciate their work ethic and offer full-time, part-time and seasonal positions at the Magic Kingdom, EPCOT, Disney MGM, Disney's Animal Kingdom, plus their resort hotels and the three water parks. The water parks tend to hire more seasonal workers in the summer. Disney's Wide World of Sports also employs workers.

Employees are known as "Cast Members," and their uniforms, which are provided, are "Costumes."

## $ Disney workers:

**Bill and Jean** worked at Disney World for three and one-half months one winter. They stayed at a membership park nearby, and Jean worked about 17 hours a week there for free rent. At Disney World they each worked from 24 to 45 hours a week, but after the first of January, hours were cut. Before that you could work as many hours a week as you wanted. Jean notes, "Disney is very flexible; some RVers worked only three weeks." One perk they enjoyed was seeing the dress rehearsal of the Christmas shows and parade, complete with snow and no one else around. They also watched the Spectro Magic parade from the balcony of the Castle and met Tinkerbell. Jean worked in Costumes, taking care of Cinderella and the girls. As a result she got autographed shirts for family who visited.

**Paul and Stephanie** worked for Disney MGM for two winters. Explains Stephanie, "The first winter we worked in crowd control for the Indiana Jones show. We would greet the guests, answer questions, get them into the theater, pack the theater (fit as many guests in as possible), and then get them out of the theater and prepare the theater for the next show. We also worked on some special assignments like crowd control when the Disney Christmas Parade was filmed for TV.

"The second year the Indiana Jones show was shut down for rehab so we worked some holiday specials: "Honey I Shrunk the Kids" and "Hunchback of Notre Dame." Paul also worked the Indiana Jones Street Show and Star Tours. The diversity the second year made our jobs even more enjoyable.

"It is wonderful to be able to meet people from all over the world and help them have a magical time. The perks at Disney are wonderful, which brings a lot of RVers to Disney. What some RVers forget, however, is that this is a real business and you are taking on a real job when you work for Disney."

## Working for the Mouse — Stephanie Bernhagen © 2001, 2007

Disney World in Florida employs between 51,000 and 57,000 people. Disney offers several categories of employment:

| | |
|---|---|
| food and beverage | culinary |
| custodial | merchandising |
| attractions | transportation |
| housekeeping | office, technical, reservations |
| life guard | |

Employees are called "cast members" and uniforms are called "costumes." This goes hand in hand with cast members being "on stage" when they are in the park. When "on stage," Disney has set guidelines cast members must follow.

There are three levels of employment—full-time, part-time and seasonal. Full-time positions include paid benefits. Part-time positions, referred to as Casual Regular (CR), do not pay benefits. CR's must be available two days a week and must not exceed 24-hours a week for more than six months of the year.

Seasonal positions, referred to as Casual Temporary (CT), are employed during peak tourist season but may be hired anytime. These positions may last from a few days to a few months. CRs and CTs receive overtime when they exceed eight hours in a shift.

A benefit to being a cast member is the ability to enter Magic Kingdom, Epcot, Disney MGM and Animal Kingdom with your ID. Once you work eight hours, you receive a Main Gate Pass good for one year, which allows you to take a three guests into the parks six times per year. CTs also receive two Complimentary Gate Passes good for two years, which can be used by anyone. Your Gate Pass is good as long as you work at least one day a year and leave in a re-hire status. You work with your assigned scheduler when you want to return to work.

Cast members who are hired before the end of October normally receive a Christmas package that includes discounts in stores and restaurants on Disney property, plus guest passes.

The hiring process starts with an interview with a Casting Representative. Once hired, you attend a class called Traditions, which provides background on the Disney Corporation. Next you attend a training day for the park or resort area where you will work. Finally you are trained in your specific area.

**Jay and Sandy** also worked at Disney World in outdoor foods, opening up Animal Kingdom. "How often do you get to be an Opening Crew Member in a new theme park for Disney?" enthuses Jay. "We signed on and had a blast! We worked with kids young enough to be our own, laughed every day we went to work, shared the magic, played for free all over Disney and met others older than ourselves who had found this great place to work in the winter months."

**Dan and Sue** also had fun. Quips Sue, "They paid me to stand around and talk to strangers! It was perfect." Sue's job entailed standing outside with one of the characters, such as Winnie the Pooh, Tigger, Woody or Buzz Lightyear, and making sure the guests got autographs and photos. Her job included "holding the Disney line," saying things like, "Piglet is not here today because he and Eyore are off looking for Eyore's tail." Dan, having previous experience with boats, trained for and then piloted a 600-passenger ferry between the Transportation Center and the Magic Kingdom.

**Skip and Virginia** enjoyed working at Disney World, but they did learn that you have to be insistent on where you want to work. Food and Beverages was short-handed so their recruiter steered them to that department. They would have preferred Attractions. Foods involved standing (not leaning) for your entire 6- or 8-hour shift, though Virginia eventually was able to work as cashier where she was able to sit. **Betsy and John** echo their remarks: "When you are hired, make sure you get the job you want." They too worked in Food Service before transfering to Merchantainment at the Disney MGM Studios. "It was a much better fit for us." They can return to these jobs by notifying their scheduler.

## BRANSON, MISSOURI

Silver Dollar City in Branson, Missouri, as well as other employers in Branson, make it attractive for RV workers. If you like country western shows, here's your opportunity to see your fill for almost nothing. Shows cost from $19–$40 so this is quite a value. Many establishments give generous discounts to full-time and seasonal employees in town.

$  **Working at Silver City: CC** likes to go to Branson around Christmastime for the Veteran's program and to see the Christmas lights. Before he began working during his visits, he would stay 7-11 days and see three shows a day. Working, he can stay six-seven weeks for the usual price of one and one-half weeks. At that time of year, there are also free or discounted programs for veterans, which cuts his expenses.

Silver Dollar City is a family destination and a big seasonal and short-term employer. It has a live play, and multiple live entertainers that put on shows throughout the day. It also has crafter demonstrations and several restaurants as well as an RV park.

During one visit CC applied at both the largest theater and largest employer and got job offers from both. Each provided free or standby passes to 99 percent of the shows and attractions and a 10-50 percent discount at most restaurants. The wages were at $6.50 and $7.00/hour, which about covered his meal expenses, while his badge and pay stub saved him $40-$75 per day in show fees. CC only worked about 15 hours a week, leaving plenty of time to see the shows.

Working at other employers in the tourist industry in Branson will give you the same discounts to shows and attractions.

## WORKING/VOLUNTEERING OVERSEAS

216. *Teacher overseas*
217. *Support worker at Antarctica*
218. *Short-term laborer*
219. *Manager for RV park in Mexico*
220. *Property caretaker*

Many countries have laws restricting foreign workers, so earning money to support yourself overseas is difficult unless you have a particular skill that is in demand. An RV couple who are psychologists were able to work in New Zealand and other countries because their position couldn't be filled by psychologists within those countries.

Teaching overseas is possible with a college degree. You do not have to have teaching credentials for most positions. Agencies of the federal government also hire teachers for overseas locations and for other positions. See the USAJOBS website at *(www.usajobs.opm.gov).*

**Teach English in Japan! BA/BS degree required. Japanese language ability not required.**

For a real adventure, consider working in Antarctica! Ratheon Polar Services is the primary support contractor for the National Science

Foundation's U.S. Antarctic program and hires approximately 800 employees to work in various jobs. Most jobs are from four to six months during the *austral* (southern) summer season, from October to February. Check their website for positions needed.

You may also be able to pick up laborer jobs in other countries like harvesting crops, waitressing, bartending or other similar positions.

> **Couple wanted to manage 30-space luxury RV park in Cabo San Lucas, Mexico. Full-time. House with utilities plus salary.**

*Caretaker Gazette* has overseas exchanges and caretaking positions listed. Occasionally you'll see an ad for Mexico.

Volunteering in another country can be a way to see it. Although you may be charged a fee and be expected to pay for your travel expenses, the cost is usually lower than a tour or vacation to the same country. In many overseas volunteer positions, you can stay with a local family and get a whole different experience. See Chapter 22 for ideas and resources.

$ **Overseas teachers:  Bill and Marna** left their motorhome on the mainland and took teaching jobs in Japan for a year. They taught conversational English in a junior college in Hiroshima. They were furnished a house and car and only worked 14 hours a week. They had plenty of time to explore the area and visit hot springs. Bill climbed Mt. Fuji. Since they were already in Asia, after their assignments ended Bill visited China and Marna traveled to Indonesia.

Resorts and travel destinations are good places to look for jobs. There is a high demand for seasonal workers. Many jobs are closer to minimum wage but that isn't always the case. There's a reason people like to go to these places and they pay lots of money to do so. You'll get paid for being there.

*Jobs 221-266*

# Chapter 20
# How to find temporary jobs and work at special events

Temporary jobs can be found through a number of sources. Agencies specializing in placing temporary workers are an excellent source for these jobs. Holiday season work can be found through agencies and local classified ads.

## TEMPORARY JOBS

221. *Office work: clerical, accounting, computers*
222. *Factory or assembly work*
223. *Professional*
224. *Construction work: carpentry, plumbing, electrical, sheet rock, block work*
225. *Product demonstration*
226. *Tax season work: accounting*
227. *Tax season work: clerical*
228. *Substitute teacher*
229. *Temporary medical jobs: nurse, therapist or physician*
230. *Fruit or vegetable picker*
231. *Work during a grape harvest: grape sampler, weigh master*
232. *Worker for wheat harvest*
233. *Corn detasseler*
234. *Agent at reservation center for campgrounds*
235. *Flagger for highway construction projects*
236. *Deliver telephone books*
237. *CDL driver, long or short haul*

## HOLIDAY-SEASON WORK

238.   *UPS driver or warehouse worker*
239.   *Christmas retail salesperson or giftwrapper*
240.   *Mall sales for See's Candy or Hickory Farms*
241.   *Santa Claus at mall or department store*
242.   *Bell ringer collecting donations*
243.   *Fireworks sales*
244.   *Post office temporary worker*
245.   *Post office contract worker*
246.   *Baggage handler for cargo aircraft*
247.   *Sign twirlers*
248.   *Usher at holiday cultural events*
249.   *Flower shop drivers, designers, salespeople*
250.   *Phone workers at call centers for catalog orders & surveys*
251.   *Worker at a Renaissance fesitval*

### Temporary agencies

Temporary agencies provide other employment opportunities. According to the American Staffing Association (ASA), more than two million people per day are employed by staffing companies and 90 percent of companies use temporary help services. Employers, not you, pay the fee to the agency.

> **Costumed characters**
> **$8/hour**
> **Fun, Fun, Fun!!!**
> *Manpower*

If you have a trade or professional skill, the wages earned can be much better than many temporary or seasonal jobs. The average assigned worker earns more than $12 per hour according to ASA. A quick stint with an agency might add a bit of traveling cash to your pockets.

Usually you find temporary or staffing agencies in mid-sized to larger towns. There are specialty agencies that place only accounting or financial type workers; others place strictly day labor. Nurses have their own agencies and physicians can work as a "locum tenen," getting placed at hospitals and practices around the country.

There are agencies with branches in cities throughout the U.S. and world like Manpower or Adecco. If you register and work regularly through these agencies, you may be able to get health insurance and other benefits. You won't need to re-register or take tests when you move to a new location. Your records are available by computer or can be transferred.

## How to locate agencies

If you are planning to stay in a location for a while and want to find a temporary agency, you can look in the employment section of the classified ads and in the Yellow Pages. The American Staffing Association website allows you to search for member agencies in each state. Many have their own websites. You can also search the websites of more well known agencies like Manpower, Adecco, and Ameritemps for locations in your area. You

> **Immediate openings!
> $7 per hour and up.
> Over 100 openings
> available.**
> *Tops Staffing*

can even make contact ahead of time. Larger newspapers are often found on the Web. Yellow Page directories are listed on the home page of most search engines. Before traveling check ahead to find out possibilities.

Unless you have previously registered with another branch of that agency, you will need to go to the office with your résumé, references, and copies of any professional or trade licenses. You may need to take a test. Most agencies that place secretarial help require a typing or word processing test to determine words per minute.

## How it works

✔ **Landing assignments:** You will need a telephone number where you can be reached. If your cell phone is out of range, then be sure to call your voice mail regularly or plan to call in at the times they might call to see if you have an assignment. Most agencies line up their temps the afternoon before the assignment, but they may also have last-minute cancellations or requests, so if you are eager for work, an early morning call as well is a good idea. The agency will give the job to the first person they can contact so keep that in mind.

✔ **Hourly pay:** You can also specify a minimum wage you are willing to accept. You don't want to price yourself out of the local job market, but you also want to cover your costs.

✔ **When paid:** Since you are employed by the agency, not the employer where you work, you will be paid by the agency, usually once a week.

✔ **Your choice:** You can also decide whether you want a specific assignment. Perhaps the location isn't convenient or they want too long a commitment. If you have a doctor's appointment scheduled, you can let the agency know you won't be available that day. Keep in mind that if you turn down or are unavailable for too many assignments, you are less likely to be the worker who gets the call.

✔ **Free training:** Since 90 percent of staffing companies provide free training, check into acquiring new skills to make you more valuable.

✔ **Reference letters:** You can ask for reference letters from both the agency and employers at job sites.

The nice thing about temp work is that you can set parameters. If they are realistic and you are a good worker, you'll get plenty of assignments. If the parameters are too high or you aren't getting good evaluations from employers, you won't get many calls.

### What you can earn

Many companies today are turning to the temporary market to find employees as a cost-saving measure. They pay a little more to an agency, but save on benefits and paperwork. They can build up their work force when needed and don't have to worry about paying unemployment when the work force drops. Plus, the agency does the screening for them and if one worker isn't what they are looking for, they can request another.

> **IMMEDIATE OPENINGS**
> **Housekeeping, production,**
> **assembly, shipping & receiving**
> *tops® Staffing*

What you earn will depend on the position and the job market. Check the help wanted ads and talk to the agency counselor to find out the going rate for your type of work. The agency will give you an idea if your desired earnings are realistic.

If there is more than one staffing or temporary agency in the area, check to see if any offer benefits such as health insurance, vacation or sick leave and what the requirements are.

**$  Temporary workers:**
  **Wally** is a trained electrician. **Patsy** saw an ad on the website Monster.com *(www.monster.com)* for a special project. One hundred electricians plus numerous helpers were being hired for a six-month project. Helpers were being paid $12/hour. Says Patsy, "Don't overlook this resource."

**Skip and Virginia** worked at temporary agencies while parked at their son's home. They only took jobs paying at least $8/hour. Advises Virginia, "There's nothing that says you can't sign up with more than one agency at once." Their first agency was not a match; the other was great to work for. Skip signed up for "light industrial," and Virginia for clerical. Both were given some basic tests. After Skip's first assignment at a warehouse, Virginia added light industrial work to her job availability — more exercise than sitting at a desk. She ended up working first for an interior design company filling in for the receptionist (boring), then for a company that managed seven parking garages and later for a small manufacturing company. One advantage of this type of work was that they could decline an assignment on days they had medical appointments scheduled.

**Tax season worker: Bea** has been working for H&R Block during tax season for eleven years, six while full-timing. H&R Block has an initial training for tax preparers, taking place over three months. She also took other pre-work training required of first-year preparers. Each year thereafter, about 40 hours of training is required, learning about changes and more advanced tax law. Tax preparers earn a commission on each tax return they prepare and she figures she now averages around $29/hour. Bea has transferred twice to a different location after a telephone interview.

While in Kissimmee, Florida, husband **Ken** ended up working for a rental equipment repair place. He found that position by calling places in the Yellow Pages after a promised job at Camping World fell through. They had gotten an RV spot near Camping World, so did have to get a second car.

## Related sources

Locate temporary job openings through local classified ads and employment publications in larger cities; search Internet job sites using the terms "seasonal" or "temporary."

**EVENT/CONCERT STAFF**
**Join T.E.A.M. for New Year's**
**Eve Block Party. Holiday pay!**

You may be able to register and use the state job service, particularly if you apply for unemployment. (See state government pages in the telephone book.)

## Things to consider

There are a couple of drawbacks to temporary work that may affect you.

✔ **No RV site:** The agency will not provide an RV site. You may have other options besides a costly RV park. If you are lucky enough to have relatives or friends with room in their driveway, like Skip and Virginia, this is a low-cost option. You will want to pay them for any expenses incurred such as electricity or telephone calls. If you don't have this option, check with mobile home parks. They often have a lower monthly or long-term rate than RV parks and can accommodate an RV or two. You might also be able to combine a temporary job with a site-sitting or house-sitting assignment. While I worked for an accounting firm during tax season, Bill volunteered for the Forest Service for our site.

✔ **Transportation:** If both you and your travel partner are working, transportation to job sites may be a challenge. If you have to purchase a second vehicle or pay for bus fares, this will lower your wages.

✔ **Attire:** Some types of work require professional attire or at least not jeans. You don't have to be a fashion plate, just neat and clean. When I worked during tax season as a secretary at an accounting firm one winter, I told the gal I was working for that my wardrobe was limited because of my RV lifestyle. I went to a local thrift store and purchased a couple of skirts plus a nice blazer, all for under $10. When finished, I donated them back to the thrift store, since I didn't need them or have room to carry them.

## Other seasonal temporary work

Other industries hire workers for their busy season. Some ideas:

$ **UPS:** United Parcel Service hires drivers and other workers during the Christmas season. Check at their websote or locally in employment guides or help wanted ads in larger towns. UPS hires about 95,000 seasonal workers nationwide.

$ **Airport:** Ramp agents and other additional help for loading and unloading cargo aircraft may be needed during the holiday season. Check local employment guides or help wanted ads.

$ **Retail sales:** Christmas-help in retail stores is always needed. You might also find a gig as a Santa Claus.

$ **Charities:** Paid bell ringers for Salvation Army and other charities collect money at Christmas.

$ **Usher:** Ushers are hired for holiday cultural events.

$ **Postal work:** A test is required but this is another source of work during the holiday rush.

$ **Post office contract work:** Post offices often contract out hauling mail from one post office to another. The contractor might need holiday or vacation relief help. Check with the Postmaster to find out the name of the contractor.

$ **Tax season:** Accounting firms hire tax preparers and clerical help for approximately three months.

$ **Public and private schools:** If you have a college degree, you might be eligible to substitute in public or private schools. Pay varies by school district.

$ **Fruit or vegetable picking:** Usually strenuous work, but it doesn't last long. Apple picking involves less bending and stooping than most harvesting jobs. You can usually find at least one employer in *Workamper News* recruiting workers.

$ **Fruit processing:** Work in a processing plant in Florida. Jobs include the Juice Room, retail, order-taking by phone, shipping and warehouse, food service.

> **Substitute teachers needed. $125 per day Hawthorne School District**

$ **Wheat harvest:** Follow the harvest in several plains states. A Commercial Driver's License is helpful.

$ **Corn fields:** Earn $1,400 to $2,200 in three weeks detasseling corn in the Midwest.

$ **Campground reservations:** Work in a call center for camping reservations like Reserve America.

$ **Flagging** for highway road construction projects. You need to take a short training course. The Laborers' International Union of North America includes these workers. If no union hall is located in your area, check with the road construction company to find out who does the hiring or provides flaggers.

$ **Delivery of telephone books:** Use own vehicle to deliver locally. Check local papers or call phone book company to find out who delivers.

$ **Selling fireworks:** Sales of fireworks in roadside stands.

$ **Delivery of flowers:** Before holidays like Mother's Day and Valentine's Day, flower shops often need extra help. They may need other workers too in sales and design.

$ **Call centers:** Catalog centers and phone survey companies often need extra help at holidays.

$ **Renaissance Festivals:** Some hire workers for the run of the festival, usually on weekends.

**$ Temporary fruit processors: Ken and Jan** worked for Sun Harvest in south Florida. Ken worked in the Juice Room, keeping an eye on the machinery that squeezes and bottles the juice. Jan took orders by telephone and typed them up. Says Jan, "Patience and tact is a must." Besides working in the mail order department, Jan worked at other times in retail or serving ice cream cones.

**$ Apple picker: April** worked picking apples one fall in Washington state. This company only hires retired RVers and even has an RV park with full hookups for them. April described the work as strenuous and not for anyone with a bad back. However, the owners included time in the schedule to take tours and explore the area. Pay depended on the variety and quantity picked. April found the listing in *Workamper News*.

**$ Winery workers: Charlie** worked two seasons for Beringer Wine Estates as a grape sampler during the fall harvest. His job was to drive to designated grape vineyards and pull off a sampling of grapes so the lab could determine if they were ready for harvest. The first season **Norma** got a position through Manpower Temporary Agency in Sonoma. The second season she was hired on as a weigh master for Beringer. Using a computer program, trucks were weighed both full and empty to figure tonnage delivered. In 1999/2000, Charlie was paid $12/hour, while Norma earned $11 and had lots of overtime. The season is approximately three months long. They were able to park their RV at a family member's house.

**$ Sell fireworks: CC** saw an ad in the *El Paso Times* newspaper for selling fireworks for Fourth of July. Working about two and one-half weeks, you could earn between $3000 and $4000 dollars. Since it is illegal to sell fireworks within the city limits, stands ring the city. The stands are adjacent to a power pole for light and for electricity for your RV. The seller gets 20-30% of total sales.

## CONTRACT WORK AND TEMPORARY WORK FOR PROFESSIONALS

252. *Computer project consultant*
253. *Technical writer*
254. *Engineer*
255. *Medical short-term assignment: nurse, therapist, physician*
256. *RN or LPN at family or children's camp*
257. *Teacher*

### Contract work

If you have specialized computer skills, Web design skills, copyediting or technical writing skills, or other "high-tech" skills, there is whole market out there for your services. You may be able to do all or part in your own RV, in which case you will need a telephone line or satellite Internet. You may travel to the company or provide your services via the Internet. You will also work as an independent contractor, rather than an employee. It does mean you will need to pay full social security tax. And if you get your jobs through agents, they will collect part of your fee as their cut. (See discussion of employee vs independent contractor in Chapter 13.)

> **Find high tech jobs online today!**
> ***www.dice.com***

*$* **Computer consultant: Byron** is a traveling computer consultant. He has taught himself several computer programs which he uses to help clients either onsite or from his RV. He specializes in Crystal Reports development, MS Access development, and Interactive Voice Response development. Most of the time Byron finds his jobs through one of hundreds of consulting companies. Byron sets his fee, normally at least $60/hour, and the consulting company adds their fee on top of that. He needs a computer, the development software (tax deductible as a business expense), and telephone contact if he is performing the work in his RV. He now has satellite Internet when working in his rig. Onsite, he uses the company's equipment. Says Byron, "It's truly fun to be able to go, at a moment's notice, anywhere in the country, to get the best-paying opportunities which wouldn't be available to those with more traditional lifestyles."

$ **Contract consultant: John** has associate degrees in Journalism and Broadcast Electronics and finds short-term work as "technical editor," "technical writer," and "technical illustrator." He earns from $20 per hour in communities with a moderate cost-of-living and $45 to $100 per hour in major cities with high costs of living. He mainly uses Monster.com for finding assignments since it is one of the few online job search sites that does not limit your search to one city or state. If he wants to work in a particular area, he locates an agency there and sends his resume. *C.E Publications Directory of Contract Service Firms* is a good resource, as is the *U.S. Register of Technical Service Firms* available from National Technical Employment Services. Agencies like Manpower, Aerotek/Maxim Group and CDI have offices nationwide and assignments for contract consultants. In any case, the employers pay the fee. One advantage of being an RVer is that if you travel more than 50 miles from your domicile, you are often eligible for per diem pay and deductions, and no lease hassles if your job ends early. Some employers also reimburse travel expenses to get there. Says John, "There are literally millions of high-tech consultants world-wide, working in a multi-billion dollar industry."

### Training

If you don't already have these computer or technical skills, you can acquire them as Byron did. You can take an online computer course if you will have Internet access while the course runs. Some courses are also self-paced where you can work at your own speed and take the final exam whenever you are ready.

For those interested in copyediting, *The Well-Fed Writer*, by Peter Bowerman, offers guidance in getting started. (See **Resources**, Ch 21.)

### Temporary work for professionals

Professionals like accountants, nurses and physicians can find agencies that specialize in their discipline. During tax season, many accounting firms hire extra tax help: tax preparers and clerical and data-entry workers.

Travel nurses and physicians take short-term assignments. For nurses, according to wannabee RVer Maryanne, "Critical care, such as cardiac ICU or surgery, or ER or neonatal ICU are the most in demand, because there is currently a shortage of nurses in those areas in particular."

**$ Registered nurse: Mary** is an RN and accepts assignments through an agency in Salt Lake City. **Tony** picks up one or more jobs where Mary's assignments are. While in Page, Arizona at Lake Powell, Tony put together a series of ways to earn money. He did grant writing, tutored a woman on computer software, sold advertising, did substitute teaching, taught at the community college, and guided float rafts from Glen Canyon Dam to Lee's Ferry. Mary receives a housing allowance when she takes a temporary assignment and this pays for their RV site.

**$ Nurse without a Purse: Dave,** who calls himself the *Nurse without a Purse,* has worked as a nurse at a number of children's camps, sometimes staying in his RV. He also took a year off to work on a wagon train that went from Pennsylvania to Florida and back. Dave says the nonprofit camps pay the best and have better food. He rates the Girl Scout camp food the best, although he had to help with the dishes.

## SPECIAL EVENTS
258. *County or state fairs*
259. *Sports events*
260. *NASCAR events in a support capacity: security, parking, cleanup, souvenirs, food service, admissions, tickets*
261. *Home and garden shows*
262. *Shows in Quartzsite, Arizona*
263. *Golf tournaments*
264. *Events at stadiums or convention centers*
265. *Race tracks: horse, dog races*
266. *Swap meets: booth sales, parking*

Home and garden shows, county and state fairs, RV shows, festivals, dog shows and golf tournaments are all possibilities for picking up some short-term work. Often exhibitors hire local help onsite for these events. Some will advertise in the local newspaper, but most hire a few days before the event right onsite. The most effective way is to stop at booths and ask if they are hiring. You will probably get minimum wage unless you have a special skill. If you work in sales, you might work on commission or a combination of hourly wage plus commission.

A number of RVers have found that selling products at fairs and other shows is lucrative. You can work for someone else on commission or sell your own product. You are often able to park your RV where you sell, though you may pay almost as much as a regular campground for it. See **Resources,** for information on locating shows and products to sell.

---

**Ushers, ticket-takers & Guards
$8-$16/hr Del Mar Fair
$6.25-$8.50 Padres Baseball
*Elite Show Services***

---

If you are interested in selling at shows for an employer, one good way to find an employer is to spend some time at fairs and shows. See what products seem to be selling well. Talk to workers in the booths when they aren't busy and find out more about the industry and their product. Ask other vendors about the reputation of perspective employers. Some employers are difficult to work for and have a bad reputation.

In working the show circuit, you usually start out doing the less lucrative shows. As you get experience, you'll find opportunities to move into more lucrative shows. Since employers nearly always have someone working the better shows, it can be a matter of waiting for turnover.

Also use your network to find other RV workers who are making money this way. You can learn a lot about the questions to ask and situations to avoid. Some considerations to get you started:

✔ **Driving distances and costs:** What area of the country will my shows be in? Consider that it will cost you each time you drive from show to show. A route that minimizes driving distances is preferred.

✔ **Delivering product to shows:** Will I need to carry product or will you ship it? One RV couple found they had to buy a van to carry all their product; another was able to work out getting shipments to the site.

✔ **Booth set-up:** Who is responsible for setting up the booth and getting it there? Will I need to carry that in my rig from show to show? Consider the space it will take up, plus the weight, which adds premature wear and tear to your rig.

✔ **Compensation:** How will I be paid? If another worker also shares the booth or a related booth, will we be splitting the commissions or each keep what we earn? Consider the abilities of this other salesperson. Will you come out with less if commissions are split?

✔ **RV site:** Will I be able to park on site and will there be any charge? If there is charge, who will pay for it?

✔ **My needs:** Does the show schedule meet my needs — for income, time off, and travel locations?

## Related

$ **NASCAR races** also provide temporary employment. *Workamper News* advertises event employment in their publication. Vendors also hire people to follow the circuit, working at each event.

> **New Hampshire Intern'l Speedway. Positions in security, parking at several major events.**

$ **Quartzsite, Arizona** is the scene of one of the world's largest flea markets. Over one million RVers spend some time here in winter. Quartzsite has acres of shows and flea markets in January and February. Some vendors hire help. Besides working in sales for a vendor, RV workers have gotten jobs at restaurants and installing solar panels.

$ **Ushers and food service.** Check with temporary agencies, and local newspapers and employment guides for local events hiring help.

$ **Quartzsite, Arizona: Terry and Joe** were in Quartzsite, Arizona. Another RVer was looking for a couple to sell their product at RV shows. Terry and Joe were looking for a different way to make money and decided to give it a try. "The product was good and the owner excellent to work for. However, we realized selling was not for us. It worked out well because we earned some money and had a chance to try it out without traveling out of our way." Another time they were boondocked in New Mexico and noticed a road project in progress. They talked to the supervisor and were hired for two weeks.

$ **NASCAR race workers: Ron and Val** picked up four-day jobs at the NASCAR Winston Cup Race at Talladega after working first at the Formula I Grand Prix at Indy and enjoying it thoroughly. Both events were listed in *Workamper News*. With tight security, they were instructed to check everyone coming through for proper tickets or credentials. Days were long, usually from 7 a.m. to 6 or 8 p.m., but they were in "spitting distance of the track." Says Val, "We got to see everything going on." They were paid $6.75 an hour plus given a free dry-camping space. Dale Earnhardt, Jr., Ricky Rudd, Dale Jarrett and other drivers got a kick out of the lady at the south tunnel entrance who insisted on checking out their credentials because she didn't recognize a one of them! Officials were so delighted to get such good workers, they practically begged them to come back and work the race in the spring. They recently worked in Las Vegas at another NASCAR event.

Temporary positions can be well-paying jobs. You decide when you want to work and for how much. You can turn down assignments that aren't a match. Temporary jobs at special events can be a way to pick up some quick cash. Rarely does an RV site come with a temporary job, but you may find you make more money even after paying for your site. A temporary agency may have specialized training you can use to improve your job skills and marketability while you gain experience in a new field.

*Jobs 267-311*

# Chapter 21
# How to operate your own business on the road

Approximately 70 percent of U.S. businesses are run by self-employed entrepreneurs. Operating your own business on the road may give you the income and flexibility that you want. Many working RVers are doing just that. The new technology available to RVers — computers and cell phones — makes having a business on the road more feasible.

The type of business you run is limited only by your imagination and willingness to make it happen. Several areas seem to lend themselves to working for yourself.

## SALES OF RV-RELATED PRODUCTS AND SERVICES

267. *Solar panels*
268. *Upholstery and carpet cleaning*
269. *Solar ovens*
270. *Laptop computers and related equipment*
271. *GPS devices*
272. *Brake assists and other RV accessories*
273. *Windshield repair*
274. *RV repair or handyman work*
275. *Hair cutting, sewing, massages*
276. *Badges*
277. *Redwood signs*
278. *Satellite dishes and antennae*
279. *Satellite Internet equipment or Wi-Fi cards*
280. *Pet grooming*

281. *Sharpening knives and scissors*
282. *Locksmithing*
283. *RV detailing*

The list of products and services above are ones that RVers might need or want. Your business could cater strictly to other RVers. You could use these ideas to pick up some extra money, or work harder and make a living from them. Often RV entrepreneurs combine several ways to bring in money on the road.

### Finding customers

One of the best ways to find customers is to park where other RVers are located. RV parks and campgrounds are good spots, or in boondocking areas where RVers congregate at certain times of the year like Quartzsite, Arizona in January and February. A sign on your vehicle may bring inquiries. If you are outside working on your business, for example making signs, other campers may ask you about your business. Use every opportunity to let people know about the product or service you provide. Carry your business cards with you at all times.

> **Make money repairing windshields. Unlimited potential.**

If you are parked in an RV park, check with management about their rules for conducting your business in their park. There may be local licenses or permits required. The park owner could be liable if you do not follow these local regulations and incur liability if someone is injured on their property. You may be able to negotiate an agreement with the owners. For example, one dog groomer pays fifty-percent of her fee to the RV park. She makes money while the park offers a service to their guests.

Attending RV rallies or educational events brings you in contact with potential customers. You could have a booth or you may be able to find customers without one (if allowed). Offering a seminar is a way to create interest in your product or service.

 **Carpet cleaning and windshield repair: Gene** has found he prefers to work for himself rather than for an employer. He and **Kathy** have gone back to an area they know well and fixed up houses and then sold them. They have also cleaned RV carpets and upholstery. Now Gene repairs chips in windshields. They find customers by parking in strategic places and by attending some rallies. Gene also assists people in getting started in the windshield repair business. In addition, they have sold Christmas trees in Texas and Kathy has worked for her former employer in the town where they lived before hitting the road.

$ **Solar power: Tom and Nancy** have been committed for years to solar energy and alternative technologies. They left northeast Pennsylvania where the sun rarely shined and traveled in Mexico for two years, promoting solar solutions. Infected with the traveling spirit, they wanted to find a way to help support their dreamed-about nomadic lifestyle. After trying a couple of other businesses, Tom came back to his earlier fascination: solar. It required a lot of initial research but Tom has been successfully marketing solar ovens and solar electric systems. Nancy has also picked up extra cash with her sewing business, doing sewing repairs for RVers.

## OTHER RV-BASED BUSINESSES

284. *Engraving*
285. *Selling advertising and producing RV park maps (own business)*
286. *Carving*
287. *Artist or craftsperson: painting, beading, photography, weaving, jewelry etc.*
288. *Offering guided tours*
289. *Teaching classes in exercise, dance or crafts*
290. *Photographer — digital photo imaging*
291. *Word processing or medical transcription*
292. *Desktop publishing*
293. *RV book publishing and sales*
294. *Newsletter publication*
295. *Musician or performer*
296. *Giving massages*

Other businesses are not aimed particularly at RVers, but can be done on the road because location doesn't matter, bulky supplies or equipment are not needed, or you may travel from one location to another to conduct your business.

## Selling at RV and other shows and fairs

Products of a more general nature can be sold at RV shows as well as Home and Garden Shows, state and county fairs or flea markets. You can pick your "circuit" and hit the shows in a particular area you like to travel or where your product does well. RVers we know sell clothes, redwood signs, digital photos transferred onto shirts and cups, cleaning products, and more. Several RVers make and sell badges and pins at RV and other shows.

Others cater to the RV market, selling and, in some cases, installing RV accessories, satellite TV and Internet equipment and laptop computers.

A number of publications and websites are available to locate shows that dovetail with your product and provide sources of saleable products.

 **Sales at shows: Wally and Patsy** have sold electric barbeques, a wood cleaning product, clothes and a needle threader at fairs, home and RV shows.

After an initial two years on the road, Patsy and Wally decided their dream was to stay on the road for as long as possible, be debt free and have money to do the fun things they enjoy. At first they sold products for other owners on a percentage basis. Then they decided to work for themselves. "Now," says Wally, "we sell what needs to be sold." Patsy and Wally have looked at many ways to earn money. Sales has the best income potential, Patsy observed, and has enabled them to reach their goals.

 **Redwood signs and digital photo imaging: Tom and Nancy** made and sold redwood signs traveling a show circuit in Michigan in the summer, as well as other shows in their travels. After several years they sold the sign business and began a digital photography business. They travel to many of the same shows, taking photos and then putting them on t-shirts, mugs, mouse pads and other items they stock. They do stock. They do their work and transport their equipment in a small trailer they tow behind their motorhome.

## INTERNET-RELATED SERVICES

297. *Sales of products on the Web through eBay or other online auction sites for yourself or others*
298. *Website sales*
299. *Produce an electronic magazine (e-zine)*

### Internet

RVers maintain websites and sell products like books and newsletters. They make money through affiliate programs where they earn money each time someone at their site clicks on a link and goes to the affiliate site. In some cases, merely going to the new site earns money; in other cases, a portion of any resulting sales is earned.

> **Have your own online mall!**
> **Only $39 a month.**
> **Ready-to-use professionally designed Web site.**

Participating in Internet auctions has developed into a moneymaker. RVers sell products on eBay, the biggest Internet auction site, or act as agents for other sellers. Web design is another service that RVers can provide.

$ **Auctions on eBay: Ernie and Nancy** sell items on eBay while traveling in their RV. According to Ernie, "Requirements are a computer, digital camera or scanner, and e-mail accessibility." They use library computers or take their laptop into a truck stop when a telephone hookup is not available in the campground where they are staying. In order to start selling, you first set up an account with eBay. Small fees are charged. Then you post the item. Auctions run from three to ten days. Then you notify the highest bidder who sends check or money order to you. "We've had people send checks for as much as $1,400 in care of General Delivery!" reports Ernie. Since carrying inventory is cumbersome in an RV, they are branching out by selling items for antique stores for a commission.

*$* **Web sales: Bryce and Lisa's** two-year travel dream to see the U.S. by RV started to fizzle short when they ran out of money. They were having too much fun to settle down so they needed to find a way to earn money on the road. For a while, they worked for American Guide Service (AGS), a company that makes maps and guides for RV parks and resorts.

When Bryce discovered the Web, that opened up a whole new world and additional ways to make money. Bryce and Lisa have their own website at *(www.webworker.com)* with all sorts of free information on creating and using your own website to have a home-based business, and making money from affiliate programs. This has branched out into several other businesses, such as eBay sales and e-books.

*$* **Website design and a travel website: Carl and Rhonda** left high tech computer jobs when they were in their mid-thirties. Now they are using these skills to earn money while traveling. Carl is writing a book on Web hosting for beginners and reviews technical manuscripts for publishers. Rhonda designs websites and also does nature/rock animal painting. They also have a popular travel website *(www.southpoint.com)*.

*$* **Web sales: Stan** was a computer programmer and started a side computer business five years before hitting the road. Now he and **Connie** travel and earn money from several different computer ventures. These include selling shareware programs through his website *(www.CottonwoodSW.com)*, and selling screensavers at *(http://AwesomeScreens.com)*. Stan has also developed a low-cost campground reservation system.  In addition he has a couple of other sites where he makes money through advertising. Links to all his ventures are at *(http://StanAndConnie.com)*.

Stan shares these methods he has used for increasing sales:

- ✔ **Offer free trial versions** of his shareware good for 30 days as an incentive to buy.
- ✔ **Use press releases** to get free media coverage in computer magazines.
- ✔ **Advertise on other Internet sites.** This is usually a free listing on other shareware websites or exchange links.
- ✔ **Run a website** to sell your programs.
- ✔ **Use Google AdWords** to send targeted visitors to your site.

Most marketing for their program is still via the web. Says Stan, "As we grow, more and more it is word-of-mouth. We've tried some licensing and commission arrangements, but so far they haven't been worth the effort. Nobody is going to be more enthusiastic about selling your product than yourself!"

When they started, one of the most difficult aspects of running an Internet-related business on the road was connectivity. "Now we use a Motosat Datastorm system (a roof-mounted auto-pointing 2-way satellite system). This can be quickly set up anywhere (as long as we're not parked under a tree), and provides constant unlimited access. This is crucial for timely responses to inquiries, orders, and support issues.

"The other issue is phone service — it's important that we be available by phone for our customers, so we have a nationwide calling plan on a cell phone (no roaming or long distance). We've had to keep increasing the plan to cover more and more minutes per month as the business grows."

One further note, Stan advises that to succeed in this business you need computer knowledge, Internet savvy, and basic business skills. This may not be enough to make a living out of it right away. It usually takes time to build up business (and develop your products), though there are overnight success stories too. Says Stan, "Most successful programs are the culmination of a few years of constant improvements and consistent marketing efforts. And most started out as a part-time side business."

## CONSULTING/PROFESSIONAL

300.　*Innsitting business*
301.　*Business consultant*
302.　*Seminar speaker*
303.　*Computer consultant, Web page designer*
304.　*Computer "debugging" and repairs*
305.　*Freelance writer*
306.　*Freelance photographer*
307.　*Investor in stock market*
308.　*Tax preparation*
309.　*Performer at school assemblies*
310.　*Instructor — exercise programs*
311.　*Academic instructor — online courses*

## Vacation relief or short-term management

A business providing vacation-relief for businesses such as bed and breakfasts, motels and storage facilities is feasible. To be viable, you would need to have experience in this area or have made contacts.

**Jackson Hewitt Tax Service Franchise opportunities available. Small start-up fee, state-of-the-art tax software.**

Some businesses hire consultants to turn them around. One couple with a background in apartment management went to apartment complexes around the county and got them back on track. They got rid of undesirable tenants and cleaned the apartments in order to provide positive cash flow. Each job took six months to a year and paid very well. They had an excellent track record in this field prior to hitting the road, however.

$ **Innsitters: Bill and Marna** always had enjoyed staying in bed and breakfasts. They started their own business providing vacation relief or "innsitting" to B&B owners. As they traveled, they would stop and meet owners and leave their business card. Owners contacted them later when they needed short-term relief. "What was great about being innsitters was that we were able to stay in lovely places, meeting interesting people and choose when we wanted to work," notes Marna.

## Seminar speakers

Giving seminars for corporations in various locations is another way RVers make money. Usually this type of business is an outgrowth of work done before hitting the road. Generally, a client base has already been developed.

$ **Corporate trainer, motivational speaker, and nature photographer: Kay and Tom** knew they wanted to hit the road as soon as their kids were out of college in 1998. Kay began developing a business doing corporate training and motivational speaking in 1991. Her background was in corporate consulting and project management, so her business evolved out of that experience. She has broadened her topics since then and now has three separate businesses, each with a different focus. Says Kay, "My work is a forum for teaching, uplifting and inspiring." Getting into this business takes expertise and networking. She also recommends joining the National Speakers Association. Tom takes nature photographs. The RV lifestyle is perfect for visiting beautiful scenery so Tom can build his portfolio.

$ **Publishers and consultants: Annette and Larry** have two family businesses involving publishing and consulting. Annette says, "The key is planning. It took us five years of development to feel confident that we could make the same amount of money 'on the road' as before." They usually stay in one location one to two months, taking advantage of monthly rates at RV parks. Overall it costs about the same as their traditional life. Though they still work pretty much full-time, the real advantage comes with their breaks. "We walk outside into a wonderland of nature whether we're in the mountains, prairies, deserts or coastlines. It's wonderful to be able to live in a vacation setting. We take days off during the week when the parks are quiet and go biking, hiking or exploring," she says.

## Freelance writers and photographers, craftspeople

Writing — particularly about the RV lifestyle or travel — seems made for RVers. Your house on wheels takes you to new areas to explore and provide inspiration for your writing. Other writers have incorporated a facet of their lives into their writing. To name a few:

✔ Stephanie Bernhagen and her husband Paul, hit the road when Stephanie was 36. She became intrigued with the RV lifestyle and the freedom, and she wanted to share it with others. Her book, *Take Back Your Life! Travel Full-Time in an RV,* was an outgrowth of that.

✔ Betty Prange, photographer and writer, has sold many articles to travel and RV magazines.

✔ Alice Zyetz also had a dream to write. Her book, *You Shoulda Listened to Your Mother,* was written on the road. Together we have published *RV Traveling Tales: Women's Journeys on the Open Road* and three eBooks: *Retire to an RV: The Roadmap to Affordable Retiorement Living, The Woman's Guide to Solo RVing* and *Taking the Mystery out of RV Writing.*

Other RVers pick up money through arts or crafts they do on the road:

✔ Donna Ellis is an avid beader. As she has traveled she has improved her craft and now has necklaces, anklets and bracelets placed in several shops around the country.

> **Wanted: Freelance Writers Seeking nonfiction articles for *Composting News* — The latest news in composting and scrap wood management.**

✔An RVing weaver travels in a van with a small loom. She sends her work back to a co-op in Massachusetts to be sold. Another RVing woman makes framed scenes of fabric she has overpainted and dyed, and quilted wall hangings. She sells her work through several galleries in California and Arizona.

## Teaching

College professors who teach online can do so most anywhere. I met an RVer in Arizona whose online college is based on the east coast. She had gotten a phone call from a student in Japan while hiking in the mountains of Colorado! Another RV friend is certified in several water exercise programs as well as the Silver Sneakers exercise program. She can conduct classes whenever she stays for a while at a park with a pool.

## Investing in the Stock Market

RVers also make money in the stock market. That is their job — to study the stock market and invest in it to make money. Right before we went on the road, we attended an Escapade, an RV rally put on by the Escapee RV Club, which includes five days of educational seminars. One seminar was by a couple who were making their living by their investments. They were quite disciplined about tracking stocks before they bought and did their homework. Most of us would be better off consulting a licensed, practicing professional. I would urge caution with the volatility of the stock market. Day-trading is particularly risky; many investors have taken big losses. Especially during bear markets, investing in the stock market may not be the best way to make money unless you have real expertise and can withstand losses.

## GETTING STARTED WITH YOUR OWN BUSINESS

First you need to determine whether or not you have the right personality and the desire to operate your own business. It helps if you are a self-starter, self-motivated and a risk-taker. Long hours may be necessary to begin making money, and you should be well-organized and comfortable making decisions.

## Is there a demand for your product or service?

Do  market research to make sure you have a product or service that is in demand. Publications, the government, trade associations, and checking your competition can provide information about your market.

✔ Do you know how to reach your potential customers?

✔ Do you have a network of contacts to help you get started?

✔ Would you be better off considering a franchise opportunity, and if so, do you have the necessary capital?

Becoming a consultant in the field you worked in prior to hitting the road might be a viable option. In rough economic times, businesses often turn to consultants rather than hire more employees.

Two big factors in starting your own business are commitment and enough money to keep you going until income reaches the level you need. Most small businesses fail because they did not have enough capital in reserve. Fortunately there are business opportunities where minimum inventories are required.

If you haven't yet hit the road, you might develop current or related skills into a self-supporting business like Kay and Tom, and Annette and Larry. They each started several years in advance of their planned departure date. If you have lead time, gradually building up your business before you need to rely on the income makes sense.

> **Sell products for someone else while learning the business.**

Many writers, artists and photographers begin their craft as a hobby, developing it into a paying business over time. Some have no desire or need to make a living from their profession, but find the extra money a nice reward for their labors.

If you are already living in your RV and are interested in selling a product, you could start like Patsy and Wally; sell products for someone else while learning the business and finding money-making products.

If you are committed to earning a living as your own boss, you can do it. You'll be investing time and hard work and possibly some capital, but the payoffs will be great. Sharlene Minshell, RV author, was widowed suddenly. She and her husband had been planning to go on the road. She decided to go anyway and write, something her  husband and kids had encouraged her to do for years. She worked hard, persevered and has now written several books about her adventures traveling as a solo plus numerous other articles and columns. Knowing you need to make something work is a powerful motivator.

### Tax, insurance, and legal considerations

As a business owner or independent contractor, you will pay both the full Social Security and Medicare taxes, totaling 15.3% of your gross income. In addition you must send in quarterly estimated tax payments or be penalized and you will be paying for any benefits, such as retirement and health insurance, yourself.

> **You must send in quarterly estimated income tax payments.**

Owning your own business or working as an independent contractor could give you additional deductions for expenses on your income tax returns. People who use their homes for business purposes can generally deduct a percentage of expenses and depreciation. Use of vehicles for business purposes can also be deducted. It will be more difficult meeting requirements for similar deductions on your RV. You will need to talk to your tax preparer to see which, if any, expenses and depreciation can be deducted in your case, and what records you need to keep to do so.

Another consideration is that using your RV and vehicles for business purposes will probably increase your insurance rates. Not letting your agent know of their business use could jeopardize your coverage should an accident occur. Additionally, you may need higher liability coverage or you may need to purchase a separate liability policy to sell at fairs and shows, for instance.

To conduct business in a state could require licenses or permits, or a resale tax number. For example, beauticians must obtain a license in each state in which they do business.

### Business form

There are three main types of businesses: single proprietorship, partnership and corporation. Each has advantages and disadvantages. If your net income is more than $35,000 you may want to consider an S Corp or even a C corporation. Being incorporated limits your liability and you may have lower income taxes. You (or the corporation) will pay for your health insurance and you can also set up a medical savings account to pay for any deductibles, using pre-tax dollars. You will be able to save more pre-tax dollars for retirement in tax-deferred saving plans. The Small Business Administration is an excellent source of information for starting a business and choosing which form is best for you. (See **Resources.**) As always, check with a qualified accountant to analyze your personal situation.

Owning your own RV business works for many RVers. While you give up the security of steady income, you are not limited in what you can make either. You may be able to make the money you need in a shorter period of time, leaving more time for travel and leisure. You are also free to set your own schedule and you answer only to yourself. An RV business is not for everyone, but it just might be for you.

# Notes

*"The problem is never how to get new, innovative
thoughts into your mind, but how to get old ones out."*
*Dee Hock, Founder, VISA*

*Jobs 312-356*

# Chapter 22
# How to help the budget by volunteering

Volunteering is an excellent way to reduce your expenses on the road. Money saved is money in your pocket. Volunteers have the satisfaction of contributing to a worthwhile cause, helping others or helping the environment. If you volunteer in exchange for your RV site or other privileges, you will have a lot more freedom than in a 40-hour, nine to five job. You will probably have a lot more say in when you work and what you are willing to do. Often you can volunteer for a short period of time rather than a whole season.

### Savings
Volunteering with a federal or state agency usually includes a place for your RV. If your expenses are higher than normal, or your income is slumping due to economic times, eliminating your campground expense saves a chunk of money. You may also save by:

✔ **Gas expense:** Driving your toad instead of your motorhome should save you money on gas. You might get better gas mileage with your pickup when not towing your RV. You can also save wear and tear on your vehicles when you aren't putting as many towing miles on them.
✔ **Recreation and entertainment:** Without having to pay admission fees, you'll have plenty to do. Often you get training or experiences that regular visitors don't get. You may even be invited by area attractions to visit at no charge so you can let visitors know about them. While employees for the federal government are prohibited from accepting these invitations, volunteers are not.

## Exchange - commercial vs. agency or nonprofit

Normally when an RV site is involved, you are doing an exchange for services that you provide. You work a certain number of hours per week in exchange for your RV site. The number of hours required varies tremendously. Agencies and commercial employers that offer this arrangement set their own time requirements.

If you are volunteering for a nonprofit or a government agency like the National Park Service, then it is similar to a charitable contribution in that you are giving your time instead of money to assist the agency in their work. You are working for a good cause and not expecting "payment." You may be able to take some charitable deductions on your federal income tax return and have a place to park your RV while you provide this service.

> **Work 20 hrs/wk in exchange for site with full hookups.**
> **Sam's RV Resort**

When it comes to volunteering or an exchange of service for a commercial RV park, private individual or enterprise, then you need to look at your time differently. Make sure you are working a fair amount in exchange for your site and not being exploited. Reread "What is a site worth?" in Chapter 11 (page 112) and determine if you are "paying" a fair amount. Here is an extreme example of a listing for a commercial exchange:

RV worker Phyllis saw a posting at a website by an RV park in New Mexico offering an RV site in exchange for 48 hours of work per week (two 12-hour days each for a couple). The sites rent for $110 a month plus electricity. During the winter the park is filled. Let's say your electricity brought the value up to $150/month. You are working at least 192 hours/month. If you figured the equivalent hourly rate, it would be about $.78 per hour. Need I say more!

If this were an agency or nonprofit, the difference between $.78/hour and a fair wage would be the contribution you are willing to give. For a commercial operation, I believe the employer is taking advantage of you. Bottom line, however, only you can decide if you have made an equitable trade. Go into it with your eyes open and remember, if employers who are in business to make a profit can get people to work for $2/hour, why should they pay more? Indirectly, you hurt RV workers who need to earn decent money to live.

You'll find plenty of options for volunteering. In **Resources** are additional websites and contacts.

## NATIONAL PARKS, FORESTS AND OTHER FEDERAL AGENCIES

312. *Campground host*
313. *Environmental educator*
314. *Videographer or photographer*
315. *Construction worker*
316. *Grant writer*
317. *Visitor center attendant or naturalist*
318. *Interpreter (of resources)*
319. *Law enforcement desk officer*
320. *Search and rescue (SAR)*
321. *River patrol*
322. *Ranger in the back country permit office*
323. *Assistant on archaeological digs*
324. *Fire tower lookout*
325. *Worker on the Trash Tracker houseboat*
326. *Worker on the GRIT houseboat*
327. *Lighthouse tour guide*
328. *Carpenter and other tradesmen*
329. *Special project worker*
330. *Campground host at military Fam camps*

Government agencies like National Park Service, USDA Forest Service, National Wildlife Refuges, Bureau of Land Management and U.S. Army Corps of Engineers rely heavily on volunteers and not just as campground hosts. Agencies can use volunteer help in maintenance, the office, and in fact, almost any area imaginable. If you have a skill, you can probably find a volunteer match. Not all locations have RV sites for volunteers; however, if a site is available, you will have a minimum number of hours to work each week.

Several publications and websites listed in the **Resources** section identify opportunities in many different locations. Volunteer.gov/gov provides federal agencies a place to list their volunteer needs. You can search by state or by type of position. Many areas are needed besides camp hosts. See *(www.volunteer.gov/gov)*.

Another option is to contact agencies directly or check the agency website. Stopping by the agency you are interested in is an excellent way to be selected, especially if volunteer spots are competitive. You can meet and talk to the selecting official, which improves your chances greatly.

The National Park Service calls their volunteers VIPs for Volunteers in Parks. They have a print brochure so named, available from most any NPS unit. The excellent map of the park system is a handy reference whether you volunteer or not, and contains an application and contact information for the coordinator of each unit. You can also contact any unit directly about volunteering.

> **Photograph recreation activities and forest scenes. Expenses negotiable. Boise National Forest**

For Forest Service volunteer opportunities, check at the regional offices' websites (See **Appendix 3)** or write or call the volunteer coordinator where you want to volunteer. You will need to complete Form 301, Volunteer Application, available online or at any Forest Service office .

*$* **VIPs: Bob and Sylvia** have volunteered at three National Parks and one National Wildlife Refuge. Acadia National Park was their first "job" and they have been back three times. Sylvia worked for Interpretation in the Visitor Center and Bob worked in maintenance on some interesting and rewarding projects. Sylvia also offered a weekly Historical Art Walk in the park. In exchange for their full hookup RV site, Bob worked 32 hours/week and Sylvia from 20-25. As perks, the concessionaire offered them free admission to their activities on a space-available basis.

At Grand Teton National Park, Sylvia worked in the Back Country Permits Office while Bob hiked or drove into the back country, testing the water supply. In Everglades National Park one winter, they were caretakers at Hidden Lake Environmental Camp, assisting with canoeing lessons to 5th graders. Bob and Sylvia also volunteered for St. Marks Lighthouse National Wildlife Refuge south of Tallahassee, planting 10,000 trees with a local elementary school and built bluebird boxes, among other things.

Sylvia and Bob agree, "These experiences have been rewarding and have also helped out with the budget. We consider the RV site 'free,' and have lots to see and do without driving the RV, saving on gas. We have made lasting friendships with other volunteers as well as many wonderful rangers."

 **Camphosts and community volunteers: Tom and Nancy** volunteered in Prescott National Forest close to Nancy's mother while she adjusted to a new living situation in nearby Prescott, Arizona. Their duties as campground hosts entailed answering visitor questions, checking permits and a daily walk of the trails and loops of the campground to pick up litter. Since they set their own schedule, they had plenty of time to visit regularly with Nancy's mother during the week.

Tom also signed up as an "elder-mentor" with Big Brothers/Big Sisters and worked on a site development committee for the local Natural History Center by conducting research, surveys and whatever needed doing. Remarks Tom, "We've had a very blessed life on the road and feel it is important to share wherever we can. We get to feel good about whatever we do, but the benefits go beyond ourselves. It takes many caring communities to build a world we can all be proud to live in."

**National parks and military Fam camp volunteers: Jim and Barb** have volunteered four different seasons at Casa Grande Ruins National Monument in Arizona. They answered visitor questions and occasionally gave a short tour. They also did some special projects. This national monument has only five hookup sites for volunteers so positions were competitive. They kept in touch and note, "Timing and staying in contact with the Volunteer Coordinator seems to be the key to getting a position." One winter Jim and Barb also volunteered as camphosts at a military Famcamp. These are camps for military and retired-military families.

## Unusual jobs with public agencies

$ **Passport in Time** is a volunteer archaeology and historic preservation program of the USDA Forest Service (USFS). You work with professional archaeologists and historians on projects including archaeological excavation, rock art restoration, survey, archival research, historic structure restoration, gathering oral histories, or writing interpretive brochures. Passport in Time's website lists projects for the year.

$ **Fire lookout towers** might suit you. Spot fires, greet hikers or other visitors. Most are operated by public agencies. (**Resources,** Ch 17.)

$ **Lighthouses** are another unusual place to help out. The National Park Service maintains a listing of historic lighthouses. You can find out more about individual lighthouses at their site. (**Resources,** Ch 22.)

$ **Houseboat working vacation:** At Glen Canyon National Recreation Area on Lake Powell, you can sign up for a houseboat trip on the Trash Tracker picking up litter and debris along the lake shores. Their other houseboat program is GRIT — "Graffiti Removal Intervention and Intervention Team." These are fun ways to see the lake and its canyons. (**Resources**, Ch 22.)

$ **Training:** NPS VIPs may be eligible to take the two-week interpretive training when they arrive. At Big Bend, George's group went out with various park staff for an inside look at the park and took an overnight catered canoe trip down the Rio Grande with the river rangers.

$ **Leave no trace volunteers: Steve and Pam** have volunteered in national forests in Arizona and Virginia, working on trails, educating hikers to "leave no trace." Additionally, they completed projects, inventoried facilities and gave talks to groups. They received their RV site plus stipend, mileage and other perks. They are especially desirable volunteers because Steve adds magic illusions to each of the seven "leave no trace" principles. This makes learning fun and helps insure their audience remembers these important principles.

Pam and Steve say, "We enjoy the flexible schedules, working at our own pace, working together as a couple and enjoying the out-of-doors plus getting the inside track on great places to visit."

$ **Lighthouse tours: Ralph and Mary Lou** spent a month during two different summers at a lighthouse in Sleeping Dunes National Lakeshore in Michigan. Each day they gave five to seven tours of the lighthouse to visitors who ferried over in the morning and returned to the mainland in the afternoon. In 22 days, they gave 103 lighthouse tours to 1021 people, climbing 12,051 steps in that time! Ralph and Mary Lou brought all their food for eight days and lived in a historic village home, returning to their RV in the park campground on the mainland for their four days off. The park provided ferry transportation, island housing and a campsite.

## STATE PARKS MAY NEED VOLUNTEERS IN

331.  *Campground hosting, which can include a variety of tasks*
332.  *Clerical, computer and fiscal help at headquarters*
333.  *Maintenance projects*
334.  *Off-season park surveillance, minor maintenance projects, weekend campground hosting and interpretive hosting*
335.  *Fee collector*
336.  *Staff at visitor center or naturalist*
337.  *Tour guide or docent*
338.  *Period-costume guide or interpreter*
339.  *Retail salesperson in a gift shop*
340.  *Photographer, update slide collection*
341.  *Teacher of Off Highway Vehicle (OHV) and Personal Water Craft (PWC) safety classes*
342.  *Golf course worker*
343.  *Campsite construction worker*
344.  *Archaeological assistant or helper*
345.  *Backcountry patrol*
346.  *Lighthouse tourguide or caretaker*

## STATE PARKS

State parks also recruit volunteers. Campground host positions along the California coast, for example, are highly coveted. Betty and her husband, Lin, updated the park's slide collection at Patrick's Point State Park in California and gave evening programs on taking better photographs. Contact any state parks you are interested in working at as well as the volunteer coordinator or volunteer office at the state or regional level. See **Appendix 4** for contact information.

*$* **State park volunteers: Bob and Caren** found their position giving tours of the North Head Lighthouse at Ft. Canby State Park in Oregon through the National Listing For Lighthouse Employment (NLLE) subscription data base. (Now defunct.)

## GETTING A POSITION WITH A PUBLIC AGENCY

After you identify the location where you want to work, contact the volunteer coordinator there to find out their needs and procedures. Check the resources for this chapter to find contact and application information. Many are listed on the Internet. Or, contact the coordinator by phone or mail. Begin lining up volunteer opportunities as early as autumn for summer positions. Some are quite competitive and have only a limited number of slots.

You will want to ask plenty of questions, just as if you were applying for a job there. Clear expectations on both parts will make for a much better volunteering experience.

✔ **What are my duties?** Be sure to clarify what you will or will not do. If you do not want to clean restrooms, let the volunteer coordinator know. If there is a task you really want to do, perhaps take photographs for the park's slide collection, or hike in the backcountry, get a commitment that a certain portion of your time will be allotted for that task.

✔ **How many hours will I work for my site?** Can those hours be split between a couple or a family? Will I have set hours or is the schedule flexible?

✔ **What sort of time commitment must I make** in terms of weeks or months?

✔ **Will I be provided training** or have opportunities to explore the area?

✔ **Will I be provided with uniforms?** If not, must I purchase certain clothing?

✔ **Will I have an RV site?** Level? In trees or the open? Full hookups? Cable or satellite TV reception?

✔ **Can I accept free tickets** from local attractions or outfitters?

✔ **Am I covered by Worker's Compensation** or other insurance if I am injured on the job?

✔ **Will you provide a vehicle or tools** for me to use if necessary, or must I provide my own?

✔ **Can my visitors camp** or park their RVs on my site at no charge?

✔ **How far is it to shopping or medical care?** If it is a great distance, do you have a refrigerator where I can store groceries in between trips to town?

✔ **Will washers and dryers be available to use?** Any charge?

✔ **Will the IRS consider my site as income?**

If you visit a park or forest but don't have something lined up, talk to the volunteer coordinator, or to department heads to see if they need volunteers or have any short-term projects you can do.

## $ Drive-in volunteers:

**Tom** had parked the 14-day limit at one of the beach campgrounds in Glen Canyon but wanted to stay longer to drive more of the 4-wheel drive roads in the area. He approached the district ranger about staying and was allowed to stay on in return for camphosting duties.

**John,** a maintenance volunteer at the Grand Tetons, had friends visit in the middle of the season. They were enjoying the area and wanted to stay longer. His visitor, Mike, was able to work with John for a few weeks in exchange for his site.

## Family volunteering

Volunteering as a family is on the rise so RVing families have plenty of opportunities to contribute their services as a family. Hope Sykes, writer and columnist, has felt for years that having a mobile lifestyle offers the best of both worlds: travel and community service. RVers can be ideal volunteers since they can pick up at a moment's notice and travel to areas of the country where the need is highest without putting a stress on already strained community resources when housing might be in short supply. She offers some resources and tips for the mobile volunteer here:

### RV volunteer: Hope Sykes

Volunteering as a family is an ideal way to help those in need. Traveling RV families can now extend their "neighborhoods" and go where help is needed most and have familiar housing and cooking facilities onboard.

To get the most out of your family experience, I recommend you start with these five simple steps:

### Step 1: Develop an awareness of what problems or issues that you would like to involve your family's efforts in.

To be most effective, you'll want to find out what issues your family is passionate about. Did a newspaper story catch someone's attention? Did you spot a homeless person during one of your travels? Did you see litter scattered about in an otherwise beautiful state park?

### Step 2: Develop a set of questions to help tackle the project.

Examples would be:

✔ Where would we like to volunteer?

✔ How much time do we want to devote to the project? A day? A few hours? A week? Longer?

✔ What skills do we each have that would work for this situation? Remember that even young children can pick up litter, sort items by color, or pass out information.

✔ Are there any new skills that we would like to learn?

✔ In addition to giving of our time and talents, what would we like to learn from this experience?

**Step 3: Research the volunteer topic so that you will be better informed and can educate others.**

Examples would include things like the number of homeless in America or to discover how much food is wasted in the U.S. per year.

Identifying the problem can help you research the topic more easily through the Internet or will assist a librarian in your search. Don't forget to check area phone books under "Social Service Organizations" to see if an organization already exists in your area where you can get both information and an outlet for volunteer activities.

Now's a good time to see how you can integrate these activities into home schooling lessons or even résumés. If you or some of your family members want some college credit on the road, check with an area university and see if some of you can receive credit for your participation.

**Step 4: Put your family's ideas and planning into action.**

Family volunteering is on the rise; however, RVing volunteers are still uncommon in many communities. You'll want to have a list of questions prepared to determine if the facility will be able to accommodate you.

Here are some of the questions that you should ask:

✔ Are all ages able to participate?

✔ Are children allowed to work independently or are the parents required to accompany them?

✔ We have very young children. What sort of arrangements are available should we need a sitter?

✔ Will we be allowed to park at the volunteer site?

✔ Is the RV site included as part of the position? What hook-ups are available? Are they included?

✔ What is the maximum length of rig that the campsite can accommodate? Can I park my truck or van nearby?

✔ If our entire family volunteers and a campsite is included as part of the benefits, can the work be divided up so that each person's time will count collectively to the requirement?

✔ Are pets allowed? What are the rules?

✔ What is the minimum and maximum time that we will be allowed to volunteer?

Once you accept a volunteer position, make sure to arrange your schedules so that you can trade off volunteer work and other activities if you have young children. Children often aren't interested in intense volunteer activity for the entire day so break up the time by other enjoyable sessions. Make sure that you have planned your activities so that the entire family can end on a happy note rather than feeling rushed, cranky, or exhausted.

**Step 5: Make sure that you decide on how you want to record your efforts.**

Picture taking and journal writing can be fun and educational. Websites can often be set up for free or at low cost and allow others to follow your progress.

Documentation is also a great way to discover how much impact you've really had on the world. How many homeless did you feed in one day at the soup kitchen? How many aluminum cans equal one pound? How many pounds of cans did you collect?

If the activity was really fun and productive, recording your efforts will then give you a template for what to look for in another adventure:

✔ What did you like best about the experience?

✔ What made it so successful and rewarding?

✔ How could the experience be improved?

✔ Who at the facility made an impact?

Volunteering as a family, you'll find, is a great way to have quality family time. See you there!"

## Working vacations

Recently working vacations have become popular. You pay a fee and then work on a project of some sort. You'll find a variety of humanitarian, environmental and archaeological projects both in the United States and overseas. In most cases you would leave your RV and travel to the site to complete the project. Some projects might be able to accommodate RV parking or permit you to stay in it. Volunteers on Lake Powell's Trash Tracker or GRIT houseboats can leave their RVs in a parking lot while out on a houseboat picking up trash or removing graffiti.

A number of organizations are listed in **Resources** that specialize in working vacations both in the U.S. and in other parts of the world.

## NONPROFIT VOLUNTEERS

347. *Construction of a Habitat for Humanity build*
348. *Office or computer work for a Habitat for Humanity affiliate*
349. *Disaster relief work*
350. *Maintenance or office work at a church camp*
351. *Maintenance, office work, tour guide, programs at YMCA camp*
352. *Volunteering overseas - environmental, construction, health and education projects*

### Habitat for Humanity

Habitat for Humanity's goal is to provide affordable housing for those who are in need. Recipients of housing must contribute a certain number of hours. Jimmy Carter is perhaps the best known worker for this organization. Habitat has offices in many towns across the U.S. They also have international builds. Their RV-Care-A-Vanners is just for mobile volunteers. You may or may not get an RV site when you volunteer (depending on the build), but you have the satisfaction of helping with a very worthwhile project that gives dignity to recipients.

**Habitat for Humanity builders: Bob and Sylvia** haven't worked with Jimmy Carter but find great satisfaction in helping this organization. The RV arm of Habitat for Humanity, RV-Care-a-Vanners, usually consisting of 10 to 12 rigs, meets at a build site and spends approximately two weeks working as a team. Some groups build a home from the foundation up, while others arrive at a site consisting of partially completed homes. In this case, they may work on tasks like roofing, siding, landscaping, and interior finish. "My husband Bob and I have done roofing, insulation, vinyl siding, electrical and plumbing, as well as the odds and ends of the job. Many times we have the opportunity to meet the homeowner as they work to complete their 300 to 500 hours of 'sweat equity' prior to moving in," explains Sylvia. The RVers generally stay in a local public or private campground at reduced fees. Lunches are often provided by local sponsors and the group socializes after work and visits local attractions." Adds Sylvia, "Each new home offers us a new challenge and many rewards."

**American Red Cross Disaster Services: Debbie and Les** have enjoyed the RV lifestyle for the past eleven years and have looked for ways to "give back." They have found volunteering for the American Red Cross (ARC) to work well with the RV lifestyle. They decided the best way to help out was to become part of the Disaster Services Human Resources system. They took classes that prepared them to be sent on assignments in any state, at Red Cross' expense, to work for a minimum of 3 weeks. These included Introduction to Disaster Services, First Aid and CPR, Mass Care, and Shelter Operations. Once on an assignment away from home, lodging is covered as are food and incidentals up to a set amount.

In September 2001, Debbie received a call from her home chapter to go to New York City because of the World Trade Center attack. Explains Debbie, "Upon reaching ARC Headquarters in Brooklyn, I attended an orientation session, was checked out by health services nurses, and received an assignment to support a mobile kitchen set up about a mile from 'Ground Zero.' I also was given the name of a hotel, one of several offering rooms to Red Cross workers. My assignment was logistics person for the mobile kitchen, acting as a liaison between the ARC and numerous service providers, including companies providing lights, Dumpsters, ice and portable toilets. In addition, I responded to dead batteries, excess food to be donated to local missions, and sudden shortages of food and supplies. Running a household and a business was excellent preparation for this type of job, which required persistence and attention to details. Other volunteers at the kitchen prepared the food, loaded it into vehicles, drove it to several feeding sites, or manned the radio."

Debbie notes, "Whatever your skills or interests, the Red Cross can put them to use. After attending the "Introduction To Disaster" class, you can choose several areas to pursue further. Classes are available at no charge and do not require local residence, so whenever we are in an area for a while we check the schedules at the local chapter office. There are about 50,000 members of the Disaster Services Human Resources System in the ARC, and it is a privilege to be a part of the Red Cross family. The feeling of camaraderie that happens when people from all over come together for a common purpose is unforgettable."

The Escapees RV Club is one RV club that offers Red Cross disaster training at its Escapades, which are five-day educational rallies.

### Volunteering overseas

Besides Habitat, a number of agencies recruit volunteers for either short- or long-term commitments at overseas locations. Volunteering overseas can be a way to travel at reduced cost. You may be helping Third World communities, working on environmental projects, or in archaeology, a couple of the many possibilities. Most projects have fees associated with them, but usually cost less than taking a tour. For some trips, the agency sets up excursions for vounteers or arranges home-stays so you get to know the locals and the area. You may see areas the average tourist never visits.

## EXCHANGE OF SERVICES
353.  Exchange work for space in an RV park
354.  Work out an exchange with a private individual
355.  Park at a business in exchange for night security
356.  Help friends or relatives in exchange for a place to park and hookups

There are many opportunities for exchanging services for an RV site and other perks. You'll find listings of employers and individuals looking for people willing to make such an exchange in both *Workamper News* and *Caretaker Gazette.*

You can also create your own opportunities for exchange of services. If you like an RV park, talk to the owner about doing a project or helping out in exchange for a free or reduced rate site. By meeting locals and asking around, you might find someone who needs a housesitter or a business that will let you park in return for keeping an eye on things at night.

$ **Work for friends: Charlie and Norma** stopped at friends while traveling through the Northwest. They stayed a month, helping with a landscaping project. Their friends gave them full hookups, plus a small amount of cash.

$ **Folksingers: Chuck and Alice** usually volunteer their services to lead or participate in singalongs in RV parks, senior centers, plus schools in Mexico, as they travel. They were at a county fair in Maine and went to the office to offer their services in exchange for an RV site on the fair grounds. As it happened, the entertainment director had just had a strolling musician cancel at the last minute. He offered them $250 to perform that afternoon!

If you are in a position to volunteer, you'll find rewards to the community and your pocketbook. You'll also have the satisfaction of knowing you are helping others and making a difference.

# Notes

*"It will be a great day when our schools have all
the money they need and the Air Force has to
hold a bake sale to buy a new bomber.'
Seen at www.coolsig.com*

# SECTION IV. RV LIFESTYLE CONSIDERATIONS

## Chapter 23
## How to manage RV expenses

Living the RV lifestyle can be inexpensive compared to living in a house though some expenses are unique to the RV lifestyle and can be greater— vehicle insurance and repairs, for example. It is easy to eat out more when you are traveling. Health insurance, which we will consider here, will probably not be provided by your employer. However, each time you reduce your expenses, you need less income.

### CAMPGROUND FEES

Any night you don't have to pay campground fees saves money. Campgrounds with only a few amenities can charge upwards of $35 a night and I've seen state parks with no hookups charge $20-25 a night. That can play havoc with a budget.

Owners of some RV parks or membership parks are open to an exchange of labor for a free or reduced site. If you will be staying at a park for at least a week, you can approach

> **Each time you reduce your expenses, you need less income.**

the owner or manager with an offer to work for free or reduced rent. In state or federal parks, you may be able to volunteer your time in exchange for a site. Usually the park requires a set number of hours to work for your site and may also have a minimum time period, such as a month. Depending on your skills, that commitment could vary, especially if you have a special project in mind. It never hurts to ask.

While you are working, a free or low-cost site might be included. When you aren't working, there are places where it is free to park, though those areas are diminishing. The past few years have seen a real push to limit areas where RVers can park free even overnight, as well as instituting fees where none were charged before. You may have to be more creative!

## RV site: weighing the costs vs. pay

You might find you earn more working for an employer who does not have or provide an RV site, even after paying for a site in another location. Some mobile home parks charge much less than RV parks. (See *What is a site worth?* Ch. 11.) However, figure costs of transportation if you drive any distance. How will you handle transportation if you have different work schedules? If one starts early and the other works late, it could be quite inconvenient. A bicycle or small motorcycle could be the solution, as could public transportation or carpooling.

## Boondocking

Boondocking is the term for camping without hookups. RVers typically use the term when that area or spot has no fee. State and federal parks do have campgrounds with no hookups and usually charge a fee. This is usually referred to as dry camping.

Much of Bureau of Land Management (BLM) and Forest Service land is open to boondocking, with restrictions. Usually there is a time limit, typically 14 days. At that point you might have to move 20 miles or so to a new location. In popular areas, there may be a yearly limit or a shorter time period allowed. Boondocking may be restricted to a limited distance from the road or to areas previously disturbed, and even prohibited in certain areas. With the Federal Lands Recreation Enhancement Act (REA), several government agencies were

> **"Boondocking" means camping without hookups.**

provided the authority to charge a number of fees. Former boondocking areas now have fees and that trend will probably continue.

To locate boondocking areas or "dispersed camping" areas within BLM and Forest Service lands, check with the local office of the agency. U.S. Army Corps of Engineer projects may also have dispersed camping. Locals may know of good spots. Many RVers are willing to share their knowledge about spots if you ask. If they seem reluctant it could be because they have seen many spots disappear as RVers took advantage of these areas by staying too long, bringing in more RVs than the area could handle, and destroying vegetation or leaving trash.

If you do find an area where you can boondock, please use simple courtesy so this area is preserved for future boondockers:

✔ **Use existing cleared areas to park.** Do not cut or damage vegetation.

✔ **Dispose of your black and gray water** in proper sewage dumps and not on the ground.

✔ **Leave the area cleaner than you found it.** Pack your trash out.

✔ **Limit the time you stay there** and keep the area neat and tidy. What can frighten locals is that squatters are setting up in the area. This happened at a nice beach near Eureka, California. Now taxpayers are paying for welfare benefits and for relocation of the squatters.

✔ **Let businesses in town know you are an RVer** and you are shopping here because you are camped near town. RV parks often lead the fight against boondocking in their area because they see it as competition. We like to let businesses know we would not be there if we had to stay in an RV park but do spend money at other businesses in town.

RVers often equip their rigs to make them more self-contained and to be able to boondock for longer periods of time. Solar panels recharge batteries and allow you to run all or most of your appliances without shore power or fear of running down your batteries.

> **Leave an area cleaner than you found it.**

Generators are part of the package for many motorhomes, or at least an option. While noisy, they do provide power if there are several cloudy days and your panels don't recharge your batteries. Small generators such as the Honda EU2000i work well to supplement solar panels and are much quieter than usual factory installed generators. If you run your generator, please respect other RVers in the vicinity. Don't aim your generator towards them. Turn your generator off by 10 p.m. at the latest and don't start it again before 7 a.m. If you're meeting other RVers, park away from those who don't run theirs. The noise, even from small generators, can be annoying. When parked near others, limit generator time to a minimum.

Catalytic or ceramic heaters also make boondocking easier. These heaters are much more efficient than the propane heaters RVs come with. Be sure to have a qualified person install your heater and follow all safety precautions.

One limit on boondocking is the capacity of your gray and black water tanks. In some places, emptying your gray water (dish water, shower water, etc.) is legal. In most it is not. Dumping your black water on the ground is never legal. Two items could help you extend your stay. If you are near a sewer outlet but not hooked up to sewage, a macerator could be useful. Rather than drive your rig to a dump, the macerator pump grinds up the solids in your black water tank so they will run out through a garden hose. We used this weekly as campground hosts in Alaska. No dump was available at our rig, but there was a small sewage outlet about 50 feet away. We have also used our macerator pump to empty our tanks at my sister's house.

> **Dumping your black water on the ground is never legal.**

Other RVers carry Blue Boys® or similar tanks. These are blue plastic tanks on wheels. You drain your holding tanks into the container (sizes vary) and then transport the Blue Boy® to the RV dump, enabling you to stay in your boondock site for a longer period of time.

Before assuming it is permissible to dump your gray water on the ground, check with the agency, town or owner to make sure you are not violating any laws. Otherwise, a hefty fine could result. Keep in mind that gray water has a strong odor. Dump daily and choose a time when you won't disturb your neighbors.

### Long term visitor areas (LTVAs)

BLM has created seven LTVAs in the deserts of Arizona and California. On most BLM land, camping in one spot is restricted to 14 days and then you must move at least 20 miles to a new spot. To camp in a LTVA, you purchase a permit, either by the week or for the entire season, and you may park at any of the sites for as long as you want from mid-September through mid-April. BLM provides some services in central locations like water, trash Dumpsters and RV dump stations in exchange for the fee. You can move from one LTVA to another with the same permit. At the time of this writing, the season pass was $180 and a weekly pass was $40, a bargain in any book.

## Desert Ecology: A reminder by Chuck Wright

Many of us are concerned about losing the right to park on national forest, the Bureau of Land Management (BLM) and other "free" lands. We must be mindful of the impact our parking has on these areas, especially in the desert.

Escapees chapter and BOF (Birds of Feather) group gatherings are becoming larger, and many are held in the desert. We must not lose sight of how easily this delicate environment can be damaged. Even the smallest plants have a role in anchoring the soil, and they have a hard time establishing themselves once driven on or simply stepped on.

We all have a responsibility to do as little damage as possible to these lands. Some of us are new to the desert and are not aware of this. I'm afraid others of us forget when we get together, to treat the desert with the respect it deserves. I, too, have been guilty.

A number of us have been parking in winter in Arizona near Ajo on BLM land. Our presence was largely ignored. Our numbers grew as several Escapees groups held gatherings in the area. Damage was done to the desert. Now there is a ranger there to enforce the 14-day limit. Will it be posted "No Camping" next?

We mean well. Most of us try not to disturb the environment. We usually don't leave trash; in fact, many of us pick up trash after others have left the area. We usually don't build firepits or burn desert wood. We do drive over or trample plants occasionally.

We are required to park off the desert roads and tracks, but we should confine this parking to previously disturbed areas. Then we must restrict our driving to existing roads, or it seems certain we'll lost the right to use these areas. For the sake of all of us, please be careful. Every plant and animal in the desert has the right to coexist.

Of course, this is not only true of the desert. It's just that the desert is particularly vulnerable. If we fail to heed these concerns — do our part and also speak up if we see someone being abusive — I fear we will lose the rest of the wonderful places we like to park. We're likely to have to host our gatherings in less attractive places.

So please, folks, don't damage our deserts, do treat them responsibly. Let's share in the stewardship of the land so we may be able to continue to use it.

*© Chuck Wright. Originally published in* Escapees *Magazine.*

## Free overnight parking

Many RVers save money when traveling from one location to another by camping overnight at rest areas, truck stops or large parking lots. While some states prohibit overnight parking in rest areas or limit the number of hours you can stay, generally that is not enforced unless a vehicle is there for more than one night. You are likely to have an 18-wheeler parked nearby with engine running all night plus lights shining outside your rig, but the price is right. Some rest stops do have separate areas for RVs, such as the ones along I-70 in Kansas, but they aren't the norm.

> **Follow "boondocking etiquette" when parked overnight on Wal-Mart parking lots.**

Truck stops generally will accommodate RVs; however, they are noisy. If possible, look for a spot away from where trucks seem to be parking. As a courtesy, ask permission from the owners and spend some money there. Buy fuel or eat a meal and most owners will be happy to give permission to park overnight.

You have probably noticed a number of RVs parked in WalMart parking lots. WalMart is usually RV-friendly, though more and more towns are pushing to revoke this privilege. Again, while shopping in WalMart, request permission from the manager. Park your rig out of the way and do not use extra parking spaces. Do not put out your awning or set up your chairs. Limit your stay to one night, otherwise it is camping and gives RV park owners just cause to complain. If you see an RVer abusing this privilege, leave a copy of Boondocking Etiquette (found at the Escapees website, *www.escapees.com*) tucked in their door, or under their windshield wiper. The letter reminds RVers that we could lose this privilege if we don't follow common-sense guidelines.

## Other parking

- ✔ **Driveways or in front of houses of friends and relatives:** Don't overstay your welcome and contribute a fair dollar amount for water and electricity used. (Some towns and homeowners' associations have ordinances against parking RVs on city streets.)
- ✔ **RV club friends:** Some RVers have a house or RV lot with room for visitors and invite others to stay a night or two if their travels take

them to the area. The Escapees RV Club, for example, publishes names and addresses of members who invite visitors to stop by.

✔ **Work out an exchange of services:** In *Home is Where You Park It* Kay Peterson relates how they were able to find places to exchange services and obtain a site while Joe was working. A business might like someone parked on the premises to keep an eye on things. A home or farm owner may want a housesitter to bring in the mail, feed pets and water plants in exchange for water, electricity and a place to park.

## FOOD

Your food expenses will probably be similar to what they were prior to hitting the road. Eating out can knock your budget for a loop, yet eating regional foods adds enjoyment to traveling. Terry and Connie eat out for lunch rather than dinner, or eat later in the afternoon at lunch prices.

Some restaurants offer early-bird specials too. Casinos often have moderate prices to pull in customers. A late lunch buffet can easily be the main meal of the day at a lower cost than dinnertime. Check local newspapers for coupons. Usually a mid-week issue features restaurants.

> **Towns with more than one supermarket usually have better prices.**

Towns with more than one supermarket usually have better prices than a small town with one grocery store. Stock up.

Janice Lasko developed a generic form on the computer for her grocery list to use in any store, no matter what the layout. Having a list keeps the grocery bill down, and I can attest to the difference the list makes in finding items quickly. (See **Appendix 7**.)

## FUEL AND VEHICLE COSTS

Driving techniques can affect fuel use. A heavy foot on hills consumes more fuel and lowers the life of your engine.

Working for part of the year will reduce your gasoline or diesel consumption, since you will not be traveling to new locations as frequently. Your truck probably won't be used as much and may get better mileage when not towing. If you have an RV site where you work, you'll save commuting costs, or you might be close enough to walk or ride a bicycle.

Catalytic or ceramic heaters are much more efficient than RV furnaces. They must be installed correctly and safety precautions taken, but you will use much less propane and there is no draw on your battery. When we are working and have an RV site, if utilities are included, we plug in a small electric heater and use that as our main source of heat.

## HEALTH INSURANCE

Can you afford health insurance? Can you afford not to have health insurance? This is probably the most difficult issue full-time RVers have to face, unless they are lucky enough to have continued coverage included with their retirement package. Due to the expense, some RVers go without. Others must choose such a high deductible that they are effectively covered only for catastrophic illness or accident.

The real challenge, if you are not eligible for Medicare, is finding coverage that is adequate and doesn't break your budget. Rates will vary by state, and can be a factor in choosing a domicile. A resource I recommend is *The New Health Insurance Solution: How to Get Cheaper, Better Coverage Without a Traditional Employer Plan* by Paul Zane Pilzer. (See **Resources.**)

The 2010 Patient Protection and Affordable Care Act has brought changes to obtaining health insurance and will make health insurance available to everyone. Many provisions are being phased in, taking full effect in 2014. Not all of the details have been ironed out at this writing.

### Some ideas:

✔ **Employers:** A few seasonal and temporary employers do offer health insurance, though it may be reserved for employees who work all or most of the year. National temporary agencies may have policies and a couple of national park concessionaires likewise offer limited health insurance to employees.

✔ **COBRA:** If you are just hitting the road, you may be eligible to convert your health insurance policy under your employer to COBRA. You can keep your group coverage by paying the full premium (by law, no more than 102% of the cost of group coverage) for 18, 29 or 36 months, depending on your situation. (Note: Smaller businesses do not have to continue health insurance coverage through COBRA.)

✔ **Low income:** If your income is low enough, you might qualify for Medicaid, a Federal/state program. Each state has different eligibility and benefits. Check the Georgetown University (Health PolicyInstitute) website. *(http://healthinsuranceinfo.net)*

✔ **Veterans:** If you served in the Armed Forces, you could be eligible for health care through the Veterans Administration (VA).

✔ **Join an association for a group rate:** Civic organizations may have a group rate. Business or trade organizations may also offer insurance to members. *Word of warning:* Make sure it is actually a group rate and not just a carrier with a low premium but poor coverage. Check also to see if the insurance company is regulated by your state, otherwise the company could increase premiums or drop coverage at any time. RVer Shaneen learned the hard way; after dealing with breast cancer, her company raised her premiums to more than $1,800 a month.

✔ **High-risk insurance pool:** Many states have a high-risk insurance pool for those who cannot find coverage elsewhere due to a preexisting condition. The federal government also has a high-risk pool.

✔ **High deductible:** Policies usually offer a variety of deductibles. For many RVers policies with high deductibles are the only option. Under some policies, you may have full coverage for one physical examination or routine tests like mammograms and pap smears each year. You are covered if something catastrophic occurs, but may have to shell out a lot before you reach that point. One broker we spoke to recommended that Bill and I each get an individual policy as opposed to a couple's policy. Together they cost only slightly more. However, if one of us were to become ill, we would have a lower amount out-of-pocket before coverage kicked in.

✔ **Stop-loss limit:** After you meet the deductible, the company pays a percentage, usually 50% or 80%, up to another amount, called the stop-loss limit. After you exceed that amount, they pay 100% of additional expenses (up to any limits on single illness or your lifetime limit). The lower your stop-loss limit, the less you pay out-of-pocket.

✔ **Canada and Mexico:** Often, prescriptions are less expensive in Canada or Mexico. Do some comparison shopping because the costs vary by medication. One RVer with no health insurance successfully took her treatment for breast cancer in Mexico because it was more affordable. It was comparable to U.S. procedures, not an alternative treatment.

## Things to check in a policy

For an article which appeared in *Escapees* magazine, Alice Zyetz interviewed two Texas insurance agents, David Loring and Roger Thomas. Their advice for RVers seeking health insurance coverage is summarized here:

✔ **Coverage where you travel:** Buy a quality plan that provides coverage everywhere you travel. Be sure you have coverage in other countries if you travel outside the United States. If you are working or spending time in a location away from the state where your policy was written, remember that the amount allowed for a doctor's visit or procedure is based on the usual rates for the home area, not where you receive treatment. In a high cost area you will have to pay the difference.

✔ **Rating:** Find out the insurance company's A.M. Best rating, an impartial assessment based on a company's financial stability and ability to pay claims. *(www.ambest.com)* Ask the company for its rating.

✔ **Be a shopper:** Compare the different plans. Make sure the coverage is in plain English. Ask questions.

✔ **Fees to agent:** A reputable insurance broker can be invaluable in understanding the "fine print" of your policy. However, don't pay a "policy origination" fee to an agent. There may be a small dollar fee to process the paperwork, but nothing else.

✔ **Deductible**: Check to see how the deductible is written. Some companies will have your deductible start over for each new illness. Instead, it should start again each year.

✔ **Pre-existing conditions:** Be clear about the definition of a pre-existing condition. A good company will describe it as a condition "for which you have received treatment, medication, or advice in the past six months."

A bad company may define it as a condition that manifested itself for a particular time before the policy began. For example, you have coverage as of February 1 and visit the doctor on February 3. Cancer is discovered that may have been growing for more than six months. The plan could label this as a pre-existing condition, even if you had no knowledge of it.

✔ **Evaluate coverage:** Don't just compare premiums. Carefully evaluate the coverage. A low premium may indicate poor coverage.

Check with the State Insurance Department in your state to make sure this company is regulated there. Horror stories abound where an out-of-state company has either jacked up premiums or dumped members who file substantial claims and the state insurance commission could do nothing about it. (Check **Resources** for the Georgetown University Institute (Health Policy Institute) website for contacts for each state's insurance department. Insurance companies, where permitted, play games to get rid of policy holders that cost them money.)

Make sure you have a proper address in the state where you have coverage. One RVer couple had been covered in Oregon prior to hitting the road. The insurance company continued their coverage when they began full-time RVing and agreed to bill them through their mail-forwarding company in another state. When one of them had a major claim, the insurance company balked at paying, saying the couple no longer had an address in Oregon. They were able to rectify this, but were lucky. Of course the company didn't raise any objections until a claim was actually filed.

## No health insurance

If you do not have health insurance, there are a few resources and ideas that can help you get affordable treatment:

✔ **Check into state programs.** You may be eligible. Some states provide free mammograms and pap smears to women who meet age and income qualifications.

✔ **Planned Parenthood** provides some free and low-cost tests to women. Some states provide similar services to women who qualify.

✔ **Health fairs** are another source of free and low-cost tests as well as useful health information. We have seen them sponsored by a chain of supermarkets.

✔ **Clinics run by a nurse practitioner** may be less expensive for routine tests or minor illnesses and injuries. Some drug stores have walk-in clinics now for treating common illnesses.

> **In most cases, you can take time to do research before treatment.**

✔ **Many hospitals will work with you** to pay your bill through no-interest loans or a payment plan. Always attempt to negotiate a lower amount. Some hospitals must provide free or low-cost care for low income patients. See (*www.hrsa.gov/ hillburton/default.htm*)

✔ **Drug companies have assistance** for patients with low-income and drug trials. Check Center Watch *(www.centerwatch.com)* or company websites. See **Resources** for additional help.

## DeAnna's Story

At a fairly young age, DeAnna found herself suffering painful arthritis in her knees. Doctors advised her she would need knee replacement surgery on both knees soon. At such a young age, there is a good chance you will need a second knee replacement operation in your lifetime and the second one usually doesn't work as well. DeAnna was also without health insurance.

She began researching. A librarian told her about the *U.S. News and World Report* annual July issue that rates hospitals. She contacted hospitals that had high ratings in orthopedics, and was then referred to orthopedic surgeons who practiced there.

A friend then told her about partial knee replacement and the doctor who operated on her. From there DeAnna found a webpage of the procedure, called Repicci II, or unicompartmental knee joint replacement. The site gave listings of doctors who do the procedure as the main part of their practice. The doctors she found through the hospitals ratings did not do this procedure as frequently, preferring total knee replacement. DeAnna felt, in the long run, she'd be better off having the partial done first, since she will likely need a full knee replacement in the future.

Next she researched prices. The cost of the surgeons ranged from $4,000 to $8,000 for one knee. DeAnna found a doctor who does 150 of these procedures each year and would do each knee for $2,000, since she was having both done. He also helped her obtain the Medicare rate for the hospital, X-rays, lab and anesthesia.

Some of the steps DeAnna took:

✔ **Contacted her network** of RVing and other friends to see if they had any knowledge that could help her.

✔ **Research, research.** She used the librarian and the Internet.

✔ **Contacted hospitals** about charges and payment plans. Usually a person in Billing is designated to handle special problems and would know of any financial assistance. (For example, I found out that a Utah hospital had a source for no-interest loans to pay off hospital bills.)

✔ **Check out the hospital** to see if it is accredited. Find out when it was evaluated and talk to the infection control nurse about what their "infections in surgery" rating is.

✔ **Take time to research.** Remember, unless it is a matter of life
or death, even if you have cancer, you have time to research.
DeAnna was surprised at how many people simply do what their
doctor or HMO recommends without doing any research. RVers
often have the flexibility to go wherever they can get the best
treatment or best price.

Unless you need immediate emergency treatment, in most cases, you
can take time to do research before having a procedure. This is true even
in the case of cancer. By checking prices of physicians and hospitals, you
can save a great deal of money.

## OTHER FINANCIAL CONSIDERATIONS
A few other issues may also have a financial impact.

### Unemployment
If you work sufficient time and have sufficient earnings, you could be
eligible for unemployment compensation. You
can collect unemployment payments from a
state even if you are no longer physically there.
If you decide to apply, contact the
unemployment office nearest to where you are
now located (in any state) and they will help

> **You may be eligible
> for unemployment.**

you determine if you are eligible and whom to contact if another state
handles your case. (Or check the website of the state where you will
collect it.) In many states, you file your weekly or biweekly report via
telephone and checks are deposited directly into your account.

### Investments
The Securities Investor Protection Corporation (SIPC) and the National
Association of Investors Corporation (NAIC) teamed up to survey
investors in 2001, reporting that 85 percent failed a "survival" quiz
gauging their awareness of what to do in times of market downturns and
other financial difficulties. This is a complex field.

If you will be obtaining part of your income from investments, or are
planning to use that income or principal for later years, I recommend
you consult with a licensed, practicing professional who understands

the unique needs of RVers. According to Dave Loring, licensed financial consultant, the time to consult with this advisor is in the planning stage, before going on the road full-time. Says Dave, "Your advisor should integrate investments, financial planning and estate planning concerns so you preserve, as well as increase your funds for your retirement years." Look for an independent agent who is a member of both the National Association of Security Dealers (NASD) and (SIPC). These organizations should be listed right on their business cards. You should not have to pay for advice and it never hurts to get a second opinion.

## ATM fees and other expenses

Avoid ATM fees: Getting charged $2.50 or more each time you get cash from a "foreign" (not your bank's) ATM can make a big dent in your account over the course of a year. You can avoid these fees by:

✔ **Credit unions:** Use an ATM at a credit union. Only 50 percent charge a fee as opposed to 94 percent of banks.

✔ **Cash back:** Get cash back using your debit card at point-of-sale terminals at grocery stores and other retail stores.

✔ **Alliances:** If you use a credit union or small bank, see if they are a member of an alliance where customers do not get charged fees at other member banks. Some banks and credit unions will allow a certain number of free withdrawals per month or reimburse ATM fees.

✔ **Online banking**: Only 11 percent of Internet banks charge customers to use another institution's ATM. Some even reimburse customers for a limited number of foreign ATM charges.

✔ **Debit card:** You should be able to go into a bank or credit union and use your debit card to get a withdrawal with no fees. Check with your bank to see if they will assess any fees on the other end. You can use your debit card in place of cash in many business establishments.

✔ **Brokerage account:** If you have an account with Charles Schwab and maintain a certain balance, there is no service charge for using your ATM card to make a cash withdrawal inside the bank or credit union.

## OTHER EXPENSES

To enjoy RVing, you need to be at a point in your life where material things aren't as important. If you need your "stuff" or have to keep acquiring "things," you probably aren't going to be happy RVing for very long. It is a different mind set. Many RVers do keep things in a storage unit somewhere, but they are usually past acquiring more things.

## Purchases

Purchasing knickknacks doesn't mean as much as experiencing a location. Besides, space is limited in an RV and who wants to dust knickknacks? Photos preserve the memory and take up much less space, and could even be stored on your computer. Some states offer sales tax holidays and waive sales tax on select items on certain days. (See **Resources.**)

## Clothes

Both a change in lifestyle and lack of space will probably trim your clothes budget. Casual clothes are the rule on most seasonal jobs. Some employers provide uniforms or at least shirts. You might save a few dressier clothes, but most of us find ourselves weeding these out of our closets after not using them in years. Some states do not charge sales tax on clothing.

## Admissions and entrance fees

Initially you may spend more on admissions and entrance fees when you first hit the road. You naturally want to see some of this country. You'll probably find these decreasing over time as your pace slows down. When you arrive in an area, check the newspaper for coupons, or ask at the visitor center or chamber if they have discount coupons. Members of Good Sam, AARP, or automobile clubs get discounts on certain attractions. Museums or attractions may offer free days or discounts. In San Diego's Balboa Park, for example, each museum has free admission one day a month.

If you have some idea of your travels, request state or regional travel planners. Festivals, fairs, parades and other events can add enjoyment to your visit and give you a real flavor of the area and are usually inexpensive. (See **Appendix 1** for state contact information.)

Some employers have access to free admission tickets as well. That might be part of your decision making when choosing a job. When Adrienne was hired by an RV park near San Francisco, she was given a "get lost" kit: $20 in change, bus schedules for the two nearby routes, a BART schedule including a booklet for sites to see near each BART station, a Muni F line route map, a map of San Francisco and a map of the nearby Pacifica businesses. She was told to take the money, purchase a bus ticket, a round-trip BART ticket, go to San Francisco, get lost and have fun, returning in the evening. She could not only be more helpful to guests, but had fun. Ron and Val received a free glacier flight-seeing tour and many other free tours while working in Haines, Alaska.

### Ideas for saving money from working RVers

✔ Get cash back when shopping, rather than using an ATM.

✔ Exchange services, such as sewing or repairs, or barter for a site during off-season.

✔ Check discard bins or give-away shelves at libraries for good reading materials.

✔ Stock up on food and clothing when in states that do not tax these items.

✔ Work in places you want to visit. Save travel time and expenses.

✔ Stay out of debt. If you don't have lots of money going out, you don't need a lot coming in.

✔ Buy prepaid phone cards. Shop for the best price, as they vary widely.

✔ Eat at home.

✔ When you eat out, go to the late lunch specials or breakfast.

✔ Check credit card bills carefully to make sure charges are accurate.

✔ Review insurance policies regularly to make sure you don't encounter expenses you thought were covered or that you aren't paying for coverage you don't need.

---

**Key points**

✍ **There are many ways to reduce expenses on the road.**

✍ **The change in lifestyle is a money-saver in some budget categories like clothing.**

✍ **There are many free or low-cost activities and places to stay that can help control your budget.**

---

*He who waits for the roast duck to fly into his*
*mouth must wait a very, very long time.*
*Chinese proverb*

# Chapter 24
# Lifestyle considerations

The ranks of full-time RVers, once the province of older, retired couples, are becoming diversified. Single men and women, families, and the physically challenged are also out on the road. There are some issues we face, or may face, at one time or another as we travel. The first is perhaps most critical to sticking with the full-time RV lifestyle.

## YOUR NEW COMMUNITY

A difficult aspect of becoming a full-time RVer can be that you lose contact with people who were once your friends. Long distance relationships are hard to maintain and many people won't want to do that. E-mail can keep you in touch, but you may have limited access, and it isn't the same as face-to-face visits. RVers find they have less in common with friends who choose to stay in one place.

> **It is important to build a new community.**

It is important to find or build a new community. It can be lonely traveling by yourselves from place to place. Contacts you meet on the road can become your new community. If you seem to have a connection with someone you meet, stay in touch. When you are traveling or in your off season you may be able to meet.

For Bill and me, the Boomer BOF (Birds of a Feather group) of the Escapees RV Club was our primary community and still is for me. As the name implies, it caters to the younger RVer, though the group has no age restrictions. We stay in touch by a newsletter, Internet bulletin board, and e-mail. I participate in RV working forums and discussion groups. We meet working RVers at our jobs and on the road. I have also acquired RVing Internet friends whom I've never met in person. If you are new to this lifestyle, you'll find the vast majority of RVers are more than willing to help out a fellow RVer.

Other clubs like FMCA or Good Sam have rallies and chapters with chances to make lasting friends and form a community. If you belong to and use membership parks, you'll run into the same people over time.

## WORKING TOGETHER

Many of the jobs or moneymaking opportunities could find you spending a lot of time on the job with your spouse or partner. Then you come home to your RV and spend more time in a small space.

RV workers Jack and Sylvia worked as a "team" in maintenance, primarily janitorial, at one state park. It was an adjustment working together as well as living together. At an RV dealership, they worked for the same employer and were in the same building but not always together. Advises Sylvia, "The first step is to identify what's happening, then make the decision not to let it affect your relationship."

Kay Peterson, who along with husband Joe Peterson founded Escapees RV Club, gives talks at Escapades about the full-time lifestyle. A blessing for us was to hear her talk about "Kay Days." Telling Joe she needed a "Kay Day" was a signal to Joe she needed a day to herself. She would go do something she wanted to do: shopping, go to the library or the movies. Bill and I often worked together. When I felt like I needed some space, I told Bill I needed a "Jaimie Day." He knew I meant I needed some time alone. I had a great time and came back recharged.

> I need a "Jaimie Day."

## THE SOLO WORKER

Not everyone travels as a couple and, in the case of a couple, both may not work. Even though many ads for working at RV parks specify couples, there are plenty of jobs and moneymaking opportunities for the solo worker.

Many RV parks advertise for couples because they get two workers per site, which is more cost-effective for them. However, if the situation is one that interests you, don't hesitate to approach the owners. An employer may require that you work a number of hours for your site. As a solo RVer, you may have to work the full amount, where a couple would split it. The hours required of solo RVers may also be negotiable.

The majority of jobs and moneymaking opportunities described in **Section III** apply to the single worker.

✔ RV worker April travels on her own. She has gotten many jobs in RV parks and public campgrounds and has picked apples in Washington. Couples picking apples earned more, but she was still hired.
✔ RV worker Phyllis often works in RV parks, though her husband is on disability and is unable to work. She prefers working as an activity director and has had no problem getting jobs.
✔ RV volunteer Jerry has volunteered in several national forests.
✔ RV volunteer Betty worked for her site and use of the facilities at a clothing-optional resort. She also worked for pay at a state park.

$ **RV writer: Joei Carlton Hossack** has been on the road since 1989. She and her husband traveled by RV through Great Britain, Europe, and parts of Africa. In 1992, during their travels, her husband died at the young age of 52. Joei has continued traveling. She has worked on three archaeological digs in England and has traveled solo through Turkey, the Greek Islands and Cyprus. She also drove her RV to Alaska. Joei supports herself through writing and speaking about her adventures and has written seven books. She currently has five in print plus three mini-reads.

A number of groups for singles provide activities where singles can meet and travel with other singles.(See **Resources.**) Use these groups as opportunities to network for job information.

## TRAVELING WITH FAMILIES

You may run across families traveling together full-time in their RV. Often the children are homeschooled. Resources for the homeschooler and groups provide curricula, support and assistance. Other RVers with families make it a point to stay in one location for the school year. Still others enroll their children in a variety of schools as they travel.

Traveling with young children could make it difficult for both parents to work unless they had different schedules or had affordable child care available. Resort areas and concessionaires in national parks have positions with evening shifts in food service, security, and retail.

We have worked in a couple of towns where pre-teens and teens were welcome additions to the work force. Busing tables, pet walking, and yard work were a few ways enterprising young people made money.

> **Jeff and Susan travel with daughter Samantha and have worked at Disney World.**

If parents have a business such as selling items at shows, children can be involved in all aspects of the business. Judith Waite Allee in *Educational Travel on a Shoestring* describes how her daughter learned to interact with customers, fill out order forms and make change as they traveled with the family photography business. *(www.angelfire.com/on/shareddreams)* Some organizations seeking volunteers welcome families as well.

Kim Goza, part of the Activated Storytellers family, has taken over the Families on the Road website. The site focuses on networking, traveling, working and homeschooling children. Kim, her husband Dennis and son Zephyr have traveled in their RV since 1988 performing professionally at schools and libraries across the U.S. They first traveled in a large RV but have downsized to a smaller one. *(www.familiesontheroad.com)*

Advise your employer you are traveling with children if you will be staying onsite in case there are restrictions. Some RV parks are adults-only parks also. The employer may be able to accommodate families scheduling parents on different shifts. Jeff and Susan travel with their daughter, Samantha. They have worked at Disney World several winters, working different shifts so their daughter was never alone. Samantha recently turned 16 and joined her parents working at Disney too.

$ **RV worker: Brandy** began traveling with her children many years ago. Says Brandy, "Working on the road takes no special skills or talents, except flexibility." Her accounts of the few times she had difficulty finding jobs show determination as well. Once in Seattle she had spent a week looking for a job and was still not working. She decided on the job she wanted and approached the owner. He told her there were no openings. She said, "That's okay, but I'm going to work for you." Wednesday she went back; he still had no openings. She reminded him she was going to work for him. Friday she stopped by again to let him know she was still interested. Monday, the same thing happened, and she told him not to forget her. On Thursday she went back again. The owner said she was so persistent, she must really need a job and want to work there, so he hired her. Months later when it was time to leave, he told her he was glad she kept trying and offered her a job if she was ever back in town.

## THE DISABLED RVER

Individuals with disabilities are discovering something wonderful: They no longer have to stay in a "fixed" home to work from home. With the advent of the RVing industry offering more accessible features on their units like wider doorways, wheelchair lifts, and barrier-free floor plans, more and more wannabe differently abled travelers are able to hit the road. Wi-Fi, satellite Internet and mobile broadband make working from the road via the Internet a viable lifestyle for RVers. Ongoing development of computer-assisted technology means more and more individuals are opting for work on the open road.

Hope Sykes, writer and volunteer, found out quickly that RVing and the Internet offered a rewarding lifestyle as well as a global network when a sudden illness struck. She is a firm believer that the RVing lifestyle along with Internet access opens a world of possibilities and taps into the depths of the imagination. To her, there are several keys to success: get an affordable rig that meets your needs, network, and build up your skills by volunteering if your résumé doesn't have the impact that you would like. She also encourages anyone with questions about accessible RVs to contact the Handicapped Travel Club. She shares her experience below. See (*www.handicappedtravelclub.com*)

### Hope's story

After RVing over 200,000 miles throughout the U.S. and Canada over the years and fully expecting no lifestyle changes, I noticed a dramatic transformation in myself one morning: I had trouble getting up and was in pain. Not long after that, I progressed to using a cane. Fortunately, a recent operation has improved my condition but I want to share with you some of the things that I learned.

Most importantly, I've learned not to be afraid of what life hands us, and that there are often ways to continue the enjoyable RV lifestyle and to be productive. That's how my writing took a more serious turn and I can honestly say that I've never enjoyed working, learning, and traveling more after this deep reflection.

"That can't always be," you say. You're right. I'm the first to admit that things aren't always rosy, but with the availability of accessible RVs and the Internet, I've found out that many individuals can actually have the dream job that they've always wanted with a future not so filled with barriers.

Even during my most difficult times, I found that with an RV and occasional Internet hook-ups, I could work from where I wanted. A beach. A forest. With a view of a lake. Yes, I was much slower than my colleagues at times, yet I seized this opportunity to decide upon what was really important in my life.

Through the RVing lifestyle, quality time with my family has been a reality. Reaching out globally via the Internet was possible at any hour when hook-ups were available and I have developed fulfilling relationships with my colleagues who are from practically any place on the planet.

I also strived to have a work area set up as I like it; where I could learn and read to my heart's content. Instead of spending wasted hours using my more limited energy reserves on cleaning and maintaining a large house on a fixed foundation, I've been productive and working with a passion on things that I really love to do.

## Getting started

Here is a suggestion for getting started. If you are currently working for a company that caters to telecommuting (working from home via computer), ask if the company would allow you to continue your job while you are on the road. For more about telecommuting, check **Resources.**

If you work on a number of projects for different clients, you may find that you only need occasional access for data uploads to an employer and can meet other communication needs by cell phone. For RV parks with Wi-Fi access, do an Internet search for "RV parks with Wi-Fi."

## Hope's advice

Once you are able to free yourself of many of the barriers, an interesting thing happens — you'll begin to dream. Suddenly your mind begins to think things like

✔ I could do that.
✔ I wonder what would happen if I...
✔ Why doesn't someone come up with...

You might start taking a few notes here and there or even keeping a journal. You begin to set your own pace. You discover things (lots of things) that you love to do. Perhaps you begin to understand that you really do have some of those talents that people had been telling you that you had all along. You used to brush off those comments. Now you reflect upon them. Hmmm. Remember what they said? "Gee, I wish that I could be good at that like YOU." Yes, you do remember. Maybe your friends weren't just trying to be nice after all.

I know, this probably won't happen overnight. It took me some time to get this far and I'm still working on it daily. So how do you get from there to here? Mostly, it takes some planning.

**Work for a while, then take some time off ...**

Pulling up roots and looking for work isn't so new these days. No job is permanent. Companies seem to be handing out pink slips or merging or going out of business at a steady rate so few of us have really any job security. Temporary workers and independent contractors are becoming more popular in the corporate world. That's where having a mobile lifestyle can be a real plus —work for a while and then take some time off, see another part of the country, or take a telecourse during a break. Remember: This is supposed to be your dream career.

If you feel that your skills aren't as sharp or your résumé is a little thin, you might want to think about doing some virtual volunteering first by using the Internet. For great resources on the topic, you'll want to visit the Virtual Volunteer Project online at (*www.utexas.edu/lbj/rgk/serviceleader/virtual/*).

Here's just a partial list of ideas from the center:

✔ Conduct online research
✔ Provide professional consulting
✔ Translate a document into another language
✔ Make sure a website is accessible for the disabled
✔ Design an agency's newsletter or brochure
✔ Help with language instruction
✔ Try distance learning: train volunteers in a subject via the Internet

Who wouldn't want some of these valuable skills on their résumé? From here, it is easier to then pursue the possibility of telecommuting where you work for a company from "home." Maybe you feel confident enough to start your own business.

If you are looking for some tools and resources to make yourself more marketable, stop by disAbility.gov at *(www.disability.gov)*. Look under Employment at the section called "Self-Employment/Entrepreneurship." Several articles profile disabled entrepreneurs, provide how-to's, and FAQs. If you are beginning to have a sudden attack of I-Can't-Do-This, read some of the "Self-Employment Success Stories" at this section before you make your final decision.

Before you sign off from the Internet, take a look at a virtual community for the disabled called "Disabled Online" at *(www.disabledonline.com)*. Under Employment, they have an "Employment Resources" area that displays websites for organizations and companies that provide job skills and jobs for people with disabilities.

Indeed, the RVing lifestyle can offer more flexibility than you ever could have imagined. When looking for additional employment resources, don't forget to check out other websites and leads which may cover areas beyond your current location. You are in a unique position where you have a choice of going to a job or having it come to you. Remember that your new backyard is as big as the whole outdoors.

## Protection from discrimination

The Americans with Disabilities Act (ADA), enacted in 1990, is a comprehensive civil rights law for people with disabilities. The Department of Justice enforces the ADA's requirements in three areas: the employment practices of state and local government; programs, services and activities of state and local government; and public accommodations and commercial facilities. Under the Act, you have the right to ask your employer for reasonable accommodations for your disability, like extra breaks or an adjustable desk. Small employers are exempted from these regulations, though many will accommodate you.

Federal and state employers keep statistics on numbers of disabled workers hired and so seek qualified help from their ranks. However, in any employment situation, be honest if you need accommodation due to your disability. If for instance you need rest periods, a stool when at a counter, or minimal periods on your feet, let the employer know beforehand.

## TRAVELING AND WORKING WITH PETS

Working RVers who travel with pets will encounter employers and park owners who do not permit pets or prohibit certain breeds. National Parks have restrictions on pets running loose in the park, though workers with their own RVs can usually have pets if they keep them on leash.

Always make sure the employer is aware of your pets prior to accepting the position. Some RV workers include a photo of their pet and letters of recommendation with their own résumé. If the employer cannot or will not allow your pets on premises, it could be quite costly for both of you if a pet agreement hasn't been reached be-

> **Make sure the employer is aware of your pets prior to accepting a position.**

forehand. If you have multiple pets or large dogs and have trouble getting a position, try visiting a potential employer as a guest. Let them get to know you and your pets. If your animals are well behaved, kept under control, and you clean up after them, the employer may relax the rules for you.

 **Solo with horses: Carol** loves to trail ride. She sold her home and her business in Florida and travels the USA with two horses, a dog and a cat. As she travels, she locates places to ride and work, planning ahead before moving on to her next adventure. She uses the Internet, first looking up the state, then searching the site for equine usage places. At one job on a ranch in Texas, she worked between 20–24 hours/week for her full hookup site, laundry, and some meals. She did mostly miscellaneous repairs, mowing and painting. Working about four hours a day left her plenty of time to ride. She often trailered the horses out to other areas to ride and explore.

## Short-term assignments

Many RVers need or want to work or volunteer but would rather not be stuck in one place for more than a few weeks or a couple of months. Many seasonal employers want you to stay for the entire season; it's expensive to keep training new workers. However, if you focus on finding short-term jobs, you can find them. Here are some ideas:

✔ Volunteer positions usually run from one month to three months.

✔ Some businesses hire for opening, closing or just the busy months.

✔ Seasonal businesses up north have shorter seasons.

✔ Events like NASCAR and fairs are much shorter. (Ch 20)

✔ Some jobs involve traveling from location to location. *Workamper News* usually has several positions of this type in each issue.

✔ National park concessionaires and other businesses often have mid-season openings.

✔ Don't be afraid to ask. The worst that can happen is they say no!

---

### Key points

✍ **Individuals can successfully find work on the road.**

✍ **There are work and volunteer opportunities for disabled RVers.**

✍ **Advise your employer if you are traveling with children or pets if you will be staying onsite or if their care will impact your job.**

---

*"Life is not a dress rehearsal."*
*Joe Lacey, Escapees RV Club member*

# Chapter 25
# Conclusion

Congratulations! You have all the tools to successfully find the job you desire. You can find jobs that meet your criteria for pay, location, duties, and good employers. You likely have dozens of useful ideas too, on how you can earn or make money on the road. Put that together with the résumé you created and your job search skills, and you are on your way to new adventures.

Keep up your **Job Notebook.** You never know when you'll need a different job or be ready for a change. One of the joys of this lifestyle is trying new things and seeing new places. Take advantage of your mobility and flexibility while you have time. Circumstances could change and that opportunity could fade away. When you need or want to make a change, your **Job Notebook** and this book will have invaluable resources.

Websites are notorious for changing or disappearing. If you cannot open a website listed in **Resources,** please advise me. I would love to hear about your work experiences as well. Please feel free to send me an e-mail at *CalamityJaimie@gmail.com.*

Your turn! This is your life and your time. Now it is time to write your own stories. I hope to hear from you!

# SECTION V. APPENDICES

# Appendix 1
# State tourism offices

**Alabama Tourist Bureau**
800/ALABAMA
www.touralabama.org

**Alaska Division of Tourism**
800/327-9372
www.travelalaska.com

**Arizona Office of Tourism**
866/275-5816
www.arizonaguide.com

**Arkansas Department of Parks and Tourism**
501/682-7777
www.arkansas.com

**California Office of Tourism**
877/235-4367
www.visitcalifornia.com

**Colorado Tourism Board**
800/COLORADO
www.colorado.com

**Connecticut Tourism**
888/CTvisit
www.tourism.state.ct.us

**Delaware Tourism Office**
866/2-VISITDE (284-7483)
www.visitdelaware.com

**Florida Division of Tourism**
888/7-FLA-USA
www.visitflorida.com

**Georgia Dept of Industry**
800/VisitGA
www.exploregeorgia.org

**Hawaii Visitor & Convention Bureau**
800-/GoHawaii
www.gohawaii.com

**Idaho Travel Council**
208/334/2470
www.visitidaho.org

**Illinois Tourist Information**
800/2CONNECT
www.enjoyillinois.com

**Indiana Tourism Division**
800/457-8283
www.in.gov/core/tourism.html

**Iowa Department of Tourism**
800/472-6035
www.traveliowa.com

**Kansas Tourism Div**
785/296-2009
www.travelks.com

**Kentucky Depart. of Travel**
800/225-8747
www.kentuckytourism.com

**Louisiana Tourism Office**
800/99-GUMBO
www.louisianatravel.com

**Maine Tourism Division**
1/888-624-6345.
www.visitmaine.com

**Maryland Office of Tourism**
866-MDWelcome
http://visitmaryland.org

**Massachusetts Div. of Tourism**
800/227-MASS
www.massvacation.com

**Michigan Travel Bureau**
888/784-7328
www.travel.michigan.org

**Minnesota Office of Tourism**
888/TOURISM
www.exploreminnesota.com

**Mississippi Div. of Tourism**
866/SEEMISS
www.visitmississippi.org

**Missouri Div. of Tourism**
800/519-2100
www.visitmo.com

**Montana Travel Bureau**
800/VISIT-MT  (847-4868)
www.visitmt.com

**Nebraska Travel/Tourism**
888/444-1867
www.visitnebraska.gov

**Nevada Tourism Commission**
800/NEVADA-8
http://travelnevada.com

**New Hampshire Travel**
603/271-2665
www.visitnh.gov

**New Jersey Tourism**
800/VISITNJ
www.state.nj.us/travel

**New Mexico Tourism**
505/827-7400
www.newmexico.org

**New York Travel Information**
800/CALL-NYS
http://iloveny.com

**North Carolina Tourism**
800/VISIT-NC
www.visitnc.com

**North Dakota Tourism**
800/HELLO-ND
www.ndtourism.com

**Ohio Office of Tourism**
800/BUCKEYE
http://discoverohio.com

**Oklahoma Tourism Depart.**
800/652-OKLA (652-6552)
www.travelok.com

**Oregon Tourism Division**
800/547-7842
www.traveloregon.com

**Pennsylvania State Travel Bureau**
800/VISIT-PA
www.visitpa.com

**Rhode Island Dept. of Tourism**
800/250-7384
www.visitrhodeisland.com

**South Carolina Tourism**
803/734-1700
www.discoversouthcarolina.com

**South Dakota Div. of Tourism**
800/SDAKOTA
www.travelsd.com

**Tennessee Depart. of Tourism**
800/GO2-TENN
www.tnvacation.com

**Texas Tourist Agency**
800/8888TEX
www.traveltex.com

**Utah Travel Council**
800/200-1160
www.utah.com

**Vermont Travel Division**
800/VERMONT (837-6668)
www.travel-vermont.com

**Virginia Division of Tourism**
800/VISIT VA
www.virginia.org

**Washington Tourism Division**
800/544-1800
www.tourism.wa.gov

**West Virginia Tourism**
800-CALL WVA
www.wvtourism.com

**Wisconsin Division of Tourism**
800/432-8747
www.travelwisconsin.com

**Wyoming Travel Commission**
800/225-5996
www.wyomingtourism.org

# Notes

*Those who say it cannot be done should not
interrupt the person doing it.*
*Chinese proverb*

# Appendix 2
# National Park Service Offices

**National Park Service**
Headquarters
1849 C St. NW
Washington, DC 20240
202/208-6843
*www.nps.gov/*

**Alaska Area Region - NPS**
240 West 5th Avenue
Anchorage, AK 99503
907/644-3510
*www.nps.gov/akso/*

**Northeast Region - NPS**
U.S. Custom House
200 Chestnut St., 5th Fl
Philadelphia, PA 19106
215/597-7013
*www.nps.gov/nero/*

**Midwest Region - NPS**
601 Riverfront Drive
Omaha, NE 68102
402/661-1736

**National Capitol Region - NPS**
1100 Ohio Dr., SW
Washington, DC 20242
202/619-7222
*www.nps.gov/ncro/*

**Intermountain Region - NPS**
12795 Alameda Pkwy
Denver, CO 80225
303/969-2500

**Southeast Region - NPS**
100 Alabama St., SW
1924 Building
Atlanta, GA 30303
404/507-5600

**Pacific West Region - NPS**
One Jackson Center
1111 Jackson St., Ste 700
Oakland, CA 94607
510/817-1300
*www.nps.gov/pwro/*

# Appendix 3
# U.S Forest Service Offices

**U.S.D.A. Forest Service**
National Headquarters
PO Box 96090
Washington, DC 20090-6090
202/205-8333
www.fs.fed.us/

**Region 1 - Northern**
200 E. Broadway
PO Box 7669
Missoula, MT 59807
406/329-3511
www.fs.fed.us/r1

**Region 2 - Rocky Mountain**
740 Simms St.
Golden, CO 80401
303/275-5350
www.fs.fed.us/r2

**Region 3 - Southwestern**
333 Broadway, SE
Albuquerque, NM 87102
505/842-3292
www.fs.fed.us/r3

**Region 4 - Intermountain**
324 25th St.
Ogden, UT 84401
801/625-5306
www.fs.fed.us/r4

**Region 5 - Pacific Southwest**
1323 Club Dr.
Vallejo, CA 94592
707/562-8737
www.fs.fed.us/r5

**Region 6 - Pacific Northwest**
PO Box 3623
333 SW First Ave.
Portland, OR 97208-3623
503/808-2468
www.fs.fed.us/r6

**Region 8 - Southern**
1720 Peachtree Rd., Ste 760S
Atlanta, GA 30309
404/347-4177
www.fs.fed.us/r8

**Region 9 - Eastern**
626 Wisconsin Ave.
Milwaukee, WI 53202
414/297-3600
www.fs.fed.us/r9

**Region 10 - Alaska**
Federal Office Building
PO Box 21628
Juneau, AK 99802-1628
907/586-8806
www.fs.fed.us/r10

# Appendix 4
# State Parks

For each system of state parks, address, phone and contact for volunteer programs are listed. If a specific webpage or volunteer coordinator could not be identified, general information is listed instead. You can always contact an individual state park to find out how to apply as a campground host or find out their needs for volunteers for other tasks. Seasonal employment information is listed where available.

**All state parks:** *www.stateparks.com*

**Alabama State Parks**
Promotions Section
64 N. Union Street, Suite 468
Montgomery, AL 36130-1452
334/242-3154, 800/ALAPark
E-mail: *parkspr@dcnr.state.al.us*
Website: *www.dcnr.state.al.us*
Volunteer website: *www.alapark.com/vip*
Notes: Each of Alabama's twenty-two State Parks is looking for volunteers in areas such as campground hosting, trail improvement, interpretive lecturing, and more. Volunteer campground hosts for one month or more. Singles or couples. Call or write for or download an application form or ask at individual parks.

**Alaska State Parks**
550 W. 7th Avenue, Suite 1380
Anchorage, AK 99501-3561
907/269-8708
E-mail: *dnr.pksvol@alaska.gov*
Website: *www.dnr.state.ak.us/parks/vip/index.htm*
Notes: Apply Oct 1 through April 1. Many types of positions, some have stipend. To receive a paper copy of the Alaska State Parks Volunteer Catalog, contact the Volunteer Coordinator at the above address. Please be sure to include a complete postal address.

**Arizona State Parks Human Resources Office**
1300 W. Washington
Phoenix, AZ 85007
602/542-6919 or 602/542-6900
For volunteer opportunities, call 602/542-7152, or
e-mail *narmstrong@azstateparks.gov* for information.
Website: *http://azstateparks.com/employment/index.html*
Notes: Find jobs at AZStateJobs.gov. For State Parks jobs only, press
"Search for Jobs" button and type AZPARKS in the keyword field.

**Arkansas Department of Parks and Tourism**
**Division of State Parks**
One Capitol Mall
Little Rock, AR 72201
888/AT-PARKS (V/TT)
Job Line: 501/682-7742
E-mail: *natural.jobs@arkansas.gov* Attn: Dept. S097PT
Website: *www.arkansasstateparks.com/*
Notes: Contact the park of your choice. An RV site may not be
included. Some parks participate in the Good Sam program.
Seasonal employment information:
*www.arkansas.com/helpful-info/employment/*

**California State Parks**
Interpretation and Education Division
P.O. Box 942896
Sacramento, CA 94296-0001
916/653-9069
Website: Volunteers in parks *http://parks.ca.gov/*
*default.asp?page_id=886*
E-mail: *vipp@parks.ca.gov*
Seasonal employment: *http://parks.ca.gov/default.asp?page_id=847*
Notes: A variety of volunteers are needed. Contact the volunteer
coordinator of the district you are interested in or call the above
number for a volunteer packet. Apply early. Approval process includes
background checks and fingerprinting. For seasonal employment, first
contact the District/Park Unit office, then complete a Standard State
Application (Form STD 678) to send to District/Park unit office.

**Colorado State Parks**
1313 Sherman Street, Room 618
Denver, CO 80203
303/866-3437
E-mail: *parksvolunteerdb@state.co.us* for volunteer brochure.
Website: *http://parks.state.co.us/Pages/HomePage.aspx*
Notes: Look under "Parks:" to go to individual Parks' homepages.
Under "Jobs" find jobs, volunteer opportunities, and forms.

**Connecticut Department of Environmental Protection**
State Parks
79 Elm Street
Hartford, CT 06106-5127
860/424-3200
Seasonal employment:
*www.ct.gov/dep/cwp/view.asp?a=2699&q=323356&depNav_GID=1511*
Notes: Not all campgrounds use volunteer campground hosts. Contact
individual park.

**Delaware Dept. of Natural Resources & Environmental Control**
Division of Parks & Recreation
Attn: Greg Abbott
89 Kings Highway
Dover, DE 19901
302/739-3197
Website: *www.destateparks.com/*
Notes: See Parks Information Request, volunteering or employment links
Seasonal employment:
*www.dnrec.delaware.gov/parks/Home/Pages/Employment.aspx*

**Florida State Parks**
Coordinator of Volunteer Services
Bureau of Operational Services
Division of Recreation and Parks
3900 Commonwealth Boulevard, MS 535
Tallahassee, FL 32399-3000
850/245-2157
Website: *www.floridastateparks.org/getinvolved/volunteer.cfm*

**Georgia State Parks and Historic Sites**
2 MLK Jr. Dr., Suite 1352 East
Atlanta, GA 30334
Website: *www.gastateparks.org/volunteer*
Volunteer Resources Coordinator: *lynn.barfield@dnr.state.ga.us*
Volunteer Coordinator direct line: 404/656-6533
Notes: Locate parks at website. Contact above for more information
on volunteering.

**Hawaii State Parks**
Department of Land and Natural Resources
Division of State Parks
P.O. Box 621
Honolulu, HI 96809
808/587-0300
E-mail: *dlnr@hawaii.gov*
Website: *www.hawaiistateparks.org/*
Notes: Click on partners for information. Several agencies use
volunteers.

**Idaho State Parks**
P.O. Box 83720
Boise, ID 83720-0065
208/334-4199
Website: *http://parksandrecreation.idaho.gov/aboutus/
currentvolunteeropportunities.aspx*
Notes: Find out about parks looking for volunteers, view current
listing by park, and fill out or print application.

**Illinois State Parks**
Illinois Department of Natural Resources
One Natural Resources Way
Springfield, IL 62702
Call 217/782-6302
E-mail *dnr.volunteers@illinois.gov*
Website: *http://dnr.state.il.us/volunteer/*
Notes: Variety of positions, as well as clerical. Positions listed at
website, apply online.

**Indiana State Parks**
Campground Host/Volunteers in Parks program
Indiana Department of Natural Resources
Division of State Parks and Reservoirs
402 W. Washington, Room W298
Indianapolis, IN 46204
800/622-4931
Website: *www.in.gov/dnr/parklake/* Click on About Us, then
Volunteering.
Indianna State Park Inns' employment opportunities:
*www.in.gov/dnr/parklake/5422.htm*
Each property has a volunteer coordinator. For more information
download the volunteer brochure. Seasonal employment is handled
through the State Personnel Deptartment.

**Iowa Department of Natural Resources**
Keepers of the Land
502 E. 9th Street
Wallace State Office Building
Des Moines, IA 50319-0034
515/281-5918
E-mail: *dnr.volunteer@dnr.iowa.gov*
Website: *www.iowadnr.gov/volunteer/index.html*
Sign up for e-notification about volunteer opportunities. Find
application under Become a Campground Host.
Temporary employment listings:
*www.iowadnr.gov/employment/temp_seasonal.html*

**Kansas Department of Wildlife and Parks**
512 SE 25th Avenue
Pratt, KS 67124-8174
620/672-5911
Website: *www.kdwp.state.ks.us/news/State-Parks*
Notes: Contact individual state park for needs and application. Also
participate in the AmeriCorps program, a volunteer program that will
pay a living allowance and give a grant for college once you have
completed the required hours.

**Kentucky Department of Parks**
Capital Plaza Tower
500 Mero Street, Suite 1100
Frankfort, KY 40601-1974
800/255-7275
Website: *http://parks.ky.gov/*
Notes: There are about 12 different ways to volunteer. Each park recruits their own volunteers and operates their own program. Click on Become a VIP for information and an application.

**Louisiana Office of State Parks**
P.O. Box 44426
Baton Rouge, LA 70804-4426
Toll free 888/677-1400
E-mail: *parks@crt.state.la.us*
Website: *www.crt.state.la.us/parks*
Notes: Contact park manager at park you are interested in. Campground host job description and application available on website.

**Maine State Parks**
Maine Department of Conservation
Bureau of Parks and Lands

| Southern Region | Northern Region |
|---|---|
| 107 State House Station | 106 Hogan Road |
| Augusta, ME 04333-0107 | Bangor, ME 04401 |
| Telephone: 207/624-6080 | 207/941/4014 |

Website: *www.state.me.us/doc/parks/volunteer/volunteer.html*

**Maryland State Parks**
Maryland Department of Natural Resources
580 Taylor Avenue
Annapolis, MD 21401
877/620-8367
E-mail: *lmartin@dnr.state.md.us*
Website: *www.dnr.state.md.us/publiclands/volunteer.asp*
Volunteer information via phone at 443/630-9746.
Seasonal employment: *www.dnr.state.md.us/hr/jobs.asp#park*

**Massachusetts Department of Environmental Management**
Division of Forests and Parks
251 Causeway Street, Suite 600
Boston, MA 02114-2104
617/626-1250
Contact individual units.
Website: *www.mass.gov/dcr/getInvolved.htm*
Seasonal jobs: *www.mass.gov/dcr/employment.htm*

**Michigan State Parks**
Parks and Recreation
Mason Building, Third Floor
P.O. Box 30257
Lansing MI 48909
517/373-9900
Website: *www.michigan.gov/dnr/0,1607,7-153-10366_10871---,00.html*
Notes: Campground hosts plus others needed. Apply online.
Seasonal jobs: *www.michigan.gov/dnr/0,1607,7-153-10366_11866---,00.html*

**Minnesota Department of Natural Resources**
DNR Information Center
500 Lafayette Road #36
St Paul, MN 55155-4040
651/259-5249
Website: *www.dnr.state.mn.us/volunteering/index.html*
Notes: Volunteer opportunities listed at Web site or contact a unit directly. Subscribe to CyberNews Services for information on volunteering.
Seasonal jobs: *www.dnr.state.mn.us/jobs/openings.html*

**Mississippi State Parks**
Mississippi Department of Wildlife, Fisheries and Parks
1505 Eastover Drive
Jackson, MS 39211-6374
Phone: 601/432-2400
Website: *http://home.mdwfp.com/Parks/Default.aspx*
Contact individual parks.

**Missouri Department of Natural Resources**
Volunteers in Parks (VIP) Program
Division of State Parks
P.O. Box 176
Jefferson City, MO 65102
800/334-6946 for information
Website: *www.mostateparks.com/volunteer.htm* for volunteer application
and information.
Seasonal employment as a ranger: *www.mostateparks.com/rangers/
index.html*
Notes: Volunteers serve as interpreters, park aides, trail workers and
campground hosts. Four-week (consecutive) stay minimum.

**Montana Department of Fish, Wildlife and Parks, Division of Parks**
1420 East Sixth Avenue
P.O. Box 200701
Helena, MT 59620-0701
406/444-3750
Website: *http://fwp.mt.gov/parks/volunteer/default.html*
Notes: Campground hosts, naturalists, visitor center attendants,
archaeological volunteers, special projects. Call headquarters or Parks
Dvision office where you want to volunteer. Application online.

**Nebraska Game and Parks Commission**
2200 North 33rd Street
Lincoln, NE 68503-0370
402/471-0641
Request a VIP application: *suzanne.ridder@nebraska.gov*
Website: *http://outdoornebraska.ne.gov/parks/programs/vip/vip.asp*

**Nevada State Parks**

| | |
|---|---|
| Southern Region | Northern Region |
| 4747 Vegas Drive | 16799 Lahontan Dam |
| Las Vegas, NV 89108 | Fallon, NV 89406 |
| 775/486-5126 | 775/867-3001 |

For volunteer brochure and application, contact *stparks@parks.nv.gov*
Website for seasonal employment and volunteering:
*http://parks.nv.gov/job.html*

**New Hampshire Division of Parks and Recreation**
P.O. Box 1856
172 Pembroke Road
Concord, NH 03302-1856
Phone: 603/271-3556
E-Mail: *nhparks@dred.state.nh.us* Click on Get Involved.
Website: *http://nhparks.state.nh.us*
Seasonal employment: Call 603/436-1552 for information.

**New Jersey Department of Environmental Protection**
Division of Parks and Forestry
501 East State Street, P.O. Box 404 Unable to verify street address.
Trenton, NJ 08625
For more information: 800/843-6420 or 609/984-0370
Volunteers in Parks program -contact any park office
Website: *www.state.nj.us/dep/parksandforests* Click on Become a
Volunteer or Seasonal Jobs.
Notes: Seasonal employment application deadline is March 1.

**New Mexico State Parks**
1220 St. Francis Drive, P.O. Box 1147
Santa Fe, NM 87504
505/476-3355 or 888/NMParks (667-2757)
Website: *www.emnrd.state.nm.us/PRD/* Click on Volunteer or Jobs.
Online volunteer form plus information on program.
Notes: Several different types of volunteers sought.

**New York State Parks**
Empire State Plaza
Agency Building 1
Albany, NY 12238
515/474-0456
Website: *www.nysparks.state.ny.us/camping/camper-assistance-
program.aspx* See Camper Assistance Program (CAP), their volunteer
program. Contact parks directly.
Seasonal employment:
*www.nysparks.state.ny.us/employment/park-employment.aspx*

**North Carolina State Parks**
1615 Mail Service Center
Raleigh, NC 27699-1615
919/733-4181
E-mail: *parkinfo@ncmail.net*
Website: *www.ncparks.gov/Jobs/main.php*
Notes: Numerous types of volunteers needed. Contact the Volunteer
Manager at the park of choice.
Seasonal employment: *www.ncparks.gov/Jobs/seasonal.php*

**North Dakota Parks and Recreation Dept.**
1600 E. Century Avenue, Suite 3
Bismarck, ND 58503-0649
701/328-5357 Campground Host Program: 701/263-4015
E-mail: *parkrec@nd.gov*
Website: *www.parkrec.nd.gov/parks/volunteer.htm*
Seasonal Employment: *www.parkrec.nd.gov/information/employment.htm*
Notes: Volunteer four weeks, 30-hours/week. Receive full hookup site,
annual park entrance permit, and free camping at ND State Parks.

**Ohio State Parks**
2045 Morse Rd, C-3
Columbus, OH 43229-6693
614/265-6561
E-mail: *OhioStateParks@dnr.state.oh.us*
Website: *www.dnr.state.oh.us/parks/resources/supportyourparks/volunteer/
tabid/821/Default.aspx* Describes volunteer opportunities. Contact
individual parks or e-mail *jm.henanan@dnr.state.oh.us.*
Seasonal employment: *www.dnr.state.oh.us/career/summer/tabid/223/
Default.aspx*
Resorts state parks operated by Xanterra Parks and Resorts:
*www.coolworks.com/ohspr/default.htm*

**Oklahoma State Parks**
15 N. Robinson, 6th Floor, P.O. Box 52002
Oklahoma City, OK 73152-2002
800/652-6552 or 405/230-8400
E-mail: *mcossey@otrd.state.ok.us*
Website: *www.travelok.com/State_Parks/* Contact individual parks

**Oregon Parks and Recreation Department**
Volunteer Programs
725 Summer Street N.E., Suite C
Salem, OR 97301
Toll-free: 877/225-9803
E-mail: *volunteer.info@state.or.us*
Website: *http://egov.oregon.gov/OPRD/VOL/index.shtml*
Download application.
Employment: *http://egov.oregon.gov/OPRD/JOBS/jobs.shtml*

**Oregon Dept. of Fish and Wildlife**
Volunteer Host Program
7118 N.E. Vandenberg Avenue
Corvallis, OR 97330-9446
541/757-5230
E-mail: *vol.program@state.or.us*
Website: *www.dfw.state.or.us/hr*
Notes: Link to both paid and volunteer jobs. Duties could include
stocking and feeding fish, visitor contact, maintenance, carpentry,
habitat projects, clerical.

**Pennsylvania State Parks**
Bureau of State Parks
P.O. Box 8551
Harrisburg, PA 17105-8551
888/PA-PARKS
Website: *www.dcnr.state.pa.us/personnel/regular.aspx*
Notes: Several different types of Conservation Volunteer opportunities.
Call above number or contact state park directly.
Concession opportunities: *www.dcnr.state.pa.us/stateparks/business*

**Rhode Island State Parks**
Division of Parks & Recreation
2321 Hartford Avenue
Johnston, RI 02919-1719
401/222-2632
Webste: *www.riparks.com*  No volunteer program at this time.
Seasonal employment: *www.riparks.com/employment.htm*

**South Carolina State Park Service**
1205 Pendleton Street
Columbia, SC 29201
803/734-0156
866/224-9339
Website: *www.scprt.com/state-park-service/volunteeropportunities.aspx*
Seasonal employment: *www.scprt.com/state-park-service/employmentstateparks/temporaryseasonalemployment.aspx*
Notes: Many types of volunteers are needed, including campground hosts. Contact the State Parks for a volunteer application. Submit completed application to the park of your choice.

**South Dakota Division of Parks and Recreation**
Volunteer Coordinator
523 East Capitol Avenue
Pierre, SD 57501
605/773-3391
E-mail: *SDParksVolunteers@state.sd.us*
Website: *http://gfp.sd.gov/state-parks/volunteer/default.aspx*
Seasonal employment: *http://gfp.sd.gov/agency/employment/default.aspx*
Employment at Custer State Park:
*www.sdgfp.info/Parks/Regions/Custer/CSPvolunteer.htm*
Notes: Positions can include campground hosts, naturalist assistants, and visitor center attendants. Apply online. The seasonal job announcement is published in December and applications are accepted in December and January. Custer has paid seasonal positions and a concessionaire.

**Tennessee Department of Environment and Conservation**
State Parks and Recreation
401 Church Street
L & C Tower, 7th Floor
Nashville, TN 37243
888/891-8332 or 615/532-5249
E-Mail: *tnstateparks.volunteer@tn.gov*
Website: *www.state.tn.us/environment/parks/volunteer.shtml*
Notes: Applications available at parks, online or from coordinator. Send to indivicual parks or submit to volunteer coordinator.

**Texas Parks and Wildlife**
4200 Smith School Road
Austin, TX 78744-3291
512/389-4746
E-mail: *Lori.Reiley@tpwd.state.tx.us*
Website: *www.tpwd.state.tx.us/involved/volunteer/spdest*
Seasonal employment: *www.tpwd.state.tx.us/business/jobs/*
Notes: Contact the park of your choice or write, call or e-mail the above contact information. Camp hosts plus others needed. Volunteer positions may be short term, for specific events or activities, or ongoing programs.

**State of Utah Natural Resources**
Division of Parks and Recreation
1594 West North Temple Street, Ste. 116
Box 146001
Salt Lake City, UT 84114-6001
Volunteer coordinator: 801/537-3445
E-mail: *robinwatson@utah.gov*
Website: *www.stateparks.utah.gov/volunteer*
Seasonal employment: *www.stateparks.utah.gov/about/employment*
Notes: Positions/duties can include camp hosts, plus docents, golf course marshal, visitor center/gift shop, park or trail maintenance and patrol, OHV and PWC safety education, and general park operations. Call or write for an application. Temporary and seasonal employment: questions, information and to apply, contact parks directly.

**Vermont State Parks**
103 South Main Street
Waterbury, VT 05671-0601
802/241-3655
E-mail: *parks@state.vt.us* for information.
Website: *www.vtstateparks.com/htm/employment.htm* for volunteer and seasonal employment opportunities and applications.
Notes: Season generally runs from early May through mid September or October and recruiting begins in January. Campground volunteers receive free fishing licenses if they choose, propane refills for RVs, free

admission to other state parks, and free or reduced admission to many Vermont tourist attractions.

### Virginia Department of Conservation and Recreation
203 Governor Street, Suite 213
Richmond, VA 23219-2094
800/933-PARK
E-mail: *vspvolunteer@dcr.virginia.gov* or call 703/583-5497 for an application or more information.
Website: *www.dcr.state.va.us/parks/volnteer.htm*
Seasonal Employment: *http://dcrintra.dcr.virginia.gov/DCR_Public/Jobs/JobList.cfm*
Notes: A variety of opportunities. Campground and park host programs for RVers. See site for list of parks needing hosts.

### Washington State Parks and Recreation Commission
1111 Israel Road S.W.
Olympia, WA 98504-2650
360/902-8844
360/902-8583 for application/volunteer packet.
E-mail: *volunteers@parks.wa.gov* Include your mailing address.
Website: *www.parks.wa.gov/volunteers/*
Seasonal employment: *www.parks.wa.gov/jobs/* Hire Park Aides.
Notes: Send application to individual parks or one of the regional offices. Off-season volunteers/hosts needed in some parks. Volunteers needed for both long- and short-term projects. Camp hosts are used in campgrounds, marine parks, interpretive centers and programs and Environmental Learning Centers.

### West Virginia State Parks
Parks and Recreation
Volunteer Coordinator
1900 Kanawha Boulevard, E.
Building 3, Room 714
Charleston, WV 25305-0314
304/558-2764 or 800/CALL-WVA
E-mail: *parks@wvdnr.gov*
Website: *www.wvstateparks.com/community/volpark.htm*

Seasonal employment: *www.wvstateparks.com/summerjobs.html*
Notes: Volunteer park host program for RVers. Campground attendant jobs available at more than 20 state parks.

**Wisconsin State Parks**
Bureau of Parks and Recreation
P.O. Box 7921
101 S. Webster Street
Madison WI 53707-7921
608/266-2621
E-mail: *PeterBiemeier@wisconsin.gov*
Website: *www.dnr.state.wi.us/org/land/parks/voljobs/index.html*
For information: Call 608/264-6136
Seasonal jobs: *www.dnr.state.wi.us/employment*
Notes: Several types of volunteers. Find volunteer application online. Send completed application to park of your choice or the address above.

**Wyoming State Parks and Historic Sites**
Human Resources
2301 Central Avenue, 4th Floor
Cheyenne, WY 82002
307/777-6323
Volunteer coordinator: 307/777-7379
Seasonal employment: 307/777-3631
E-mail: *spcr@state.wy.us*
Website: *http://wyoparks.state.wy.us/index.asp*
Volunteer and seasonal employment information:
*http://wyoparks.state.wy.us/Employment/index.asp*
Notes: Write or call for information and application for volunteer program. Seasonal job applications downloaded online and submitted to individual parks or sites.

# Notes

*"A life isn't significant except for its impact on others."*
*Jackie Robinson*

# Appendix 5
# State revenue offices and tax information

A quick comparison chart of State Individual Income Tax rates at the
**Federation of Tax Administrators website:**
www.taxadmin.org/fta/rate/ind_inc.pdf

**Alabama Department of Revenue**
www.ador.state.al.us

**Alaska Tax Division on Line**
www.tax.state.ak.us
(No state income taxes)

**Arizona Department of Revenue**
www.azdor.gov

**Arkansas Department of Finance and Administration**
www.dfa.arkansas.gov

**California Franchise Tax Board**
www.ftb.ca.gov

**Colorado Department of Revenue**
www.colorado.gov/revenue

**Connecticut Department of Revenue Services**
www.ct.gov/drs

**Delaware Department of Finance, Division of Revenue**
http://revenue.delaware.gov

**Florida Department of Revenue**
Information for new residents:
http://dor.myflorida.com/dor
Call Taxpayer Services, Monday through Friday, 8 a.m. to 7 p.m., ET,
at 800/352-3671.

**Georgia Department of Revenue, Income Tax Division**
https://etax.dor.ga.gov

**Hawaii State Department of Taxation**
www.state.hi.us/tax

**Idaho State Tax Commission**
http://tax.idaho.gov

**Illinois Department of Revenue**
www.revenue.state.il.us

**Indiana Department of Revenue**
www.in.gov/dor

**Iowa Department of Revenue and Finance**
www.iowa.gov/tax

**Kansas Department of Revenue**
www.ksrevenue.org

**Kentucky Revenue Cabinet**
http://revenue.ky.gov

**Louisiana Department of Revenue**
www.rev.state.la.us

**Maine Revenue Services**
www.maine.gov/revenue

**Maryland - Comptroller of Maryland**
www.comp.state.md.us

**Massachusetts Department of Revenue**
www.mass.gov/dor

**Michigan Department of Treasury**
www.michigan.gov/treasury

**Minnesota Department of Revenue**
http://taxes.state.mn.us/Pages/index.aspx

**Mississippi State Tax Commission**
www.dor.ms.gov

**Missouri Department of Revenue, Taxation and Collection**
http://dor.mo.gov

**Montana Department of Revenue**
http://revenue.mt.gov

**Nebraska Department of Revenue**
www.revenue.state.ne.us

**Nevada Department of Taxation**
http://tax.state.nv.us
(No state income tax)

**New Hampshire Department of Revenue**
www.nh.gov/revenue
(Taxes interest, dividends, inheritance)

**New Jersey Division of Taxation**
www.state.nj.us/treasury/taxation

**New Mexico Taxation and Revenue Department**
www.tax.newmexico.gov

**New York Department of Taxation and Finance**
www.tax.state.ny.us

**North Carolina Department of Revenue**
www.dor.state.nc.us

**North Dakota State Tax Department**
www.nd.gov/tax

**Ohio Department of Taxation**
http://www.state.oh.us/tax

**Oklahoma Tax Commission**
www.oktax.state.ok.us

**Oregon Department of Revenue**
www.oregon.gov/DOR

**Pennsylvania Department of Revenue**
www.revenue.state.pa.us

**Rhode Island Division of Taxation**
www.tax.state.ri.us

**South Carolina Department of Revenue**
www.sctax.org/default.htm

**South Dakota Department of Revenue**
www.state.sd.us/drr2/revenue.html
South Dakota has no personal or corporate income tax.

**Tennessee Department of Revenue**
www.state.tn.us/revenue

**Texas Comptroller of Public Accounts**
www.window.state.tx.us
No state income tax. See above for other types of taxes including inheritance.

**Utah State Tax Commission**
http://incometax.utah.gov

**Vermont Department of Taxes**
www.state.vt.us/tax/index.shtml

**Virginia Department of Taxation**
www.tax.virginia.gov

**Washington Department of Revenue**
http://dor.wa.gov
No state income taxes

**West Virginia State Tax Department**
www.wvrevenue.gov

**Wisconsin Department of Revenue**
www.dor.state.wi.us

**Wyoming Department of Revenue**
http://revenue.state.wy.us
No personal income taxes

# Notes

*"He [or she] who is overcautious will accomplish little."*
*J.C.F. von Schiller*

# Appendix 6
# State motor vehicle and
# driver's license bureaus

**DMV.org** has links to departments of motor vehicles in all 50 states.
www.dmv.org

**Alabama Department of Public Safety, driver's licenses**
www.dps.state.al.us
**Alabama Department of Revenue, motor vehicle registration**
www.ador.state.al.us/motorvehicle/index.html

**Alaska Department of Administration, Division of Motor Vehicles**
http://doa.alaska.gov/dmv

**Arizona DOT, Motor Vehicles Division**
www.azdot.gov/mvd

**Arkansas Department of Finance and Revenue, Office of Motor Vehicles & Drivers Services**
www.arkansas.gov/dfa

**California Department of Motor Vehicles**
www.dmv.ca.gov/dmv.htm

**Colorado Department of Revenue, Motor Vehicle Group**
www.colorado.gov/revenue/dmv

**Connecticut Licensing Information Center**
www.ct.gov/dmv/site/default.asp

**Delaware Division of Motor Vehicles**
www.dmv.de.gov

**Florida Department of Highway Safety and Motor Vehicles**
www.flhsmv.gov

**Georgia Dept of Motor Vehicle Safety**
www.dds.ga.gov/Drivers

**Idaho Division of Motor Vehicles**
www.itd.idaho.gov

**Illinois Secretary of State**
Information for new residents:
www.sos.state.il.us/services/new_residents.html

**Indiana Bureau of Motor Vehicles**
www.in.gov/bmv

**Iowa Department of Transportation**
www.iowadot.gov

**Kansas Department of Revenue, Division of Motor Vehicles**
www.ksrevenue.org/vehicle.htm

**Kentucky Transportation Cabinet**
www.kytc.state.ky.us

**Louisiana Office of Motor Vehicles**
http://omv.dps.state.la.us

**Maine Bureau of Motor Vehicles**
www.state.me.us/sos/bmv

**Maryland Motor Vehicle Administration**
www.mva.maryland.gov

**Massachusetts Registry of Motor Vehicles**
www.massdot.state.ma.us/rmv

**Michigan Department of State, Driver and Vehicle**
www.michigan.gov/sos

**Minnesota Department of Transportation**
www.dot.state.mn.us/cars.html

**Mississippi State Tax Commission**
Motor vehicle registration:
www.dmv-department-of-motor-vehicles.com/
MS_Mississippi_dmv_department_of_motor_vehicles.htm
**Department of Public Safety**
Driver's license: www.dmv-department-of-motor-vehicles.com/
MS_Mississippi_dmv_department_of_motor_vehicles.htm

**Missouri Dept of Revenue, Motor Vehicle and Driver Licensing**
http://dor.mo.gov

**Montana Department of Justice, Motor Vehicle Division**
www.doj.mt.gov/driving

**Nebraska Department of Motor Vehicles**
www.dmv.state.ne.us

**Nevada Department of Motor Vehicles and Public Safety**
http://nevadadmv.state.nv.us

**New Hampshire Department of Safety, Division of Motor Vehicles**
www.nh.gov/safety/dmv

**New Jersey Motor Vehicle Services**
www.state.nj.us/mvc

**New York Department of Motor Vehicles**
www.nydmv.state.ny.us

**North Carolina Division of Motor Vehicles**
www.ncdot.org/DMV

**North Dakota Department of Transportation/ Driver, Vehicle, Fleet Services**
www.dot.nd.gov

**Ohio Bureau of Motor Vehicles**
www.bmv.ohio.gov

**Oklahoma Tax Commission Vehicle registration:**
www.tax.ok.gov/motveh.html
**Oklahoma Dept of Public Safety -Drivers licenses:**
www.dps.state.ok.us/dls

**Oregon Driver and Motor Vehicle Services**
www.oregon.gov/ODOT/DMV

**Pennsylvania Department of Transportation**
www.dmv.state.pa.us

**Rhode Island Division of Motor Vehicles**
www.dmv.ri.gov

**South Carolina Department of Motor Vehicles**
www.scdmv.org/DMVNew

**South Dakota Motor Vehicles Division**
www.state.sd.us/drr2/motorvehicle/index.htm

**Tennessee Department of Revenue, Vehicle Title and Registration**
www.tn.gov/revenue/vehicle/
**Tennessee Department of Safety, Drivers Services**
www.state.tn.us/safety/dlmain.htm

**Texas Department of Motor Vehicles**
http://www.txdmv.gov

**Utah Division of Motor Vehicles**
http://dmv.utah.gov

**Vermont Department of Motor Vehicles**
http://dmv.vermont.gov

**Virginia Department of Motor Vehicles**
www.dmv.state.va.us

**Washington Department of Licensing**
www.dol.wa.gov/

**West Virginia Department of Transportation**
www.transportation.wv.gov

**Wisconsin DOT Division of Motor Vehicles**
www.dot.wisconsin.gov/drivers

**Wyoming Department of Transportation**
www.dot.state.wy.us/wydot

# Notes

*"Every thought, decision, and action moves you
closer to or further from achieving your goals -
Everything counts!"*
*The Goals Guy at www.goalsguy.com*

# Appendix 7
## Janice's grocery shopping list

When my husband, Gabby, and I became full-time RVers in the mid-1980s, a situation occurred that was totally unexpected: Grocery shopping in a different market, in a different city every time supplies were needed.

Now, I knew I wasn't on a different planet and many stores were laid out in a similar fashion. Nonetheless, I became frustrated with my usual style of keeping a grocery list. I had to come up with a better method than simply jotting down an item on a piece of scrap paper whenever I thought it was needed and ending up with a list that jumped from one type of product to another.

What I designed was a list with headers in alphabetical sequence by shape or style of items. For example, the first column of the list is titled, Boxes, followed by Cans. Next I had columns for Dairy, Freezer, Fruits, Jars, Meats, Starches, Vegetables, and last, Miscellaneous, such as cleaning products, paper goods or pharmaceutical supplies.

Now, when I run out of, say, cereal, that item is written down in the Box column. If I happen to have a coupon for that product, an asterisk is plugged in next to the item, and the coupon is immediately attached to the list.

Once my list is full (or near-full), it automatically becomes market day no matter where we are. The list, with coupons attached, and a pen, accompany me. As I cruise each aisle, I simply shop by shape. No more scanning a piece of scratch paper from top to bottom each time I come to a new item on the shelf. When each product goes into the shopping cart, it is crossed off the list and I don't have to look for it again. A quick glance down each column indicates whether the columns are complete, and, of course, when they are, shopping is done.

## Sharing the list

The way the list is made up, it can be split down the middle and if there are two of you shopping, each of you can take half the list and shopping is accomplished in half the time.

If you stick to what is on the list, you'll avoid impulse buying, and consequently, save even more money. I've shared the list with friends and have been told they are still using this method after making changes to suit their own shopping needs.

One added suggestion is to permanently add the names of your favorite products and the chain that carries them. Listing the city wouldn't hurt.

Another way to save time and money is to prepare master lists of your favorite company or holiday meals. Reverse the shopping procedure by circling only those items you need.

For me, this is shopping made simple and is a system that has worked well for us for many years. Now, if we could only remember where we parked the car in that strange parking lot.

*Author's note:* Janice Lasko shared her grocery shopping list with me in 1994. This list was a lifesaver the three seasons we worked at Bull Frog marina at Lake Powell, Utah. We shopped four hours away in Grand Junction every four to six weeks. If we forgot something, we were out of luck until the next trip. The little grocery at the marina was expensive and had few items we needed. I kept the list handy and immediately wrote down anything we ran out of or would need on the next trip.

Since I was planning meals for a month or more, I would list my menu on the back and as I decided on a meal, I would record any ingredients I needed in the appropriate column. That way I didn't plan lasagna and get home with no ricotta cheese.

Our boss made a refrigerator available for us to freeze bread and meat. We were able to supplement our diet with fresh fruit and vegetables locally. We ate once or twice a week at the concessionaire dining room, which had an excellent salad bar. Fellow workers shared produce from their gardens and fruit trees planted in the housing area produced peaches and apricots.

To take into account my shopping patterns, I modified the headings Janice used slightly to the ones you see on the following page. Feel free to do the same.

| FRUIT/ VEGETABLES | BOXES/ JARS | CANS | PASTA BEANS | BAKING/ SPICES | BREADS/ MEAT | DAIRY/ FROZEN | HOUSEHOLD /MISC/WLMT |
|---|---|---|---|---|---|---|---|
|  |  |  |  |  |  |  |  |
|  |  |  |  |  |  |  |  |
|  |  |  |  |  |  |  |  |
|  |  |  |  |  |  |  |  |
|  |  |  |  |  |  |  |  |
|  |  |  |  |  | HEALTH FOOD |  |  |
|  |  |  |  |  |  |  |  |
|  |  |  |  |  |  |  |  |
|  |  |  |  |  |  |  |  |

# Menu/notes

**Note:** If you have a convection oven and have wondered how to use it, what pans or dishes to use or how to convert your recipes, *I Have a Convection Oven in My RV. Now What?* by Adrienne Kristine can help. Available in print or e-Book format at RVLifestyleExperts.com.

# Appendix 8
# Budget worksheet

| (Per month) | Now | Full-timing |
|---|---|---|
| **RV payment/housing** | $ _____ | $ _____ |
| **Food, including restaurants** | $ _____ | $ _____ |
| **Health** | | |
|   Medical insurance | $ _____ | $ _____ |
|   Other medical expenses | $ _____ | $ _____ |
| **Camping Fees** | | |
|   Membership parks & campground fees | $ _____ | $ _____ |
| **Transportation** | | |
|   Fuel | $ _____ | $ _____ |
|   Insurance, incl. towing | $ _____ | $ _____ |
|   License & reg. | $ _____ | $ _____ |
|   Maintenance | $ _____ | $ _____ |
| **Communication** | | |
|   Telephone and Internet | $ _____ | $ _____ |
|   Mail service | $ _____ | $ _____ |
| **Other** | | |
|   Clothing | $ _____ | $ _____ |
|   Gifts | $ _____ | $ _____ |
|   Laundry | $ _____ | $ _____ |
|   Life insurance | $ _____ | $ _____ |
|   Memberships- clubs | $ _____ | $ _____ |
|   Federal/state taxes | $ _____ | $ _____ |
|   Propane | $ _____ | $ _____ |
|   TV/satellite | $ _____ | $ _____ |
|   Misc. | $ _____ | $ _____ |
| **Total** | $ _____ | $ _____ |

X 12 = _____/yr    x12=_____/yr

# Notes

*"There ain't no free lunches in this country. And don't go spending your whole life commiserating that you got raw deals. You've got to say, 'I think that if I keep working at this and want it bad enough, I can have it.'"*
Lee Iacocca

# Appendix 9
## Stephanie Bernhagen's
## Budget worksheet

This worksheet will help you evaluate your expenses today, help you determine what your expenses will be in the full-timing lifestyle and help you make a decision if you have enough money or will need to work on the road. The categories listed are typical categories, but may not include all of your expenses, so don't forget to add your unique expenses. Be sure all your dollar amounts are for the same period, i.e. monthly, quarterly, or annual.

|  | TODAY | FULL-TIMING |
|---|---|---|
| **Camping** | | |
| · **Campground Fees** | $_____ | $_____ |
| · **Membership Fees** | $_____ | $_____ |
| **Clothing** | | |
| · **Laundry** | $_____ | $_____ |
| · **New Clothing** | $_____ | $_____ |
| **Communications** | | |
| · **Phone** | $_____ | $_____ |
| · **Calling Card** | $_____ | $_____ |
| · **Postage** | $_____ | $_____ |
| · **Mail Service** | $_____ | $_____ |
| · **Internet Access** | $_____ | $_____ |
| · **Message Service** | $_____ | $_____ |
| **Entertainment** | | |
| · **Cable/Satellite TV** | $_____ | $_____ |
| · **Admission Fees** | $_____ | $_____ |

- Movies                      $_____          $_____
- Books/CDs/
  Newspapers                  $_____          $_____
- Crafts/Hobbies              $_____          $_____
- Entertaining Others $_____                  $_____
- Other                       $_____          $_____

## Fuel
- Towed/Tow                   $_____          $_____
- Motorhome                   $_____          $_____

## Food
- Groceries                   $_____          $_____
- Dining Out                  $_____          $_____

## Health
- Health Insurance            $_____          $_____
- Dental Insurance            $_____          $_____
- Vision Insurance            $_____          $_____
- Prescription
  Insurance                   $_____          $_____
- OTC Drugs                   $_____          $_____
- Out-of-Pocket
  Medical Expenses            $_____          $_____
- Long-term Health            $_____          $_____

## Home/Vehicle Insurance
- Homeowners                  $_____          $_____
- Renters                     $_____          $_____
- Vehicle                     $_____          $_____
- RV                          $_____          $_____
- Road Service                $_____          $_____

## Housing/RV
- House Mortgage              $_____          $_____
- Property Taxes              $_____          $_____

- Home Owners
  Dues                  $_____        $_____
- Home
  Maintenance           $_____        $_____
- Rent                  $_____        $_____
- RV Loan               $_____        $_____
- RV Maintenance        $_____        $_____
- RV Registration       $_____        $_____

## Pets
- Food                  $_____        $_____
- Veterinarian          $_____        $_____
- Kennel                $_____        $_____

## Savings
- RV/Vehicle
  Replacement           $_____        $_____
- Medical
  Deductible            $_____        $_____
- Property Purchase     $_____        $_____
- Care Facility         $_____        $_____
- Burial                $_____        $_____

## Taxes
- State                 $_____        $_____
- Federal               $_____        $_____

## Utilities
- Electric              $_____        $_____
- Propane               $_____        $_____
- Natural Gas           $_____        $_____
- Sewer/Water           $_____        $_____
- Other                 $_____        $_____

## Vehicle
- **Loan**            $_____          $_____
- **Registration**    $_____          $_____
- **Maintenance**     $_____          $_____

## Work
- **Work Related Expenses**    $_____          $_____

## Miscellaneous
- **Storage Unit**     $_____          $_____
- **Gifts**            $_____          $_____
- **Life Insurance**   $_____          $_____
- **Other**            $_____          $_____

|                    | **TODAY** | **FULL-TIMING** |
|--------------------|-----------|-----------------|
| **Total Expenses** | $_____  | $_____        |

The following one-time expenses will deplete your savings. Be sure to account for one-time expenses and subtract them from your savings before you determine what you can earn on your savings. (Unless you plan to raise additional money for these expenses before making the purchase.)

**FULL-TIMING**

## One-Time Expenses
- **RV Purchase Without Loan**       $_____
- **Vehicle Purchase Without Loan**  $_____
- **Solar Panels**                   $_____
- **Heater**                         $_____
- **RV Accessories**                 $_____
- **Initial Membership Costs**       $_____
- **Other Expenses**                 $_____

| | TODAY | FULL-TIMING |
|---|---|---|
| **Income** | | |
| · **Investments** | $_____ | $_____ |
| · **Interest** | $_____ | $_____ |
| · **IRA, 401K, etc.** | $_____ | $_____ |
| · **Pension** | $_____ | $_____ |
| · **Social Security** | $_____ | $_____ |
| · **Work** | $_____ | $_____ |
| · **Other** | $_____ | $_____ |
| | TODAY | FULL-TIMING |
| **Total Income** | $_____ | $_____ |

# Budget notes

*Some couples go over their budgets very carefully*
*every month. Others just go over them.*
*Katherine Mansfield*

*"Find a job you love and add five days to
every week."*
H. Jackson Brown

# Appendix 10
# Three RV worker stories

In this appendix we have stories of the work experiences of three RV workers. They are expanded to give you some ideas of the variety available and more details on how some working RVers have put it all together.

In the first story, Bill and I share how we targeted a specific geographical area in which to work and fulfilled our Alaskan dream. Normally we prefer to apply to national parks. However, to work in Alaska, we were willing to work for another employer and make less money. We share the many resources we used to put together a geographic job search.

In the second story, Janice Lasko, editor of *Escapees* magazine, recounts their fascinating work history. Their preference is working in cold locations because they love to ski. They have held some unique positions while doing what they love.

Finally, Lou Schneider shares a variety of work experiences he has had on the road. He obtained his Commercial Driver's License so he could make more money on the road.

## PUTTING IT ALL TOGETHER:
## OUR ALASKA DREAM COME TRUE

When you have a specific destination or location where you want to work, and that is the overriding factor for your employment choice for the season, it is time to use all you've learned about finding jobs. You may not be as concerned about the type of job as much as the location, so the important thing is to get job offers. How we got jobs in Alaska is a review of the many techniques we have covered. If you too would like to work in Alaska, see the resources we used in **Resources** (Appendix 10).

Traveling and working in Alaska had been one of my dreams for years. Five years after hitting the road, we focused on finding summer jobs in Alaska.

Getting a job in Alaska isn't difficult; employment opportunities are plentiful. Cruise lines bring myriad tourists to ports along the Inside Passage. Many tourists visit the main part of Alaska — Anchorage, Denali and Fairbanks — in RVs or on tours connected with their cruise package. Holland America and Princess also have land-based operations, hotels and bus tours in several locations.

Skagway, where we worked, adds about a thousand seasonal workers to its year-round population of 700. Major employers include White Pass & Yukon Route Railroad, National Park Service, Princess Tours, Gray Line Tours, Skagway Street Cars, Westmark Hotel, and Temsco Helicopters. Retail stores also hire.

Wages are generally higher in Alaska, but that is offset by the cost of getting there and the higher cost of living. Weather and extended daylight are factors too. The panhandle of Alaska, along the Inside Passage, is coastal rainforest. Annual rainfall varies from 30" in Skagway, to over 150" in Ketchikan. Summer temperatures are generally cool, though occasionally temperatures can reach 90 degrees. Long daylight hours make it difficult for some people to sleep.

> **Wages are generally higher in Alaska**

We began searching for potential summer employers in November. We applied to just about any employer so we would have definite jobs before heading north. Since Seattle to Skagway is 1,800 miles and it's more than 2,400 miles to Anchorage, travel is a big expense.

## Housing

Make sure you have housing or an RV site lined up before you leave. We had heard that RVers parked the whole summer at Wal-Marts or Fred Myers and were told by an employer in Juneau that we could park at the Fred Myers the whole summer. We later found out that was not allowed. We interviewed with a Denali concessionaire who could not provide an RV site nor a place to park our RV if we stayed in their housing. He suggested a boondocking area about 20 miles away, but we were not comfortable with that option since we could not check it out beforehand.

RV parks may be limited. In Skagway, at the time, only one of the three RV parks had a monthly rate. The park was expensive and we were packed in like sardines. We found that most Skagway employers who provided RV sites or employee housing charged their employees rent.

Be alert to camphosting opportunities. Page and Ardith acted as camp-ground hosts in an Anchorage campground during off hours in exchange for a site. They still had time for full time jobs. The next year they were able to park at the RV dealership where they worked. Halfway through the season, Bill got the job camphosting at the NPS campground in nearby Dyea. We eliminated rent from our budget and had a gorgeous, quiet setting for the rest of the summer.

Ron and Val contacted Halsingland Hotel in Haines, and lined up jobs in their RV park. Their paid positions came with site, plus many other perks like free and discounted tours and transportation. A bonus for Ron — great fishing!

> **Make sure you have housing or an RV site lined up before you leave.**

Bill had fun helping visitors pan for gold at Liarsville (and telling lies!) and I gave talks and tours as a ranger at Klondike Gold Rush National Historical Park. For two summers, we took advantage of free and discounted prices offered by tourist attractions to "summer locals" at the beginning of each season. On weekends, we explored nearby Alaska, British Columbia and the Yukon Territory. We kayaked in Glacier Bay and panned for gold near Dawson City.

For us the scenery, wildlife, and history made our summers in Alaska a dream come true.

## Other tips

- ✔ **Start early:** Begin in November or December prior to the summer you are targeting. Some employers fill their positions very early.
- ✔ **Express your interest** even if there are no current openings. A former employee may not come back.
- ✔ **Keep in contact** with employers for whom you would really like to work. The more contacts you have with a potential employer, the more likely you are to be remembered for that last-minute opening.
- ✔ **Apply to many employers:** Don't put all your eggs in one basket. You can always turn down a job offer; if you didn't apply, it may be too late.

✔ **Network:** Now is the time to go back through your **Job Notebook** and see if you have any notes that would help you. Contact everyone you know who might have knowledge of jobs in this area. As you talk to employers or the Chamber of Commerce, ask them if they know of anyone else who might be hiring.

## WHISTLE WHILE WE WORK BY JANICE LASKO

I knew I was in for a fair amount of traveling when my husband Gabby proposed in early 1971 saying, "Let's fly to Jamaica to be married." We were living a good distance from Kingston, in Marina del Rey, California.

It took nearly one year of preparation and corresponding with the Magistrate of Home Affairs to gather the proper documentation. We finally married in Kingston at the Magistrate's home and honeymooned on the island in December 1971. There were three people in attendance at the celebration: the Magistrate, who performed the ceremony; his son, who doubled as our photographer and witness; and the Magistrate's house-keeper, who was the second witness, played the appropriate wedding march and served the celebratory champagne. It was intimate and special.

We have since traveled to Europe on several occasions, Mexico at least a half dozen times, taken cruises and island-hopped in the Pacific and Caribbean. One summer we self-crewed a sailboat with two other couples around the British Virgin Islands. These trips would be preludes to our eventual ease into full-time RVing because we felt RVing would be the best way to see North America in depth via the back roads.

> **"We began traveling in an RV with a bang."**

Although I say we eventually eased into full-timing, I should mention we began traveling in an RV with a bang. In 1982 we had already sold our home and had quit high-pressure jobs in the city. Gabby was a construction contractor and I was part of the exciting world of advertising in the Los Angeles area. We moved into our vacation condo in a ski resort community in the California High Sierras, promising ourselves to take only fun jobs and work just enough to support our favorite hobbies — skiing, windsurfing and traveling.

### Hitting the road full time

That all changed when one day in 1985 we saw a used class A motorhome for sale, test drove it and bought it. (The motorhome really wasn't for sale; we just kind of talked the owner into selling it to us.) Our first trip was a whopping 17 miles from our condo, and each time we thought of something we had forgotten to bring with us, we simply drove back home to pick it up and then returned to our campsite. We have become much more organized and have subsequently realized one of the biggest advantages to traveling in a motorhome is having all of our stuff with us all the time.

We eventually extended our distances and found we were spending more time in our motorhome traveling than we were in our fixed dwelling. That's when we began to think about traveling on a full-time basis. We wondered if it could be done and whether others sold everything, abandoned family and friends and hit the road for good. Our condo sold in less than one week and closed escrow by the second week. So, whether others did or didn't go on the road full-time, that's what we wanted to do and did. We soon learned we were not alone.

> **"Full-time traveling is a way of life, not a permanent vacation."**

We also discovered that full-time traveling is a way of life, not a permanent vacation. New restaurants are fun, but not three times a day. Laundry, shopping and cooking still must be accomplished and the rig needs to be cleaned on a regular basis, although it only takes about one hour to do a thorough job. Most importantly, vehicle maintenance takes a high priority. All these things can't wait to be taken care of as usually happens at the end of a vacation.

Eventually we realized we wanted and needed to divide our attention between our hobbies, traveling and maintaining an income that would allow us to remain living on the road. So we became the opposites of snowbirds (those who follow the sun and camp in southern climates all winter). We didn't run from the snow for the Sun Belt each winter. That way we could find jobs in order to pursue and support the expensive sport of snow skiing.

## Winter work

I'm an early-blooming baby boomer. Gabby is 18 years my senior and, I must add, in excellent condition. He prides himself on skiing anywhere from 50 to 100 days each season. In spite of his white hair, we are thrilled at the acceptance we've both had when applying for work.

Did I say work? That's right. We found that, in order to stay ahead of the financial game and remain on the road, the word "work" would have to reenter our vocabulary and become part of our lives again. As a result, we have added some unusual and extremely interesting skills to our experiences on the road, which come second to the people we've met and the friends we've made. Another benefit of working in this lifestyle is the network of people who are doing what we do and who share job possibilities. In a sense, one job has led to another in different parts of the country and sometimes with the same friends.

For instance, one winter season we sold lift tickets at a ski resort in Oregon. One of the couples we met also worked at the resort and were camped near us in the same RV park. We have remained in touch with this couple ever since, traveled together on several occasions and worked with them again, selling Christmas trees in central California one year, and in Texas a few years later. By the way, the perks for that ticket-selling job were numerous. In addition to a salary, there was a company bus from town to the mountain, which gave our truck a much-needed rest that winter, free skiing and a locker at the base of the mountain to store our ski gear. And that gave us oodles of extra storage space in the rig that season. We were finished selling lift tickets by 11:00 a.m. and were on the hill skiing by noon, following a discounted meal on the mountain.

Preparing the Christmas tree lots and subsequent three to four weeks of tree sales was physically demanding. However, that turned into a plus for us because the physical labor conditioned us for the slopes. Since we were through selling trees by Christmas day, we looked for the best snow conditions in the country and drove our fifth-wheel trailer to the area as quickly as possible to set up for the rest of the winter. More than one season found us back in Mammoth Lakes, California, our former homebase. It was a simple task to procure jobs amongst former neighbors and be working by mid-January. One year Gabby went into show business in Mammoth at the candy counter at the local theater. Then one of his coworkers led him to a desk clerk position at a motel in

**"One year Gabby went into show business..."**

town. We stayed past the winter that season, which gave Gabby the opportunity to work in the maintenance department of the motel.

That same year I was a nanny (nicknamed by the youngsters 'Janny the Nanny') for a four-year-old and his sister, just 13 months his junior. Being a close-knit town, word spread, and there were days when I was taking care of seven children, all under the age of six. It was exciting to watch these youngsters grow and mature as winter turned to summer and eventually autumn. Their mom and dad owned a restaurant, and from time to time I'd fill in as a hostess in the best pizza house in town. The drawback with this job was the growing attachment to the children. After eight months, it definitely was time to move on.

> **"Short visits are better than no visit at all."**

We have stayed in touch with another couple we met when we first began to travel via RV and have met up with them all over the country 42 times, some planned, other times by sheer good fortune. The shortest visit was under one hour when they happened to see our parked rig from the highway while on their way to a new job in the next state. Our motto is, "in this lifestyle, short visits are better than no visit at all." Well, this couple interested us in working for a company that produces RV park guides with area maps pinpointing local businesses. Although we didn't work for the company too long, we were rewarded with a supportive home-office staff and the ability to remain on the move, seeing new, as yet unexplored towns, in addition to complimentary campsites, plus, of course, that oh-so-thrilling-to-receive commission check.

## Time for work and play

An added challenge to our job hunting is to leave the days free to ski and play. One season I did data entry for a catalog company filling Thanksgiving and Christmas gift orders. Being willing to work the 4:00 p.m.-to-midnight shift meant time-and-a-half and sometimes double-time pay. The company provided a data entry/computer training course at no expense to new employees and superior fruit items at the end of each shift that didn't quite meet top-quality standards for shipment to customers.

One interesting time found Gabby and me sharing the rig for a mere four hours a day. Gabby was the night-shift bartender for a ski resort and didn't arrive home until midnight. I awoke at 4:00 a.m. to provide

50 radio stations with ski and weather conditions. When I was done by 9:00 a.m., I would fetch Gabby, we'd ski a few hours together and start over. Again, we were provided a salary as well as free skiing.

We have both enjoyed the challenge of waiting tables in various restaurants and have also worked in several RV parks in Texas, California, Idaho and Alabama. At these parks we maintained a balancing act of taking reservations, checking guests in and out, cleaning the bathrooms, running a grocery store, shoveling snow out of the RV parking sites and skimming leaves out of the swimming pool. Five days a week in Alabama, I even taught line dancing (now that is not work, it's just plain fun). Maintenance of the grounds at one park gave me the opportunity to freshen up a nine-foot totem pole on a miniature golf course with a new coat of paint while Gabby helped install water, sewer and electric hookups to 10 new sites.

> **"We were provided a salary as well as free skiing."**

For working in RV parks we were rewarded with a free campsite, salary, cost-of-living allowance, and, if we stayed one full year at a park in Idaho, a rather princely bonus. We stayed near beautiful ski resorts in Sun Valley.

As fun and challenging as these jobs were, time seemed to stretch slowly and it became difficult for us not to pick up and go whenever someone pulled out a map or began talking to us about their travel plans.

The jobs are out there almost for the taking. It's just a matter of attitude and willingness and honesty. We try to let our prospective employer know we are interested only in seasonal, part-time employment. This avoids hard feelings when we suffer from "hitch-itch" and begin poring over maps, something we can do for hours on end.

## Motorhome or 5ᵗʰ wheel?

By 1987 we switched from that used motorhome to a new truck and fifth-wheel trailer, which served us well for five years, followed by a second fifth-wheel (same truck). We were delighted with the space the single, 17-foot slide-out provided, which was half the length of the rig. Actually, we were not looking for another new rig, but our latest purchase was a brand-new motorhome. We decided we could always work to pay it off, which is exactly what we are doing.

The latest job offer came from the Escapees RV Club when I was asked to be editor of *Escapees* magazine, produced in Livingston, Texas, national headquarters of the Escapees RV Club. The magazine is a bi-monthly publication for the serious RVers. We had no intention of settling down to such a challenging commitment, but another lesson we've learned is to never say never to anything, even sitting in one place, because you never know what it may lead to. In 2001, I was given the opportunity to continue as *Escapees* magazine editor, but editor-on-the-go. Now, I have my cake and can eat it, too, as we travel and I edit. Gabby has a slice of the pie, too, as he worked this winter in an inn as maitre d' at a ski mountain, Taos Ski Valley in New Mexico.

There are advantages to each type of recreational vehicle, and what works for us seems to change as we age. All we ask is plenty of storage space for our bulky winter clothes and ski gear, as well as the bicycles and golf clubs. (The windsurfing equipment was donated to a younger generation of our family long ago.)

## Sticking to a budget

Because I keep copious records, we are able to account for every penny spent, by category, since day one. The categories are (1) campsites, (2) gas and truck maintenance, (3) groceries, (4) restaurants, (5) telephone, (6) laundry, and (7) gifts, museums, and entertainment. Fixed and unknown expenses, such as campground memberships, dues, insurance, medical, and dental are kept in a separate file. I analyzed six months of working versus six months on the road and found the cost of living to be slightly less while traveling. When we work, I adjust our budget higher, but we are also careful not to fall into the trap of spending what we earn. We try to live frugally so we can rebuild our surplus and be back on the road.

> **"We've traveled over 500,000 miles since 1985."**

Although we've traveled over 500,000 miles since 1985, when looking back, sometimes it seems we've been working more than traveling. But that's okay with us. It turned out better than we originally planned. We first thought we'd RV for two years, see it all and settle down again permanently. We didn't count on becoming so passionate about this way of life; we've discovered it's fun to settle for a short period of time and then hit the road again. No matter which role we're in, we are always looking forward to something new.

The years are whizzing by. We have cut our skiing back to roughly 15 or 20 days a year, and have even slowed down on crisscrossing North America in the RV. If the day comes when we are forced to hang up the keys, maybe we'll do it in some snowbird-type RV park where we can line dance, play cards, golf, take an occasional bike ride or even an airplane trip. But best yet, we'll always look forward to a vacation in any RV. If planned and timed right, the RVer can catch, for example, the Calgary Stampede, the Hot Air Balloon Festival in New Mexico, the Fryeburg Fair in Maine, and then pick up Autumn's burst of fall colors throughout New England. Well, the list of famous events and small, local festivals goes on. The more we see, the more we learn there is to see.

> **"We would not have missed this myriad of job opportunities for the world."**

We would not have missed the myriad job opportunities for the world. Each one has led to discovering a part of our country, a heritage, a way of life that would have remained alien to us had we locked ourselves into that old lifestyle of fixed dwellings and job commuting. We have learned that work is certainly not a four-letter word; it is a means to an end, and never have we faced so many stimulating choices. It's no wonder we have reason to whistle while we work.

For more information about the Escapees RV Club, see **Resources.**

## LOU SCHNEIDER'S WORKING TALES

My work career was as a radio engineer, installing and maintaining broadcast transmitters and all of the related technical equipment. I had been doing this since I was 16 and decided it was time to try something new.

Two years ago I quit my job and started full-timing at age 45. A couple of years prior to this, I moved into my RV and lived in a nearby RV park while I worked. The park rent was much less than what I had paid to rent an apartment, so I put the difference into savings. When I was ready to make the break, my rig was paid for and I had a nice little nest egg.

The first thing I did was get my Class A Commercial Driver's License (CDL). I always wanted to drive a big rig. I'd seen several classified ads from Swift Trucking Company offering CDL training, so I talked to their recruiters and told them I was exploring career options. They said

I could pay for the school up front and not be under any obligation to work for them, but if I did they would reimburse my tuition. So I spent three weeks at the school, then said, "No thanks," after I got my license.

There is an acute shortage of CDL drivers and I found job opportunities are plentiful. While spending last winter in Quartzsite, Arizona, I noticed a truck assembly plant near the California state line. I made some inquiries and applied to the company that had the contract to deliver the new trucks to customers. I was promptly hired, even though I had no commercial driving experience. The assembly plant builds both CDL and non-CDL trucks, and there was a desperate need for drivers with a CDL to deliver the larger trucks. These trucks had 24-foot van bodies, a GVWR over 26,000 lbs., dual drive axles and air brakes. Unloaded they drove about the same as a smaller truck. The pay for delivering these was almost twice as much as delivering a non-CDL truck.

> **"There is an acute shortage of CDL drivers."**

I only delivered a couple of trucks while in Quartzsite, but the money more than covered my living expenses for the three months I stayed there.

## Temporary agency

Later I was in Sacramento and signed up with a temporary agency, Link Staffing. I told them that although I had a Class A license I didn't want to drive anything larger than a Class B truck until I gained more experience. Even so, they kept me as busy as I wanted at $10-15 per hour.

The agency would call the day before an assignment, which I was free to accept or reject. Usually I would report to work at a warehouse or distribution center where there would be a loaded truck waiting. I would follow another truck to a destination or be given a map and sent out on my own. All of these were local deliveries within a 50-mile radius. At the end of the day I would return to Link's office, where they issued a check on the spot. I did this for six weeks, and when I left I was told I could start any time I wished. Link has offices in other major cities and my records could be transferred to any of them.

## Tomatoes

My goal was to find a something I could do for four to six months and earn enough money to carry me through the rest of the year. I came

344  *Support Your RV Lifestyle!*

close when I started driving the tomato harvest. I applied to a seasonal trucking company and got a job driving a full Class A rig, a tractor towing two flatbed trailers carrying tubs full of tomatoes. The loaded weight was 80,000 lbs. Drivers are paid based on the delivered weight and mileage traveled, and I was able to average $850 to $1,000 per week. The only disadvantage was it was a 7-day per week job. Once the harvest starts it doesn't let up for two to three months.

> **"They issued a check on the spot."**

I would report to the terminal in the morning, check out the truck, then head south with a set of empty trailers. At the field I would drop off the empty trailers, hitch up a loaded set, then take the load to the cannery. After dropping the loaded trailers at the cannery, I'd get another empty set and repeat the process. Each leg of the process took one to two hours, so I was able to deliver two or three loads each day.

## Don't burn your bridges

After a month I was looking forward to the end of the harvest and returning to the Arizona desert for the winter. That's when I discovered the value of not burning my bridges.

My former boss in radio installation left the company I had worked for about the same time I began driving the tomato harvest. He took a similar position across town at another group of radio stations and quickly discovered there was a backlog of work, including installing several transmitters. He contacted me via e-mail and asked if I would be willing to help him out at consultant rates.

The pay was too good to pass up — $75 per hour for three to four weeks of full-time work. So I left the trucking company with the understanding I could return and finish out the harvest after I had finished installing the transmitters. I never did go back.

I was asked to take a full-time position, and negotiated an arrangement that allows me to travel for extended periods of time plus gives me an ongoing income for the foreseeable future.

I'm classified as a full-time employee so I get company benefits like health insurance and retirement. But I get substantially more annual vacation than standard company policy. While this year the company has a backlog of work and I will only get off two weeks per quarter, in the next year, I will work about six months of the year. I'll work one or two months, then get the same amount of time off. While I am off, the company will continue paying my health insurance and I'll continue to participate in the retirement plan.

## Two things I've learned

✔ Keep your eyes open for employment possibilities. They are everywhere.
✔ Don't overlook the possibility of continuing to work in the career field you are leaving.

It's been an interesting ride so far!"

# Notes

*"If you don't make a total commitment to whatever you're doing, then you start looking to bail out the first time the boat starts leaking. It's tough enough getting that boat to shore with everyone rowing, let alone when a guy stands up and starts putting his life jacket on."*
*Lou Holtz*

# Section V. Resources
## Listed by chapter

## General resources:
### BOOKS ON FULL-TIME RVING
- *The Complete RV Handbook*, Jayne Freeman. At Amazon or Barnes and Noble bookstores.
- *Home is Where You Park It*, Joe and Kay Peterson, RoVers Press. *(www.escapees.com)*
- *Meandering Down the Highway*, Nick Russell. Account of their first year as full-time RVers. *(www.gypsyjournal.net)*
- *The RV Book*, Mark Polk. Comprehensive intro. Also training DVDs on various types of RVs. *(www.rveducation101.com)*
- *Over the Hill: An Ethnography of RVing Seniors in North America,* Dorothy Ayers Counts and David Reese Counts. Results of a study of full-timing. (Amazon.com)
- *The Woman's Guide to Solo RVing*, Jaimie Hall Bruzenak and Alice Zyetz. Print, CD or e-Book. *(www.rvlifestyleexperts.com)*
- *Take Back Your Life! Travel Full-Time in Your RV,* Stephanie Bernhagen, Bernham-Collins. Out of print, but still recommended. Find used at Amazon.com and other booksellers.
- *Retire to an RV: The Roadmap to Affordable Retirement,* Jaimie Hall Bruzenak and Alice Zyetz. Answers questions about the RV lifestyle and provides resources to get started. E-Book. *(www.rvlifestyleexperts.com)*

### BOOKS ON WORKING ON THE ROAD
- *Road Work II: The RVer's Ultimate Income Resource Guide*, Arline Chandler *(www.workamper.com)* 2004.
- *Travel While You Work,* Joe and Kay Peterson. RoVers Press *(www.escapees.com)*
- *Work Your Way Across the USA: You Can Travel and Earn a Living too!* Nick Russell. Publishing Partners. *(www.gypsyjournal.net)*

### RV PUBLICATIONS
- **RV club membership:** Membership includes a subscription to their print magazine.

## RV ELECTRONIC MAGAZINES (e-zines)

- *RV Lifestyle:* Semimonthly e-zine edited by this author. Subscribe at *www.rvlifestyleexperts.com*. Add *RVLifestyleExperts@yahoo.com* to your address book.

## CHAPTER 1: WHAT DO YOU BRING TO THE JOB MARKET?

- **Taking a look at yourself:** A number of books have been written to assist you in looking at your life, deciding on goals for your life or job, and how to achieve them.
  - *What Color is My Parachute?* Richard Bolles' classic book on looking at what careers are a match.
  - *I Could Do Anything if I Only Knew What It Was,* and *It's Only Too Late If You Don't Start Now* by Barbara Sher. All her books are helpful, especially these two.
  - *Finding Your Perfect Work:* Paul and Sarah Edwards. Geared for finding self-employment that works for you. Discover your personal style, then find a match.
  - **Look also:** The Career section of a bookstore or library should have these and other helpful references.

## CHAPTER 3: HOW MUCH MONEY WILL YOU NEED?

### Budgeting and financial management

- **Bankrate.com** has a number of useful financial calculators. At the "Home Page," click on "Calculator." *(www.bankrate.com)*
- **Dave Ramsey's Financial Peace University.** Courses available through churches, other organizations or online: *(www.daveramsey.com/)*
- **BudgetYes!** A personal financial program designed to develop a customized money plan to meet your goals. *(www.stretcher.com/resource/bkstor/ord-form.htm)* or call 954/772-1696 to order.
- **Escapees RV Club:** Discussion forum/RVing on a Budget. *(www.escapees.com)*
- **"Managing Your Money** While Living on the Road is a Breeze," by Lucy Lazarony at Bankrate.com. *(www.bankrate.com/brm/news/auto/20010507a.asp)*
- **North Dakota State University** *NDSU Extension Service.* Taking Charge of Family Finances: Family Money Manager. *(www.ext.nodak.edu/extpubs/yf/fammgmt/he222w.htm)*

- *Over the Hill: An Ethnography of RVing Seniors in North America,* Dorothy Ayers Counts and David Reese Counts. Elaborates on their 1993 study on what RVers spend. The March 2001 edition contains a new section on working RVers and an additional resource section.
- **Quicken money management programs.** User-friendly for those with minimal computer skills. There are several versions of the software available and a free online version. *(www.quicken.com)* Available at office supply stores.
- **Retirement calculator:** Use the "Ballpark E$timator" to calculate how much money you will need to retire. *(www.choosetosave.org/ballpark)*
- *Take Back Your Life! Travel Full-time in an RV,* Stephanie Bernhagen. See Chapter 2. Now out of print, used copies can be purchased at online bookstores. See also **Appendix 9** for a copy of her budget worksheet.

## Benefits
- **AARP** has information on these topics at *(www.aarp.org)*. Social Security and other related topics.
- **Benefits Check Up** is the nation's first 50-state (including the District of Columbia) online service to provide public benefit screening on benefits ranging from health coverage to supplemental income to help in paying utility bills. Millions of older adults who could benefit from a wide array of public programs if they knew about them and how to apply for them. *(www.benefitscheckup.org)*
- **Medicare benefits:** Check benefits and find out about supplemental policies and prescription drugs. Call 800/633-4227 to speak to a customer service representative. *(www.medicare.gov)*
- **Social Security benefits:** Check "Retirement" to determine how to best take those benefits. Information on disability and other benefits. *(www.ssa.gov)*

## Buying an RV
- **RV Buyers Guide:**  If you haven't purchased an RV, read the articles on things to consider, particularly about weight. Overloading your RV is one way to wear it out more quickly. *(www.rvbg.com)*
- **RV Consumer Group:** Before you buy an RV, check *(www.rv.org)*. Worth joining to get rating information on RVs.

- **RV Safety website:** Recall notices, towing laws, plus ratings of RV accessories. Useful articles. *(www.rvsafety.com)*
- **Used RV prices:** If you are considering buying or selling your RV, check prices at *(www.nadaguides.com)*. Complete an appraisal report by inputting model and features. Lemon check by VIN number.

## Income tax, financial planning, estate planning

- **Professionals familiar with the unique issues RVers face.** All are members of the Escapees RV Club.
  - **Dave Loring:** Licensed financial consultant. Free consultation, no charge for placement or management of investment. 800/260-1615. 146 Rainbow Dr., #4650, Livingston, TX 77399-1046.
  - **Alfred Lutz:** Attorney. Tax preparation for all 50 states. Wills and trusts for all except Louisiana. Will give phone advice generally without charge. 530/398-4143. P.O. Box 128, Macdoel, CA 96058. *Alutz@cot.net*
  - **Carol Richards:** Attorney in Livingston, TX. Specializes in wills, estate planning. 936/327-5764.
- **Choose to save:** The Ballpark E$timate is an easy-to-use, two-page worksheet that helps you quickly identify approximately how much you need to save to fund a comfortable retirement.
- **State income tax rates:** Compare state income tax rates at *(www.taxadmin.org/fta/rate/ind_inc.pdf)*

## Insurance - RVs

- **GMAC Insurance:** Mention RV club affiliations. 800/GMAC-123. Get a quote. *(www.gmacinsurance.com/)*
- **Foremost Insurance:** Call 800/527-6136 to find a local agent; 800/262-0170 for quote. *(www.foremost.com)*
- **Good Sam VIP Insurance:** For members. 800/234-3450 for membership information. *(www.goodsamclub.com)*
- **Progressive Insurance Company:** Mention RV club affiliations. 800/776-4737 or *(www.progressive.com)* for quote.
- **Agencies:** Miller Insurance Agency, 800/622-6347 *(www.millerrvinsurance.com/)* and Poliseek, 866/540-7335 *(www.poliseek.com/)* specialize in helping RVers find insurance.

## Membership campgrounds

- **NAM:** Before buying into a membership campground, check the National Association for members' website to see if the campground is experiencing problems. *(www.natlassoc.com)*
- **Membership RV Parks & Discount Camping Clubs:** Alice Zyetz' column for Road Trip America. *(www.roadtripamerica.com/rv/Membership-RV-Parks.htm)*

## CHAPTER 5: HOW EMPLOYERS AND FAMILY CAN REACH YOU: GETTING MAIL AND PHONE CALLS ON THE ROAD.

### Cellular service providers - national

- **AT&T:** 888/333-6651 *(www.wireless.att.com)*
- **Sprint:** 800/SPRINT1 *(www.sprint.com)*
- **Verizon:** 800/2-JOIN-IN *(www.verizonwireless.com)*

## Cellular service

- **Compare cell phone plans:** Compare plans at *(www.myrateplan.com)* and *(www.billshrink.com/?noCache=true&tv=true&_v_alrpd=3)*
- **Cellular service:** Check cell reception in an area at *(www.cellreception.com)*
- **Pick a provider:** Compare cell phone providers at *(http://reviews.cnet.com/cell-phone-buying-guide/)*
- **Compare prepaid cell phone plans:** See *(www.prepaidreviews.com/)*

## Federal Express

- **Federal Express locations:** Pick up your package at a Federal Express location. Free service. Ask at a Federal Express drop off location or see *(www.fedex.com)*. "Ship/Locations," then "Advance Search Options- hold at location." Customer service: 800/463-3339.

## United Parcel Service:

- **UPS:** Pick up your package at a UPS location. It must be one of the centers, not a retail location. Call 800/742-5877 to check.

## Voice mail

- **Cellular service:** Voice messaging is usually included.

- **Voice Connect Inc:** Provides voice mail service if you don't have it through your cell phone. Or, do an Internet search for a company. *(www.voiceconnectinc.com)*

## Zip Codes and toll-free directory
- **USPS zip code** lookup at 800/275-8777 and *(www.usps.com)*. Find general delivery zip code for a city. Type "General Delivery" on the delivery address line for lookup.
- **Toll-free directory:** *(http://inter800.com/)* or *(http://www.internettollfree.com/)* Also White and Yellow pages online.

# CHAPTER 6: HOW TO USE A COMPUTER IN YOUR JOB SEARCH
## Computers for RVers
- *Campin' and Computin' — The Second Editon: A Basic Guide for RVers New to Computers:* by Eric Anderson. Good intro. *(www.thervitguy.com)*
- *The Digital RV:* by Richard Charpentier. Covers choosing a laptop computer, computer maintenance, Internet on the road.

## Computer education
- **Online courses:** Computer Training Schools website lists schools that offer programs, including online computer schools. *(www.computertrainingschools.com)*
- **Senior Net** has learning centers in 26 states and provides adults 50+ with education in computer technology. 900 Lafayette St., Ste. 605, Santa Clara, CA 95050. 408/615-0699. *(www.seniornet.org)*

## E-mail on the road
- **Free Web-based e-mail:** Hotmail (*www.hotmail.com*), Yahoo, (*www.yahoo.com*) and GMail *(http://mail.google.com/mail)* are three popular services. Sign up at websites. You can check e-mail anytime you have an Internet connection, on any computer.
- **Discussion Forums:** InternetbyCellPhone@yahoogroups.com and InternetbyWiFi@yahoogroups.com. Sign up at *(http://groups.yahoo.com)*.
- **Peek e-mail device:** A mobile device that allows you to send and receive e-mail while you're on-the-go. *(www.getpeek.com/)*

## Wireless technology

- **Full-timer Communication website:** Options for calling cards, cellular service and Internet connections. *(www.full-timer.com)*
- **Traveling with laptop computers:** See *(www.roadnews.com)* for articles and advice.
- **Find a Wi-Fi signal:** 14 ways, including several databases for searching. *(http://webworkerdaily.com/2008/03/31/14-ways-to-find-a-wifi-signal/)*
- **Wi-Fi FreeSpot Directory:** RV parks listings. *(www.wififreespot.com/rv.html)*
- **Wi-Fi hotspots:** *(www.wi-fihotspotlist.com)*
- **Wi-Fi Planet:** Information and tutorials on this technology. *(www.wi-fiplanet.com)*

## CHAPTER 7: HOW TO PREPARE RÉSUMÉS AND COVER LETTERS FOR WORKING ON THE ROAD

### Résumés

- **AARP:** Provides help on résumés and sample résumés plus other related articles. *(www.aarp.org/work/job-hunting/info-08-2010/how-to-refresh-your-resume.html)*
- **Workamping 101:** Six-part audio-visual course on finding your first job and creating a résumé. Recorded sessions, handouts and exercises. *(www.workamper.com/WKN2008_university/workamper101/)*
- **Awesome Applicants résumés:** List your résumé for working on the road in a searchable database at Workamper.com. Sample résumé.
- **Damngood.com:** Yana Parker's thorough website with résumé tips, advice plus other resources. *(www.damngood.com)*.
- *Dynamic Cover Letters* by Hansen and Hansen. Ten Speed Press. A complete book about cover letters. *(www.quintcareers.com/dcl.html)*.
- **Resumania:** Under Career Tips, good advice for résumés from *Job Hunting for Dummies®, 2nd edition.* Lots of lines included in résumés and cover letters that did *not* help the job-seeker. Good for a laugh. *(www.resumania.com)*
- *You Shoulda Listened to Your Mother: 36 Timeless Success Tips for Working Women* by Alice Zyetz. Chapter on résumés elaborates on functional vs chronological résumés, strong words, do's and don'ts. *(www.rvlifestyleexperts.com)*

## CHAPTER 8: HOW TO DO A JOB SEARCH
### Publications for finding RV-related or seasonal jobs
- *The Caretaker Gazette*, P.O. Box 4005, Bergheim, TX 78004. 830/336-3939. *caretaker@caretaker.org (www.caretaker.org). An* online subscription is $29.95/year; print is $34.95/year.
- *Workamper News,* 709 W. Searcy St., Heber Springs, AR 72543-3761. 800/446-5627. *info@workamper.com (www.workamper.com).* Subscription is $33/year for basic; $48 for WorkamperPlus subscription and $42 for an online WorkamperPlus subscription.

**Campground directories** See Resources for Chapter 14.

### Networking
- **Workamper forums:** Open to all, Workamper Experiences forum for Plus members. *(http://forums.workamper.com)*
- *You Shoulda Listened to Your Mother* by Alice Zyetz. Chapter on networking and informational interviews. *(www.rvlifestyleexperts.com)*
- **Other resources:** Forums on working on the road at *(http://forums.workamper.com).* Other forums on working on the road at *(www.rvtravel.com)* and *(www.rv.net/forum)* and at Escapees at *(www.rvnetwork.com).*

## CHAPTER 9: HOW TO USE THE INTERNET TO FIND WORK
### Campgrounds with Wi-Fi
- **Campground listings:** See page 353, "Wireless Technology."
- **Other:** Do an Internet search for RV campgrounds with Wi-Fi. Campground directories usually indicate if an RV park has Wi-Fi.

### Job search - how to use the Internet
- **Job Hunters Bible:** Website by Richard Bolles, author of *What Color is Your Parachute?* Worth a look. An excellent resource to using the Internet for job hunting, plus links. *(www.jobhuntersbible.com)*
- **The Riley Guide:** Comprehensive gateway to job search sites, including conventions and trade shows of specific occupations and job-specific agencies. Link to key job search sites. *(www.rileyguide.com)*

## Job search - websites with seasonal jobs

- **Coolworks:** Employers and jobs are grouped by location or category. *(www.coolworks.com)*
- **Job Monkey:** Seasonal positions. Bookstore has books on jobs and careers. *(www.jobmonkey.com)*
- **Fun Jobs:** Lists fun jobs, fun companies, job fairs, events and resources. *(www.funjobs.com/)*
- **Seasonal employment:** Lists summer and winter seasonal employers, several concessionaires at national parks. *(www.seasonalemployment.com)*
- **Summer Jobs:** Lists jobs by state. Look under "More world-wide jobs." *(www.summerjobs.com)*
- **Workamper News:** Some postings. "WorkamperPlus" includes database, forums for questions and posting work experiences, along with your print subscription. Post situation wanted ads. *(www.workamper.com)*
- **Jobalot.com:** Keyword "seasonal." *(www.jobalot.com)*
- **Wiseworker.com:** Jobs and resources for older workers. *(www.wiseworker.com)*

## Job search - websites with some seasonal jobs

- **Career One Stop:** This page will help you locate alternative sites where you can search for jobs or prospective employees. *(www.jobbankinfo.org/)*
- **Career Builder:** Partners with 140 newspapers, personalized job hunting tools, skills certification, and articles. Access to more than one million jobs on the Internet. *(www.careerbuilder.com)*
- **Hot jobs:** Search by type of job, location or company. Highly rated site. *(http://hotjobs.yahoo.com)*
- **Monster Jobs:** Huge job search site. *(www.monster.com)*

## Newspapers on the Web

- **AdQuest 3D:** Database of more than 374,000 jobs, updated daily by 1600-plus newspapers. Search by geographic area or key word like "summer employment." *(http://adquest.com/search/search.asp?BRD=1&PAG=87)*
- **Newspaper Association of America:** Links to most newspapers. *(www.newspaperlinks.com/voyager.cfm)*

## CHAPTER 10: HOW TO INTERVIEW AND GET RESULTS

### Interviewing

- *Interviewing for Seasonal Positions: The Answers and Keywords That Will Help You Land a Short-Term Post: (www.hcareers.com/us/resourcecenter/tabid/306/articleid/345/default.aspx)*
- Phone interview tips: *(http://jobsearch.about.com/cs/interviews/a/phoneinterview.htm)*
- How to master telephone interviews: *(www.workfree.com/tb/IN_telephone.cfm)*
- Telephone interviews and other interview tips: *(www.jobmonkey.com/main/html/telephone.html)*
- Workamping 102: Interviewing for a Job: Three-part audio-visual class taught by Jaimie Hall Bruzenak in partnership with Workamper University. Includes recorded video plus handouts and exercises. *(www.workamper.com/WKN2008_university/workamper102/)*

## CHAPTER 11: HOW TO NEGOTIATE FOR BETTER COMPENSATION

### Negotiation

Check the Job Search websites listed in Chapter 9 for articles on negotiation.

## CHAPTER 13: LEGAL AND TAX CONSIDERATIONS

### State and federal income tax

- Tax Foundation:  Chart with state income tax by state. (States can change their tax codes at any time so check with the state revenue office for the latest information. **Appendix 5** has websites)
- Federation of Tax Administrators: Compare state tax rates for income tax, sales tax and others. *(www.taxadmin.org/fta/rate/tax_stru.html)*

## CHAPTER 14: HOW TO FIND JOBS WITH A CAMPSITE

### Campground directories

- Go Camping America: ARVC's campground information online at *(www.gocampingamerica.com)*

- *Military RV, Camping & Outdoor Recreation Areas Around The World:* Order from Military Living Publications, P.O. Box 2347, Falls Church, VA 22042-0347 or at *(www.militaryliving.com)* under Books. Website includes RV/camping links.
- *Trailer Life Directory:* Online at *(www.tldirectory.com)*. Order the directory in print or on CD at site or check magazine.
- *Wheelers RV Resort and Campground Guide*: Directory can be purchased at many RV dealers and suppliers. Order online at *(www.wheelersguides.com)* or click on "search" to locate campgrounds. 480/784-4771.
- *Woodall's Campground Directory*: Purchase at RV dealers and suppliers, campgrounds or bookstores, or online at their website. Or, contact Woodall Publications at 877/680-6155. Find a searchable directory online at *(www.woodalls.com/rvs)*.

## Campground guides: jobs
- **Wheelers Resort and Campground Guide,** 1310 Jarvis, Elk Grove Village, IL 60007. Telephone: 480/784-4771; fax: 480/784-4420. Online contact form. *(www.wheelersguides.com)*
- **Southeast Publications USA:** 4360 Peters Road, Ft. Lauderdale, FL 33317. Telephone: 954/583-3900. *(www.sepub.com/career.htm)*

## Christmas tree sales
- **National Christmas Tree Association:** At their website *(www.realchristmastrees.org)* select "find a tree near you." From there, choose a state to obtain a list of tree farms and retail lots.

## Site-sitting
- **Publications:** *Caretaker Gazette* and *Workamper News.*
- **Starkey International:** Household management certification and placement of house couples. 800/888-4904. *(www.starkeyintl.com)*

## Training
- **Escapees RV Club:** Training for members interested in becoming managers, assistant managers, hosts, activity directors for one of their RV parks. Contact Escapees RV Club. *(www.escapees.com)*

- **National Association of RV Parks and Campgrounds** (ARVC) training program: ARVC, 1455 Tenderfoot Drive, Larkspur, CO 80118. 303/681-0401. *arvc@erols.com (www.arvc.org)* See Educational Opportunities.

  The Campground Management Certificate Program is a 50-hour program conducted for one week a year over a two-year period. The course is designed for park owners, operators and managers and covers a wide array of management and operations topics including finance and administration, marketing, customer service, recreation programming, maintenance, personnel management, retail and food service operations and more. The course is held at Oglebay Resort, WV. Earn CPU credits and credits toward ARVC's Certified Park Operator (CPO) certification as well.

- **British Columbia Lodging & Campgrounds Association** Professional certification, based on national standards established by the Canadian Tourism Industry, for campground operators. 209 - 3003 St. John's St., Port Moody, BC V3H 2C4, 888/923-4678. *info@bclca.com (www.bclca.com/Home/tabid/36/Default.aspx)* See Business Resources.

- **Reservation software training:**
  - **ROS2000:** Purchase CD by calling 800/811-5988.
  - **Campground Manager:** Free download at *(www.campgroundmanager.com)*

## CHAPTER 15: HOW TO GET JOBS TRAVELING IN YOUR RV

### Caravans

- **Fantasy RV Tours**, P.O. Box 95605, Las Vegas, NV 89193-5605. Also hires travel ambassadors. Call 800/952-8496. *(www.fantasyrvtours.com)*
- **Other caravan companies:** look for ads in RV magazines. Check at RV shows for their booths.

### Carnivals and circuses

- *Circus News:* Links to U.S. circuses. *(www.circusnews.com)*
- *Workamper News* often has a carnival or circus advertising under "multiple locations." *(www.workamper.com)*

## Sales
- **Self-evaluation:** The following articles can assist you in deciding if sales is for you.
  - "Top Sellers: Characteristics of a Superior Salesman" differentiates between tellers and sellers. *(http://edis.ifas.ufl.edu/ pdffiles/SN/SN00400.pdf )*
  - "Profile of a Perfect Salesperson" describes 4 types of sales. *(www.bluinc.com/news/potps.htm)*
  - Do a search on Google.com for "self-evaluation in sales" to find companies selling instruments to help make this evaluation.

## Mystery shoppers
- **Mystery Shoppers Providers Association:** 4230 LBJ Freeway, Ste. 414, Dallas, TX 75244. 972/406-1104. Certification program. Search for assignments by state. *Info@mysteryshop.org (www.mysteryshop.org)*
- **Mystery Shopper scams:** Read this article about scams before you use a company. *(www.snopes.com/fraud/employment/shopper.asp)* See also *(www.rvlifestyleexperts.com/free-rv-info/working-and-volunteering/ mystery-shopping/).*
- **Fabjob:** An electronic, downloadable book is available at the site for $25.95. *(www.fabjob.com/mysteryshopper.asp)*

## RV transport companies
- *How to Get Paid $50,000 a Year to Travel (Without Selling Anything)* by Craig Chilton. Describes the Road Rat® lifestyle and lists over 4,000 manufacturers in the U.S., Canada, Europe and Australia, plus RV transporter companies. Workamper.com bookstore.
- **Other resources:** *Workamper News* usually has a listing for at least one company. Talk to dealers at RV shows or contact manufacturers for names of companies they contract with. Look at RV America's website *(www.rvamerica.com)* under RV Directories/Employment-RV Deliveries for a list of professional delivery services.

## Dog show judging
- **American Kennel Club (AKC):** Becoming a judge is a long process and takes experience showing dogs. The AKC also hires field personnel that go from show to show. AKC Job-Line: 919/852-3896. See

Inside AKC at *(www.americankennelclub.com).* For information on selling products at dog shows and other shows, see Ch. 20 and Ch. 21.

## Manufacturer's reps
- **MANA** (Manufacturer Agents National Association), One Spectrum Pointe, Ste 150, Lake Forest, CA 92630. *MANA@manaonline.org (www.manaonline.org)*
- **UAMR** (United Association of Manufacturers' Representatives), P.O. Box 986, Dana Point, CA 92629. 949/240-4966. *info@uamr.com (www.uamr.com)*

## Pipeline Technicians
- **Southern Cross**, Two Sun Ct., Ste. 400, Norcross GA 30092. 800/ 241-5057. *(www.southerncrosscorp.com)*

## Site guides - selling
- **AGS**, 2575 Vista Del Mar, Ventura, CA 93001. 800/245-9666. *(www.agsinternet.com/)*
- **Southeast Publications**, 4360 Peters Rd., Fort Lauderdale, FL 33317. 800/832-3292. *(www.rvingusa.com)* Online form.
- **Other leads:** Fairgrounds and towns sometimes have similar maps. Look on the map for the name of the company that produces it.

# CHAPTER 16: HOW TO GET JOBS WITHIN THE RV INDUSTRY
## Camping World - jobs
- **Camping World**, P.O. Box 90018, Bowling Green, KY 42102. Openings listed online. Download application. *(http:// campingworld.submit4jobs.com/)*

## Mechanic certification
- **National Institute for Automotive Service Excellence**, (ASE certified mechanics) 101 Blue Seal Dr., S.E., Ste 101, Leesburg, VA 20175. Toll-Free Information Line: 877/ASE-TECH, *(www.asecert.org)*. ASE certification tests measure technicians' knowledge of diagnostic and repair skills necessary for competent job performance.

## Training
- **Camping World RV Institute**, 134-A Beech Bend Rd., Bowling Green, KY 42101. The complete Service Technician training is nine weeks long, or take individual units. 800/356-0311. *rvi@campingworld.com (www.cwrvi.com)*
- **The National RV Technical Institute:** Offers certified RV Technician training through a number of community and technical colleges around the U.S. Sponsors are Recreation Dealers Association (RVDA) and the Recreation Vehicle Industry Association (RVIA). Certification is independent of training, but the training at Camping World and RVIA is designed to help prepare the applicant for the test. For information on locations for training, contact RVIA at 800/336-1054. Check their website *(www.rvia.or*g) under RV Technician Training. Or write to: National RV Technical Institute, PO Box 2999, 1896 Preston White Dr., Reston, VA 20195-0999. See also *(www.rvlearningcenter.com* - U.S.) and *(www.rvcareers.ca* - Canada) and RV Distance Learning.

  For information on the RVDA certification program and testing: 703/591-7130, *techcert@rvda.org. (www.rvda.org)*
- **The RV Industry's Training Calendar:** Lists all types of training for the industry. *(www.rvtrainingcalendar.org)*
- **Escapees RV Club** training for park managers and activity directors. See **Resources**, Chapter 14.

## CHAPTER 17: HOW TO GET SEASONAL FEDERAL JOBS
### Federal agencies
### Army Corps of Engineers
- **Bid on contracts:** Contact individual districts to get information and to be notified about upcoming solicitations. Look at "Where we are" at *(www.usace.army.mil)* for District information.
- *Camping With The Corps of Engineers* by S. L. Hinkle. Lists all COE campgrounds. (Online RV bookstores and Amazon.com)
- *RVer's Guide to Corps of Engineer Campgrounds* by Jane Kenny.
- *Workamper News:* The September/October issue each year lists projects soliciting bids as well as projects seeking volunteers. 501/362-2637. *(www.workamper.com)*

## BLM

- **Website:** A description of jobs hired at BLM can be found at *(www.blm.gov/wo/st/en/res/blm_jobs/how_to_apply/ wildland_fire_positions.html)*. Find openings at USAJOBS; sort by agency. *(www.usajobs.opm.gov)*

## Fire towers

- **Websites:** At Forest Fire Lookout Assoc. (FFLA), see Lookout Job Postings, links to agencies that employ workers and volunteers. *(www.firelookout.org)* Also, see National Historic Lookout Register. Lists fire towers and agencies. *(www.nhlr.org).*

## National Park Service

- **Website:** At USAJOBS, sort by agency. Look for temporary positions. *(www.usajobs.opm.gov).*

## USDA Forest Service

- **Website:** The USDA Forest Service website gives information about jobs *(www.fs.fed.us/fsjobs)*. Job openings with the Forest Service can be found at*(www.avuecentral.com)*. Look at website for "Fire Hire" positions. These include paid positions as lookouts for fire towers.
- **Other:** Check USAJOBS, sort by agency (Department of Agriculture). *(www.usajobs.opm.gov)*
- **Senior Community Service Employment Program:** Designed for low-income workers over 55 years of age. Contact Forest Service Headquarters of the specific forest, or write for more information to U.S. Dept. of Agriculture, Forest Service, Human Resources Program, P.O. Box 96090, Washington, DC 20090.
- **Regional offices** can supply you with a map and listing of the forests in their region plus other employment information. (See Appendix 3)

## Federal jobs-find job announcements

- **Internet:** You can search by agency, state or work series. Most, but not all, seasonal/temporary positions are grade-5 or lower. Some common temporary positions are: visitor use assistant, ranger, fee collector, maintenance worker, motor vehicle operator, forestry technician, and range technician. *(www.usajobs.opm.gov)*

- **Automated Telephone System:** Call 703-724-1850 or TDD 978-461-8404.
- **Contact the agencies** where you are interested in working for specific application instructions.

## Federal job résumés
- **Online résumés:** At each job announcement click "apply online" where ou'll be able to complete your résumé. As an alternative, you can upload the OF-612 or other résumé.
- **Obtain a copy of OF-612:** You can print out a copy of the OF-612 résumé at *(www.opm.gov/forms/html/of.asp)*. You can also fill out the OF-612 online. Save a copy for each job so you have a record and can reuse them.

## Getting your first federal job
- **Student Conservation Association (SCA).** Volunteer positions, internships, paid positions. Receive housing, small stipend, money towards tuition and experience. Provides conservation service in national parks, refuges, forests and urban areas in all 50 states. Use contact form online for questions. *(www.thesca.org)*
- **Other:** See Chapter 22 on volunteering.

# CHAPTER 18: HOW TO GET JOBS WORKING IN THE OUTDOORS
## Helicopter jobs
- **Just Helicopters:** Lists jobs for helicopter pilots and mechanics. *(www.justhelicopters.com)*

## Variety of job opportunities
- **Coolworks:** Check the following categories: National Parks, State Parks, Older and Bolder, Jobs on Water, and Other Cool Work for possible jobs in the outdoors. Several NPS concessionaires are listed here. *(www.coolworks.com)*
- *Workamper News:* See **Resources**, Ch. 8, for address and subscription information. Print edition has ads for forest service concessionaires and other types of jobs listed in Ch. 18. *(www.workamper.com)*

## Other job sources

- **NPS concessionaires:** There are more than 500 NPS concessionaires. Find out concessionaire information for a park by contacting NPS there. If no concessionaires, ask for names of "gateway" or nearby cities. Contact the chamber of commerce or tourist/visitor center for lists of employers. Information about park locations and contact information can be found at *(www.nps.gov)*.
- **Forest Service concessionaires:** Contact USDA Forest Service regional or a specific forest headquarters to find out who operates their campgrounds. See also **Appendix 3** for contact information for regions. Several concessionaires advertise in *Workamper News*.
- **Operate a concession in a national forest:** Contact the individual forest(s) you are interested in. When a concession comes up for bid, the forest will first publish a prospectus and solicit bids. Contracts run from 1-5 years. Find contact information at *(www.fs.fed.us)*.
- **State and county concessions:** If you have an area in mind, contact state and county parks to find out names of any concessionaires.
- **Firefighter support:** State and federal forests may contract out firefighting support services. Your best bet is to check with an individual forest to find out the contractor. See also *Workamper News*.
- **PA State Parks:** Bid on concessions in Pennsylvania State Parks. *(www.dcnr.state.pa.us/stateparks/business)*

## State and city parks

- See **Appendix 4** for contact information for state parks.
- **Other:** Look at Coolworks.com and *Workamper News*.

## CHAPTER 19: HOW TO GET A JOB AT RESORTS AND TRAVEL DESTINATIONS

### Amusement parks

- **International Association of Amusement Parks and Attractions:** (IAAPA) 1448 Duke St., Alexandria, VA 22314. 703/836-4800. *iaapa@iaapa.org (www.iaapa.org)*
- **Other:** Check *Workamper News* and Coolworks.com for jobs.

## Bed and Breakfasts

- **Professional Association of Innkeepers International** (PAII) has books and training. Join to be listed as an innsitter. List is circulated to all PAII members. 207 White Horse Pike, Haddon Heights, NJ 08035. 856/310-1102. *(www.innkeeping.org/)*
- **Other:** Find jobs working for a B&B by contacting directly or through local help-wanted classified ads.

## Casinos

- *American Casino Guide* for $13.56 plus s/h lists details of more than 700 casinos in 36 states, including riverboat and Indian facilities. Their online directory includes links to casino web pages. In some cases, you can apply right online or download an application. Call 954/989-2766 to order or order online. *(www.americancasinoguide.com)*
- **Non-dealer positions:** Go to the casino personnel office or check local help-wanted ads.

## Cruise lines/maritime jobs

- **Find cruise lines:** Check at Coolworks under Alaska and Jobs on the Water to identify cruise line. Check at their website or call their toll-free number. For dance host positions, contact individual cruise lines. *(www.coolworks.com)*
- **Maritime jobs:** Find concessionaire positions on cruise ships such as beauty shops, gift shops, massages. Also work in ship's casinos, Alaska fishing boats or processing. *(www.maritimejobs.com)*

## Dude ranches

- **The Dude Ranchers' Association**, P.O. Box 2307, Cody, WY 82414. Telephone: 866/399-2339. Obtain a directory of member ranches or access online. For $10, you can place an employment-wanted ad directly in their biweekly newsletter. *(www.duderanch.org)*
- **Workamper News:** Find some listings in the print publication.
- **Guest Ranches of North America,** P.O. Box 191625, Dallas, TX 75219-8503. Employment openings of member ranches by state. Post your employment-wanted ad at no charge. *(www.ranchwork.com)*

## Overseas work

- *Transitions Abroad Magazine:* Articles and advertisements for working overseas. Many are open only to students who can obtain a student visa, as countries often restrict foreigners from seeking employment in their countries. (That is not to say you can't find work in another country.)  At (*www.transitionsabroad.com*) look under "Work" for categories like: Work Abroad Resources, Short-term Work Abroad, Internship Programs, Volunteer Programs, and Teaching English Overseas. Copies available at newsstands.
- **Peace Corps:** Volunteer in other countries for two years, plus three months training. Receive stipend plus $6,000 when you return. 800/424-8580. (*www.peacecorps.gov*)
- **Work at Antarctica:** Many support workers are hired by Raytheon Polar Services. Most work from October to February. Take a look at their website. (*http://rpsc.raytheon.com*)

## Resorts

- **Coolworks:** Lists resort jobs. (*www.coolworks.com*)
- **Resorts and Lodges:** Sort by area and resort types. (*www.resortsandlodges.com*)

## Resorts/attractions that hire RV workers

- **Adventureland Park:** Located in Des Moines, Iowa, this amusement park hires upwards of 200 Workampers. Write to: Adventureland Personnel, P.O. Box 3555, Des Moines, IA 50316. Call 515/266-2121 or e-mail *hr@adventureland.com. (www.adventureland-usa.com)*
- **Branson, Missouri:** Order a travel planner from the Chamber of Commerce plus find a list of shows, attractions, and RV parks at (*www.explorebranson.com*) or call 800/214-3661.
- **Disney World Jobline:** 407/828-1000. They like to hire RVers. RV site not included. (Jobline for Disneyland is 818/558-2222.)
- **Silver Dollar City:** *employment@silverdollarcity.com,* 417/338-8212, fax. (*www.bransonsilverdollarcity.com/employment*)
- **Wall Drug**, 510 Main Street, P.O. Box 401, Wall, SD 57790. 605/279-2175. (*www.walldrug.com*) Check for employment information at Coolworks. *Workamper News* may carry an ad.

## Ski resorts

- **Go Ski:** Lists ski resorts all over the world. Under USA, search by region or state for ski resort. Obtain contact information, or link to resort's website. Find employment opportunities at individual websites. *(www.goski.com)*
- **Skiing Jobs:** Source for ski jobs. Job lists, resume posting, and employer posting. *(www.skiingjobs.com)*
- **Coolworks:** See "ski jobs" category. *(www.coolworks.com)*

## CHAPTER 20: HOW TO FIND TEMPORARY JOBS AND WORK AT SPECIAL EVENTS

### Computer assignments (short-term), high-tech assignments

- **Resources for short-term computer jobs:** Check jobs and post résumés at *(www.dice.com)* and *(www.net-temps.com)*.
- **Contract Job Hunter:** Specializes in job openings for *serious* contractors and consultants in engineering, IT/IS, and technical disciplines. Print magazine, *Contract Employment Weekly*, available. Website subscription $25/year. *staff@cjhunter.com*. *(www.cjhunter.com)* Contract Job Hunter is a service of C.E. Publications, Inc., 425/806-5200.
- **National Technical Employment Service** (NTES) Also has contract listings. Links to resources under "Hot Flash." *(www.ntes.com)*
- **Other:** Check Internet job sites, local classified ads, and temporary agencies.
- **U.S. Register of Technical Service Firms:** Directory online at National Technical Employment Services. *(www.ntes.com/directory)*

### Motorsports/NASCAR

- *Workamper News:* Check for ads in this sport as well as the print publication. *(www.workamper.com)*
- **Other leads:** Contact tracks that have NASCAR events for job openings during races. At *(www.nascar.com)* click on Races, then Schedule to find a list of upcoming races, dates and track.

### Road construction - flagging

- **Flaggers:** Flaggers on DOT road construction sites must be certified. Find local courses and job openings through the National American Traffic Safety Services Association (ATSSA).

*(www.atssa.com)* Click on Education & Certification, Webinars, National Flagger Database.

## Special events
- **Flea Market Guide:** Events plus wholesalers. *(www.fleamarketguide.com)*
- **Special Events Directory:** The most complete source for North American fairs, craft shows, festivals, indoor & outdoor shows. More than 150,000 events and attractions online. *(www.eventcrazy.com)*
- **International Association of Fairs and Expositions (IAFE):** *(www.fairsandexpos.com)* Click on Find a Fair to locate fairs and expositions by state. Check dates, employment opportunities.
- **Trade Show News Network:** Website listing trade shows. Sort by type, date or location. *(www.tsnn.com)* Calendar of trade shows.
- **ASD/AMD Trade Show-Las Vegas:** View and purchase merchandise to sell. Resale number/tax identification number required to attend. *(www.asdonline.com)*
- **Other ASD/AMD shows:** Find additional shows to purchase merchandise for resale at *(www.asdonline.com/info/show-dates-hours)*.
- **Wholesale merchandise:** Do a computer search for "wholesale merchandise." One website is *(www.wholesaledir.com)*,which offers a comprehensive online directory of wholesalers by type of merchandise.
- **Renaissance Festivals:** Calendar of festivals. Contact individual festivals for employment information. *(www.renaissancefestival.com)*
- **Vacation planners:** Order vacation planners from states where you want to travel for events calendars. See **Appendix 1**.
- **Other:** Check for jobs at special events at Internet job sites, local classified ads, and temporary agencies.

## Temporary agencies
- **National Association of Temporary and Staffing Services:** (NATSS) At website search for temporary agencies and contact information under "Job Seeker." Search by area, type of work and whether you are looking for a temporary position, temporary to permanent or permanent position. *(www.staffingtoday.net)*

- **Temping.com:** This free service allows you to search for temporary staffing agencies and positions by geographic area. *(www.temping.com)*
- **Nation-wide agencies:** May offer employees benefits and the ability to transfer records from one office to another:
  - **Adecco:** Over 6600 offices in 70 countries. Service bonus, paid holidays, 401K program. *(www.adecco.com)*
  - **Manpower:** Provides jobs that are full-time, part-time, long-term, contract or short-term assignments. Benefits available. More than 1,500 online training courses through their Global Training Center. *(www.manpower.com)*
  - **Kelly Services:** Offices in 30 countries. *(www.kellyservices.com)*
- **Specialty agencies** place accountants and financial personnel, medical personnel, and others. Larger cities may have agencies that specialize in labor- or construction-type positions. Look in the Yellow Pages and Help Wanted ads in Sunday newspapers.
- **Travel Nurse jobs:** Jobs for RNs, LPNs and ORTs. *(www.rntravelerjobs.com)*
- **Sunshine Enterprises:** Find a job detasseling corn for three weeks at *(http://varsitydetasseling.com)* and *(www.teamcorn.com)*
- **Wheat Harvest:** U.S. Custom Harvesters is an agency that recruits workers. *(www.uschi.com/emp_opp.php)*
- **ReserveAmerica** hires call center reservation agents in Ballston Spa, NY, Madison, WI, Orlando, FL and Rancho Cordova, CA. ReserveAmerica, P.O. Box 199, Ballston Spa, NY 12020. E-mail resume to: *csacala@reserveamerica.com* (Attention: Human Resources. Mention position you are applying for.) *(www.reserveamerica.com)*

## CHAPTER 21: HOW TO OPERATE YOUR OWN BUSINESS ON THE ROAD
### Performing

- **School assemblies:** Resource for making money by putting on assembly programs in schools. *How to Make Money Performing in Schools: Definitive Guide to Developing, Marketing and Presenting School Assembly Programs* by David Helflick. (Amazon.com)

- **RV parks:** Contact individual RV parks to arrange an exchange of services or pay for performing.

## Photography

- *Photographer's Market:* Updated each year. Thousands of markets like magazines, advertising agencies and stock photography agencies. Published by Writer's Digest Books. Available at bookstores or at online bookstores. *(www.writersdigest.com)*

## Self-employment resources

- *422 Tax Deductions for Businesses and Self-employed Individuals,* by Bernard B. Kamoroff, C.P.A. Useful information for small business owners and independent contractors.
- **Are you an entrepreneur?** Excellent checklist by Robert Sullivan, author of *The Small Business Start-up Guide.* Entrepreneurial aptitude test. *(www.thealternativebookshop.com/busn0001.html)*
- **Chambers of Commerce:** Check with the Chamber of Commerce where you plan to register your business for local resources for assisting businesses. You may find funding sources, support groups and opportunities for networking when you are in that area.
- *Entrepreneur Magazine:* Geared to small business owners. Website has numerous articles on starting and growing a business, electronic newsletters. Find magazine at newsstands or subscribe at website. *(www.entrepreneurmag.com)*
- **"How to Form a Corporation**, LLC, or Partnership in ..." Guides by W. Dean Brown for each state leading entrepreneurs through the incorporating process in their own state. Includes necessary forms and step-by-step instructions. Available through the Independent Publishers Group at *(www.ipgbook.com)*.
- **National Association for the Self-Employed (NASE):** Resources for the self-employed. Includes discounted services, legal issues, and health insurance. *(www.nase.org)*
- **Service Corps of Retired Executives Assoc. (SCORE):** A resource partner with the U.S. Small Business Administration. Aides in the formation, growth and success of small businesses. Offers e-counseling, workshops and other information. *(www.score.org)*
- **U.S. Small Business Administration (SBA):** Government agency that helps small businesses. Povides counseling and training. Helps

with financing and other aspects  starting in your own business. Obtain a *Small Business Resource Guide* or Start-Up Guide from your local office, or download it, at *(www.sba.gov)*.

- **SBA resources for women:** Office of Women's Business Ownership of the Small Business Administration has free online courses.  Directory of local Women's Business Centers. *(www.sba.gov/aboutsba/sbaprograms/onlinewbc/index.html)*

## Seminars and public speakers

- **National Speakers Association:** Provides professional development, a Certified Speaking Professional (CSP) designation program, plus other resources. Find local chapters. NSA, 1500 S. Priest Dr., Tempe, AZ 85281. 480/968-2552. *(www.nsaspeaker.org)*
- **Toastmasters International:** Toastmasters clubs meet in 70 countries worldwide to help people improve their communication skills and lose their fear of public speaking. Find local chapters in the local telephone book. Toastmasters International, P.O. Box 9052, Mission Viejo, CA 92690, 949/858-8255. *(www.toastmasters.org)*.
- **Fabjob.com Guide to: Become a Motivational Speaker** by Tag Goulet. E-book or CD available at *(www.fabjob.com)*.
- **Hot Tips for Speakers:** Book by Rob Abernathy and Mark Reardon on how to get ideas across to an audience with maximum effect. Independent Publishers Group at *(www.ipgbook.com)*.

## Sales

- See **Special Events**, Chapter 20.

## Telecommuting

- American Telecommuting Association. Resources for the telecommuter. 800/ATA-4-YOU. *(www.yourata.com)*
- **Find postings:** *(www.tjobs.com)*

## Windshield repair

- **Start-up kits:** Contact Gene and Kathy Thaden for information on starting your own windshield repair business at12772 E 37th Pl., Yuma AZ 85367. 515/360-9444. Or e-mail at *ekthaden@juno.com* with your contact information.
- **Other:** See business opportunity magazines for franchises.

## Web-based businesses

- **Bryce and Lisa Jackson's Webworker.com** has information for the beginner about affiliate sites. Includes information on selling on eBay. *(www.webworker.com)*
- **See also:** magazines and books geared to Web-based businesses.

## Writing and publishing

- *Writer's Market:* A Writers Digest book listing thousands of markets and useful advice for writers. Also, *Writer's Online Marketplace* for Internet markets. The monthly magazine, *Writer's Digest*, is an excellent resource for writers too. Magazine available at newsstands. *(www.writersdigest.com)*
- *Taking the Mystery Out of RV Writing* by Jaimie Hall and Alice Zyetz. Sections on the writing process, publishing articles, writing a book, self-publishing and marketing. Available in CD or e-Book format. *(www.rvlifestyleexperts.com)*
- **Internet newsletters:** Several electronic newsletters provide invaluable information for those wanting to sell articles or publish books and e-books. A few of my favorites are:
  - **Publishing Poynters:** Dan Poynter is known as the guru of self publishing. Subscribe at *(www.parapublishing.com)*.
  - **Writers Weekly:** Angela Hoy's freelance writing ezine. Subscribe at *(www.writersweekly.com)*.
  - **Writing World:** A world of writing information. Moira Allen's e-zine. Subscribe at *(www.writing-world.com)*.
  - **Funds for Writers:** Paying assignments, grants. Subscribe at *(www.fundsforwriters.com)*.
- *Well-Fed Writer*: *Financial Self-Sufficiency as a Freelance Writer in Six Months or Less* by Peter Bowerman. How to make good money copywriting. (Review at RVLifestyleExperts.com)

## CHAPTER 22: HOW TO HELP THE BUDGET BY VOLUNTEERING
### Volunteer opportunities - volunteer websites/publications
- **RV Volunteers Make a Difference:** One-hour audio-visual CD. How-to's plus resources on RV volunteering. *(https://store.workamper.com/index.cfm?det=128&AID=103803)*

- **The RVing Volunteer:** Information about volunteering by Hope Sykes. *(www.escapees.com/care/vto.asp)*
- **Family Matters:** Excellent resource for families looking for a volunteer project. *(www.pointsoflight.org)*  Look under Programs.
- **Habitat for Humanity:** RV-Care-A-Vanners. *rvinfodesk@habitat.org (www.habitat.org/rv)* Also find affiliates and information about international needs. *(www.habitat.org)*
- **Disabled Online:** Disability community online. *(www.disabledonline.com)*
- **Idealist:** Database of nonprofits both nationwide and worldwide, including volunteer opportunities. Search for positions that match your interests. *(www.idealist.org)*
- **Passport in Time:** Volunteer archaeology and historic preservation program of the USDA Forest Service. Current projects online. *volunteer@passportintime.com. (www.passportintime.com)*
- **Random Acts of Kindness:** Free resources especially useful for parents who are homeschooling or want a project idea. Lots of good ideas for all for short ways to help out. *(www.actsofkindness.org)*
- **RVLifestyleExperts.com:** See Working/Volunteering pages. *(www.rvlifestyleexperts.com)*
- **Servenet:** Find volunteer projects by zip code. *(www.servenet.org)*
- **Service Corp of Retired Executives:** (SCORE). Volunteer to help small business owners succeed. *(www.score.org)*
- **Volunteer Match:** Search database for short and long term volunteer opportunities by zip code. *(www.volunteermatch.org)*
- *Vehicles of Hope* by Carol Tebo with Larry Tebo recounts their experiences volunteering for Habitat for Humanity and disaster relief. *(www.tebotales.com)*
- **Volunteer.gov/gov:** Search by state or type of opportunities with federal agencies. *(www.volunteer.gov/gov)*
- **YMCA camps:** YMCA Trout Lodge & Camp Lakewood offers 3-12 week opportunities. Includes RV site, meals, benefits. *(www.ymcaoftheozarks.org)* By state at *(www.stwmd.com/y-camps.php)*

## Virtual volunteering

- **OnlineVolunteering.org:** Volunteer internationally without leaving home. Use your computer to write grants, fund raise or Web design. *(www.onlinevolunteering.org/en/vol/index.html)*

- Virtual Volunteering Project: (*www.utexas.edu/lbj/rgk/serviceleader/virtual/*)

## Volunteer vacations

- **American Hiking Society:** Volunteer vacations are $130 ($100 for members). (*www.americanhiking.org*)
- **Archaeological Fieldwork Opportunities Bulletin:** Comprehensive listing about almost 300 excavations and field schools throughout the world with openings for volunteers and students. Updated yearly. Order from *(www.oxbowbooks.com)* or 800/791-9354. Searchable database at (*www.archaeological.org/webinfo.php?page=10015*)
- **Earth Watch Institute:** An international nonprofit organization. 4,000 members volunteer their time and skills to work with 720 research teams each year on Earthwatch field research projects in more than 50 countries around the world. Programs are 1-3 weeks. 800/776-0188; *info@earthwatch.org. (www.earthwatch.org)*
- **Global Volunteers:** Two- to three-week programs, most of fee is tax deductible. Nonprofit, nonsectarian organization. Call 800/487-1074. *(www.globalvolunteers.org)*
- **GRIT:** Graffiti Removal Intervention Team at Glen Canyon. See *(www.nps.gov/glca/supportyourpark/grit.htm)*. See contact information for Trash Tracker, below.
- **Trash Tracker:** Write Glen Canyon National Recreation Area, Trash Tracker, P.O. Box 1507, Page, AZ 86040. 928/608-6200. *(www.nps.gov/glca/supportyourpark/trashtracker.htm)*
- **Volunteer vacations:** *Volunteer Vacations: Short-Term Adventures That Will Benefit You and Others* by Bill McMillon, Edward Asner.

## International volunteer opportunities

- **Cross-Cultural Solutions:** A nonprofit organization that sends volunteers abroad to provide humanitarian assistance with volunteer work programs in Africa, Asia, Eastern Europe and Latin America. Fees are associated with each program, however you can obtain a fund-raising kit. 800/380-4777. *(www.crossculturalsolutions.org)*
- *The International Directory of Voluntary Work:* (7th Ed) by Louise Whetter, Victoria Pybus. Vacation-Work. Available at Amazon.com.

- **International Habitat for Humanity:** (See above in Volunteer section for contact information.)
- **Mercy Ships:** Write to P.O. Box 2020, Garden Valley, TX 75771-2020. 903/939-7000. *(www.mercyships.org)*
- **Student World Traveler:** Working and volunteering positions overseas. Search by country. *(www.studenttraveler.com)*
- **Transitions Abroad:** *(www.transitionsabroad.com)* (See **Resources** Chapter 19.)
- **Volunteer Abroad:** One of largest directories on the Internet. *(www.volunteerabroad.com)*
- **World Teach:** A nonprofit organization that sends people to teach in various countries. One year, six months, and summer programs. Fees cover airfare and living allowance. Financial assistance is available. B.A. degree required or its equivalent, except for China. They try to place couples. World Teach, c/o Center for International Development, Harvard University, 79 JFK St., Cambridge MA 02138. 800/4-TEACH-0 (483-2240). *(www.worldteach.org)*

## CHAPTER 23: HOW TO REDUCE EXPENSES
### Camping - free or reduced cost
- **BLM Long term visitor areas (LTVAs):** Buy an LTVA pass from the BLM Yuma Field Office located at 2555 E. Gila Ridge Rd. in Yuma, AZ 85365-2240. 928/317-3200 and BLM El Centro Field Office, 1661 S. 4th St., El Centro, CA 92243. 760/337-4400. *(www.ca.blm.gov/elcentro)* More information is available on LTVAs. *(www.blm.gov/az/st/en/prog/recreation/camping.html)*

### Purchases
- **Sales tax holidays:** States may waive sales tax on certain purchases at different times. *(www.taxadmin.org/fta/rate/sales_holiday.html#chart)*
- **Sales tax exemptions:** List of states that exempt food and/or drugs from sales taxes. *(www.taxadmin.org/fta/rate/sales.html)*
- *Frugal RVing or Pinching Pennies without Getting Bruised and Other Advice from the Road* by Adrienne Kristine. Available in eBook format at RVLifestyleExperts.com. (CD available from Workamper.com)

## Health insurance

- **AARP:** insurance for 50-64 year olds through Aetna. *(www.aarphealthcare.com/products/premierhealth/Aetnahome.aspx)*
- *The New Health Insurance Soltion: How to Get Cheaper, Better Coverage Without a Traditional Employer Plan* by Paul Zane Pilzer. Excellent resource. See review at RVLifestyleExperts.com. Available at Workamper Store.
- **Department of Labor:** Pension and Welfare Benefits Administration of the DOL has information and brochures on health benefits and COBRA. *(www.dol.gov/ebsa/faqs/faq_consumer_cobra.html)*
- **Georgetown University (Health Policy Institute):** Find information about insurance protections in all 50 states. Call 202/687-0880 to consult *Consumer's Guide to Getting and Keeping Health Insurance. (http://healthinsuranceinfo.net)*
- **National Committee for Quality Assurance (NCQA):** Accreditation/ rating of specific plans. *(www.ncqa.org/tabid/60/Default.aspx)*
- **High risk pools:** Information on high risk pools and the states that have them. *(www.naschip.org/states_pools.htm)* and *(www.cobrahealth.com/statehighriskpools.html)*
- **Federal high-risk insurance pool:** *(www.pcip.gov/FAQ.html)* or see the AARP article on the federal high-risk pool. *(www.aarp.org/ health/health-care-reform/info-04-2010/ health_care_reform_and_preexisting_conditions.html)*
- **Clinical Trials:** Center Watch lists thousands of clinical trials and other useful information. *(www.centerwatch.com)*
- **Hill-Burton Free and Reduced-Cost Health Care** designates some hospitals to provide free and reduced-cost service for low income patients. *(www.hrsa.gov/gethealthcare/affordable/hillburton/)*
- **MedlinePlus:** Information on all aspects of health. Includes directories and informative articles on drugs. *(www.nlm.nih.gov/ medlineplus/)*
- **Assistance with obtaining medications:**
  - **NeedyMeds.** *(www.needymeds.com)*
  - **Pharmaceutical Research and Manufacturers of America:** Patient assistance programs. *(www.phrma.org)*
  - **Together RX.** *(www.togetherrxaccess.com/Tx/jsp/home.jsp)*
- **Healthcare Blue Book:** *(www.healthcarebluebook.com/)*
- **Medical tourism:** *(www.healism.com/)*

- **Veteran's Affairs health care eligibility***: (www4.va.gov/ healtheligibility/)*
- **Government Benefits:** Eligibility: *(www.benefits.gov/)* Good Medicare overview: *(www.heinrichassociates.com/medicare.html)* Medicaid info: *(www.cms.gov/home/medicaid.asp)* State Medicaid websites: *(www.healthsymphony.com/medicaid.htm)*

## Investments
- **Licensed financial consultant:** Dave Loring offers free financial planning consultations for Escapee RV Club members and other RVers. 8w00/260-1615.
- **Securities Investor Protection Corporation (SIPC):** Articles on protecting yourself against investment fraud, links to regulatory agencies. *(www.sipc.org)*
- **Department of Labor: Pension and Welfare Benefits Administration** has articles and information on investments as it relates to pensions. *(www.dol.gov/ebsa)*

## Lose your credit cards
- **What to do:** Besides calling the credit card company, notify the anti-fraud departments of the major credit bureaus:
  - **Equifax**   800/525-6285
  - **Experian** (formerly TRW) 800/879-3752
  - **Trans Union** 800/680-7289
  - **Social Security Administration-** Fraud line at 800/269-0271.

# Chapter 24: Lifestyle considerations
## Disabilities
- **Access-Able Travel Source:** Information on accessible attractions and HTC-identified accessible RV parks. *(www.access-able.com)*
- **Americans with Disabilities Act (ADA):** For more information, go to *(www.ada.gov)*. Information line: 800/514-0301.
- **Disability.gov** has links to the federal government's resources and services. *(www.disabilityinfo.gov)*
- **Enabled RVer:** Hope Sykes at *(http://maxpages.com/enabledrver)*
- **Handicapped RV Club:** Lists accessible RV manufacturers, campgrounds and other useful resources. *(www.handicappedtravelclub.com)*

- **RV-info.net** has a list of websites for accessible RVs. *(www.rv-info.net/rvspecialty.html)*
- **Virtual Volunteer Project:** Includes online tutoring and mentoring. *(www.serviceleader.org)*

## Family travel

- **A to Z Home's Cool Homeschooling:** Articles and resources. Links to forums. *(http://homeschooling.gomilpitas.com/weblinks/traveling.htm)*
- *Educational Travel on a Shoestring* by Judith Waite Allee and Melissa L. Morgan. *(www.angelfire.com/on/shareddreams)*
- **Families on the Road:** Networking for families on the road. *(www.familiesontheroad.com)*
- *Homeschooling on a Shoestring* also by Allee and Morgan.

## RV Clubs

- **Escapees RV Club**, 100 Rainbow Dr., Livingston, TX 77355. 888/757-2582. "Sharing the RV Lifestyle." Provides services for full-time RVers. Find Boondocking Etiquette letter under "What's Hot" at the Escapees website (See Action Items). *(www.escapees.com)*
- **Family Motor Coach Assoc.:** FMCA, 8291 Clough Pike, Cincinnati, OH 45244. 800/543-3622. *(www.fmca.com)*
- **Good Sam Club:** 800/234-3450. *(www.goodsamclub.com)*

## Solo travelers

- **Loners on Wheels (LOW)**, P.O. Box 1060-WB Cape Girardeau, MO 63702. 505/546-4058. For information and a sample newsletter, e-mail *lonersreply@clas.net. (www.lonersonwheels.com)*
- **RVing Women**, P.O. Box 1940, Tempe, AZ 85217-1940, 888/557-8464. *rvingwomen@juno.com (www.rvingwomen.org)*
- **Wandering Individuals Network, Inc. (WIN)**, P.O. Box 6068, Pahrump, NV 89041-6068. *(www.rvsingles.org)*
- *The Woman's Guide to Solo RVing* by Jaimie Hall and Alice Zyetz. Pine Country Publishing. Available in e-Book or CD at *(www.rvlifestyleexperts.com)*.
- **Workamper.com** has free "Singles seeking Workamping partners" classified ads in its print edition. Also, at the website, participate in the Solo Workamping forum for solos.

- **Joei Carlton Hossack:** Order her books from Amazon.com. *Everyone's Dream Everyone's Nightmare*; *Kiss This Florida, I'm Outta Here*; *A Million Miles From Home*; *Alaska Bound and Gagged, Free Spirit - Born to Wander*; and *Chasing the Lost Dream*. *(www.joeicarlton.com)*

## Traveling with pets
- **Pet-friendly RV parks:** *(www.roamingtimes.com/Searchcamps/petfriendly.asp)*
- **Travel with dogs:** *(www.rvingwithdogs.com)*
- **Travel with horses:** *(www.travelingwithhorses.com)*

## APPENDIX 7: JANICE'S GROCERY SHOPPING LIST
- **Convection ovens:** *I've Got a Convection Oven in My RV. Now What?* Adrienne Kristine. E-Book. *(www.rvlifestyleexperts.com/rv-books/ebooks/)*

## APPENDIX 10: THREE RV WORKERS' STORIES
### Alaska job search
- **Coolworks:** Start with *(www.coolworks.com)*. Click on Alaska for links to a variety of employers.
- **Alaska's Division of Tourism:** Find links to, and addresses of, city visitor bureaus and chambers of commerce. Order a free vacation planner. *(www.travelalaska.com)*. Ron and Val saw Halsingland Hotel advertised, sent in their résumés and were hired.
- **Alaska Campground Owners Assoc.:** Links to member campgrounds. *(www.alaskacampgrounds.net)*
- **Internet search:** Search for Alaskan cities by name. Chamber of Commerce will list potential employers and RV parks.
- **Federal seasonal jobs:** For seasonal jobs with federal agencies check *(www.usajobs.opm.gov)*. Limit your search to Alaska.
- **Classified sections:** Many newspapers can be found on the Internet. Ardith and Page checked out employment ads in Anchorage prior to heading north. (See **Resources,** Ch. 9.)
- **Volunteer:** Volunteers needed for Alaska State Parks. Look at Coolworks or *(www.alaskastateparks.org)*. Contact federal agencies around the first of the year for summer volunteer positions.
- *Workamper News:* Look under Alaska listings.

# Additional resources/notes

*"Get a good idea and stick with it. Dog it,*
*and work at it until it's done and done right."*
Walt Disney

# Index — Job list

## A

Academic instructor - online courses - *Own business Ch 21*

Activity director:

    Activity director or recreation leader - *Clubs Ch 16, Resorts Ch 19*

    Activity or craft instructor - *RV park Ch 14*

Adventure/recreation tours: jobs like raft guide, stable hand, tour leader, reservations staff, cashier, mechanic, maintenance worker, driver, loader or packer - *Resorts Ch 19*

Aides or technicians in archaeology, biological, hydrological, lands, range, real estate and surveying - *USFS Ch 17*

Airport driver - *Dude ranch Ch 19*

Archaeological assistant or helper - *Federal and State volunteering Ch 22*

Artist or craftsperson: painting, beading, photography, weaving, jewelry etc. - *Own business Ch 21*

Attractions host/hostess, tickets host/hostess - *Disney Ch 19*

## B

Backcountry patrol - *Volunteering Ch 22*

Badges - *Own business Ch 21*

Baggage handling for cargo aircraft - *Holiday-season Ch 20*

Bartender - *Casinos and Resorts Ch 19*

Bell ringer collecting donations - *Holiday-season Ch 20*

Bike rental clerk, mechanic - *RV park Ch 14*

Blackjack dealer - *Casinos Ch 19*

Booking agent for a circus - *Ch 15*

Bookkeeper - *Camping World Ch 16, Non-profit Ch 18*

Brake assists and other RV accessories - *Own business Ch 21*

Breakfast preparation - *B&B Ch 19*

Bus driver/guide - *Cruise/land tours Ch 19*

Bus maintenance and cleaning worker *Cruise/land tours Ch 19*

Business consultant - *Own business Ch 21*

# C

Cafeteria worker  - *Wall Drug/similar Ch 19*

Campground-related jobs:

    Campground host - *NF concessionaires Ch 18, Federal volunteering Ch 22, Concessionaire and State parks Ch 18, State park volunteering Ch 22*

    Campground host at military Fam camps - *Federal volunteering Ch 22*

    Campground worker - *Amusement/theme parks Ch 19*

    Canoe rental clerk and livery driver - *RV park Ch 14*

Caretakers:

    Caretake/work in exchange for site, extra hours for money - *Ch 14*

    Caretaker of ranches or other property - *Ch 14, Overseas Ch 19*

    Construction sites: caretaking and security - *Ch 14*

Cartography aid or technician - *BLM Ch 17*

Carving - *Own business Ch 21*

CDL driver, long or short haul - *Temporary jobs Ch 20*

Census taker - *Ch 17*

Change person - *Casinos Ch 19*

Check gas pipe lines - *Ch 15*

Child care nanny or worker - *Ch 14, Dude ranch, Ski resorts Ch 19*

Christmas tree lot manager or helper - *Ch 14*

Circus worker - *Ch 15*

Clerical, computer and fiscal help - *State volunteering Ch 22*

Clerk or cashier at an NPS visitor center - *Non-profit Ch 18*

Computer consultant, Web page designer - *Own business Ch 21*

Computer project consultant - *Contract work Ch 20*

Computer "debugging" and repairs

Construction trades:

    Campsite construction worker - *State volunteering Ch 22*

    Carpenter and other tradesmen  - *Federal volunteering Ch 22*

    Construction - carpenter, plumber, electrician - *RV park ch 14*

    Construction -Habitat for Humanity - *Volunteering Ch 22*

    Construction work: carpentry, plumbing, electrical, sheet rock, block work - *Temporary Ch 20, Federal volunteering Ch 22*

Cook - *Dude ranch, Resorts, Disney, Wall Drug/similar Ch 19*

Corn detasseler - *Temporary Ch 20*

Environmental educator - *Federal volunteering Ch 22*
Exchanges:
    Exchange with a private individual - *Exchange Ch 22*
    Exchange work for space in an RV park - *Exchange Ch 22*
    Help friends or relatives in exchange for a place to park and hookups -
        *Exchange Ch 22*
    Park at a business in exchange for night security - *Exchange Ch 22*

**F**

Factory or assembly work - *Temporary Ch 20*
Fee collector - *NPS Ch 17, State parks and County/city parks Ch 18,
    State volunteering Ch 22*
Fire work:
    Fire suppression worker - *USFS and BLM Ch 17*
    Fire support workers - USFS, *BLM Ch 17; NF concessionaires Ch 18*
    Fire tower lookout  - *USFS Ch 17, Federal volunteering Ch 22*
    Forestry and range (fire positions) aid and technician - *BLM Ch 17*
Fireworks sales - *Holiday-season Ch 20*
Flagger on highway construction projects - *Temporary Ch 20*
Flight-seeing or helicopter tour operation workers - *Resorts Ch 19*
Flower shop drivers, designers, salespeople - *Holiday-season Ch 20*
Food related jobs:
    Cook, wait staff, busboy, bartender  - *Resorts, Ski resorts Ch 19*
    Food service worker - *RV parks Ch 14, Amusement/theme parks Ch 19*
    Food preparation and wait staff, bartender - *Casinos, Cruise/land
        tours Ch 19*
Forestry aid and technician - *USFS Ch 17*
Freelance writer - *Own business Ch 21*
Freelance photographer - *Own business Ch 21*
Fruit or vegetable picker - *Temporary Ch 20*

**G**

Game operator - *Amusement/theme parks Ch 19*
Gas pipeline inspector - *Ch 15*
Gas station jobs like cashier, mechanic, attendant  - *Concessionaire
    Ch 18, Resorts Ch 19*
Gate guard at an oil field for a security company - *Site-sitting Ch 17*
Gatekeeper - *RV parks Ch 14*

Housekeeping - *Ch 14; B&B, Cruise/land tours, Disney and Dude ranch Ch 19*
House-sitter - *Ch 14*

**I**

Innsitting business - *Own business Ch 21*
Inspect RV parks for directories - *Ch 15*
Install products - changing job locations - *Ch 15*
Instructor - exercise programs - *Own business Ch 21*
Interpreter (language) - *Amusement/theme parks Ch 19*
Interpreter (of resources) - *Federal volunteering Ch 22*
Investor in stock market - *Own business Ch 21*
IRS tax season worker - *Ch 17*

**J**

Janitor - *RV parks Ch 14, Camping World Ch 16*
Judge at dog shows - *Ch 15*

**L**

Laptop computers and related equipment - *Own business Ch 21*
Laundry worker - *Dude ranch Ch 19*
Law enforcement desk officer - *Federal volunteering Ch 22*
Lecturer or performer - *Cruise/land tours Ch 19*
Life guard, pool maintenance worker - *Disney Ch 19*
Lift ticket seller - *Ski resorts Ch 19*
Lighthouse tour guide - *Federal and state volunteering Ch 22*
Locksmithing - *Own business Ch 21*
Lot attendant - *Ch 16*

**M**

Maintenance:
　Laborer, maintenance worker, motor vehicle operator - *NPS Ch 17*
　Maintenance projects - *State volunteering Ch 22*
　Maintenance worker - *RV parks Ch 14; County/city parks, NPS concessionaires, NF concessionaires, State parks Ch 18; Dude Ranch and Wall Drug/similar Ch 19*
　Maintenance and repair worker - *Amusement/theme parks Ch 19*
　Maintenance or office work at a church camp - *Volunteering Ch 22*

Operator of a concessionaire activity - *County and city parks, Ch 18*
Operator of a hunting check station - *State parks Ch 18*

## P
Park or gate attendant at COE projects (bid) - *COE Ch 17*
Park aide - *State parks Ch 18*
Park guide - *NPS Ch 17*
Parts advisor - *Camping World Ch 16*
Performer at school assemblies - *Own business Ch 21*
Personal services like hair dresser, nanny or childcare provider, computer programmer, handyman  -*Resorts Ch 19*
Pet grooming - *Own business Ch 21*
Phone worker at call centers for catalog orders and surveys - *Holiday-season Ch 20*
Photographer - *Own business Ch 21, State volunteering Ch 22*
Playing Santa Claus - *Temporary Ch 20*
Pool operations - lifeguard, pool cleaner - *RV parks Ch 14*
Porter/porterette - *Casinos Ch 19*
Positions in biology, archeology and other fields - *NPS Ch 17*
Post office work:
    Post office temporary worker - *Ch 17, Temporary Ch 20*
    Post office contract worker - *Temporary Ch 20*
Produce an electronic magazine (e-zine) - *Own business Ch 21*
Product demonstration - *Temporary Ch 20*
Product installer - *Ch 15*
Professional - *Temporary Ch 20*
Propane service technician - *RV parks Ch 14*
Pumpkin lot manager or helper - *Ch 14*

## Q
Quality control inspector - *Ch 16*

## R
Race tracks: horse, dog races - *Special events Ch 20*
Rangers:
    Ranger - law enforcement, interpretation, general - *NPS Ch 17*
    Ranger in the back country permit office - *Federal volunteering Ch 22*
    Ranger - programs and tours, enforce rules  - *State parks Ch 18*

Sales of products on the Web through eBay or other auction sites for
   yourself or others - *Own business Ch 21*
Salesperson of advertising at campgrounds - maps or directories -
   *Ch 15*
Salesperson of products to businesses (open territories) - *Ch 15*
Selling in a gift shop - *State volunteering Ch 22*
Selling fireworks - *Temporary Ch 20*
Selling advertising and producing RV park maps -
   *Own business Ch 21*
Santa Claus at a mall or department store - *Temporary jobs Ch 20*
Satellite dishes and antennas - *Own business Ch 21*
Satellite Internet equipment or Wi-Fi cards - *Own business Ch 21*
Search and rescue (SAR) - *Federal volunteering Ch 22*
Seating host/hostess - *Disney World Ch 19*
Security personnel - *RV parks Ch 14, Casinos Ch 19*
Seminar speaker - *Own business Ch 21*
Service technician - *RV sales and service Ch 16*
Service writer - *RV sales and service and Camping World Ch 16*
Sharpening knives and scissors - *Own business Ch 21*
Shop attendant - *Camping World Ch 16*
Short-term laborer  - *Overseas Ch 19*
Shows: usher, ticket sales staff  - *Resorts Ch 19*
Shuttle driver - *RV parks Ch 14, Concessionaire Ch 18*
Sign Twirlers - *Holiday-season Ch 20*
Ski instructor - *Ski resorts Ch 19*
Solar panels - *Own business Ch 21*
Solar ovens - *Own business Ch 21*
Special events: *all Ch 20*
   County or state fairs
   Golf tournaments
   NASCAR races
   Shows in Quartzsite, Arizona
   Sports events
   Stadiums or convention centers
   Swap meets: booth sales, parking
Special project worker - *Federal volunteering Ch 22*
Staff visitor center or work as a naturalist - *State volunteering
   Ch 22*

Visitor centers:
    Visitor center worker - *State parks Ch 18*
    Visitor center attendant or naturalist - *Federal volunteering Ch 22*
    Visitor Use Assistant  - *NPS Ch 17*
    Visitor contact personnel - *County/city parks Ch 18*
Volunteer overseas - environmental, construction, health and
    education projects - *Nonprofit volunteering Ch 22*

## W

Wagon master/tail gunner for RV caravans - *Ch 15*
Wait staff - *Dude ranch Ch 19*
Wardrobe: costume assistants - *Disney Ch 19*
Warehouse worker - *Non-profit, Concessionaire Ch 18, Amusement/theme
    parks Ch 19*
Weather reporter for local radio stations - *Ski resostts Ch 19*
Website sales - *Own business Ch 21*
Webmaster or computer programmer - *Clubs Ch 16*
Wheat harvest - *Temporary jobs Ch 20*
Windshield repair - *Own business Ch 21*
Word processing or medical transcription - *Own business Ch 21*
Worker for contractor-offered services at RV parks and resorts - food,
    marina, etc. -*RV parks Ch 14*
Wrangler - *Dude ranch Ch 19*

# Index

# Notes

*"There is no wealth but life."*
*John Ruskin*

# Order form

For fax orders: 561/892-2837. Send a copy of this form.
E-mail orders: CalamityJaimie@gmail.com
Postal orders: Pine Country Publishing, 127 Rainbow Dr., #2780, Livingston, TX 77399-1027
Telephone: 928/607-3181
Credit card orders: www.RVLifestyleExperts.com

## *Support Your RV Lifestyle!*
### *An Insider's Guide to Working on the Road*
at $19.95 (U.S. funds) per copy/$29.95 with CD

Name: _____

Address: _____

City: _____

State and zip code: _____

Number of books: _____ @ $19.95 U.S.      $_____

Number of books with CD: ___ @ $29.95 U.S.      $_____

Number of CDs: ___ @ $14.95 U.S.      $_____

Media rate shipping & handling: $4.00      $_____

Priority mail shipping & handling: $5.00      $_____

Shipping & handling for additional copies: @ $2.00   $_____

Texas residents add sales tax 6.25%      $_____

   (Polk Cty- 6.75%)      $_____

**Total enclosed:**      $_____

## Payment information:
Make checks payable to Pine Country Publishing
For Visa or Mastercard orders, complete the following:
Name as it appears on your card: _____

Card number: _____ Exp. date: _____

Check digit: (last 3 digits on back in reverse italics) _____

Telephone number or e-mail: _____

Signature: _____